NATION-STATES AND THE MULTINATIONAL CORPORATION

NATION-STATES AND THE MULTINATIONAL CORPORATION

A POLITICAL ECONOMY OF FOREIGN DIRECT INVESTMENT

Nathan M. Jensen

PRINCETON UNIVERSITY PRESS   PRINCETON AND OXFORD

To Tom and Lou

Contents

Illustrations _____

Figures

Tables

I BEGAN thinking about the relationship between multinationals and domestic governments in 1998 while I was living in Budapest, Hungary and witnessing an intense campaign between the incumbent Hungarian Socialist Party and the opposition Civic Party before the legislative elections. Nine years after becoming a democratic state, Hungary's economy was rapidly improving. Having enacted liberal investment laws and transferred state assets to multinationals, Hungary stood as one of the most successful transitional economies in its attraction of foreign direct investment. Its earliest investor was GE, whose purchase of lightbulb producer (and national champion) Tungsram provided the country with a model for modern managerial techniques and also brought in advanced technology. Industrial cities such as Esztergom, Györ, Szentgotthard, and Szekesfehervar attracted investments from Audi, Ford Motor, General Motors, and Suzuki Motor, thus providing badly needed jobs. My fellow students at the Technical University of Budapest hoped for an engineering job at one of these foreign corporations.

But attracting multinationals, even given their benefits, was controversial. Most Hungarians were strongly pro-Western, passing a national referendum to join NATO by an overwhelming majority. However, Hungarians also remained suspicious of the increasing participation of foreign companies within their national political landscape. Corruption plagued Hungary's initial wave of "spontaneous privatization" as Prime Minister Gyula Horn's government was accused of selling national assets to foreign corporations well below market value. Thus, the tensions between integrating with the West and sustaining a strong national identity dominated the legislative elections of 1998. The opposition leader, Viktor Orban, and his Civic Party defeated incumbent Gyula Horn's party by running on an anticorruption platform. Not long after the elections, a scandal broke out in Orban's government when two members of his cabinet were accused of illegitimate dealings with U.S. defense contractor McDonald-Douglas. They quickly resigned.

Amid these sensationalized political scandals, the government quietly began enacting economic reforms, including massive spending cuts in subsidies to industries and transfers to individuals which it justified as a necessary means for attracting FDI and greater economic competitiveness. Hungarians benefited from this increase in FDI but also protested against the rollback of their social safety nets. Thus, the government of Hungary and its people struggled between the need for multinational corporations and the costs associated with attracting them.

Most academic scholarship on multinationals either directly tests the impact of multinationals on domestic economies or focuses simply on how mobile capital leads to a race to the bottom in levels of corporate taxation and domestic regulation. Few projects have systematically explored how multinationals react to government policies and political institutions. This is the first major focus of my project. Although I explore how multinationals respond to government fiscal policy, the central argument and empirical findings of this book are that political institutions, not government policies, are the most important determinant of FDI inflows.

It is my hope that my studies can debunk some perceived views and straw men on the relationship between multinationals and domestic governments. I show that there is very little empirical support for claims that taxes or other forms of government fiscal policy seriously affect FDI inflows. Levels of corporate taxation and government spending have almost no impact on FDI flows. Governments that maintain higher levels of government spending and corporate taxation are not punished by international financial markets.

The next major focus of this book is on the relationship between political institutions and foreign direct investment. Conventional wisdom holds that democratic regimes deter multinationals' investments. I prove this view to be false. Rather, democratic regimes are more likely to attract MNCs than any other forms of political regime. Contrary to the extensive focus on the role of fiscal federalism in promoting strong macroeconomic performance, my research shows that political federalism, not fiscal federalism, affects FDI inflows. Countries with politically federal institutions can reduce risks for multinationals, thus increasing FDI inflows. Finally, I explore the impact of international institutions on FDI inflows. Conventional wisdom holds that IMF support serves as a catalyst for private capital flows; however, I find that participation in IMF agreements leads to lower levels of FDI inflows.

This book is the culmination of years of work. I have received so much assistance along the way, I'm not sure where to begin or end in expressing my appreciation. With that caveat, I have many people to thank. Most of the research comes from my dissertation written in residence at Yale University's Ph.D. program in Political Science. Jose Cheibub, Fiona McGillivray, Bruce Russett, James Vreeland, and Leonard Wantchekon all provided guidance, insight, and mentoring. This book was completed at Washington University in St. Louis. The Department of Political Science, the Weidenbaum Center, the Center for Political Economy, and International and Area Studies Program all provided research support for further data collection and field work. Colleagues Randy Calvert, Bill Lowry, Andy Mertha, and Andrew Rehfeld all gave helpful advice on how to turn a rough dissertation into a publishable book. Daily coffees with Andy Sobel were helpful in fleshing out ideas on the relationship between political risks and international investors, and regular happy hours proved therapeutic during the final stages of writing.

The biggest contributor to this book and my academic career is Geoffrey Garrett. Geoff has been active in every aspect of this project, from my initial thoughts on the relationship between democracy and FDI, starting my dissertation at Yale to finishing my dissertation at UCLA (while learning how to surf in the process), to entering the academic job market fray, and finally publishing this book. Geoff's critical comments, advice, and patience were important contributions to the quality of this book.

The field work for this research project was conducted in 2004. As many readers know, setting up interviews spanning the globe is no easy task. Thanks to all of the individuals and organizations that have contributed to this project. Special thanks the Costa Rican Investment Board (CINDE) for their generous support.

Other scholars have also made contributions to this project. Thanks to Nancy Brune, Axel Dreher, John Freeman, Witold Henisz, Thomas König, Irfan Nooruddin, Quan Li, Layna Mosley, Jonathan Rodden, and Erik Wibbels. Thanks to Chuck Myers at Princeton University Press and two anonymous reviewers. Many of the stories about multinationals and governments come from a huge team of undergraduate and graduate research assistants. Thanks to Srijin Bandyopadhyay, Seth Cardeli, Jonathan Drucker, Abbey Hatcher, Caeli Higney, Gyung-Ho Jeong, Dan O'Neill, Katharine Ostrow, Jong Hee Park, Scott Seefeldt, Karli Sherwinter, and Natsuki Yamado.

My final acknowledgments go to the people in my life who, while not directly involved in the intellectual part of this project, have nonetheless suffered through it with me. First, thank you to Sophie Fortin for her support and for enduring the grumpiness that arose during the final stages of this book. Thank you, Scott Roecker, for always being a great listener. Thanks to the Green Bay Packers for bringing so much joy (and on occasion, heartache) into my life. Thanks to Chuck Myers and Debbie Tegarden at Princeton University Press and Karen Verde of Editorial Services. Their suggestions, support, and patience with this first-time author are greatly appreciated. Finally, thank you to my big family in Sheboygan, Wisconsin, which has grown even bigger since starting research for this book. I owe my biggest debt of gratitude to my parents, Tom and Cindy Lou Jensen. Even after I ventured off into the world, Tom and Lou always made me feel at home. I dedicate this book to them.

Abbreviations

ACLP	Alvarez, Cheibub, Limongi, and Przeworski Data Set
BOVESPA	The São Paulo Stock Exchange
CINDE	Costa Rican Investment Board
EDC	Export Development Canada
EU	European Union
FDI	Foreign Direct Investment
GATT	General Agreement on Trade and Tariffs
GDP	Gross Domestic Product
GE	General Electric
GM	General Motors
ICSDI	International Centre for Settlement of Investment Disputes
IFC	International Finance Corporation
IMF	International Monetary Fund
INC	Iraqi National Congress
ISA	Invest in Sweden Agency
LDC	Least Developed Country
MIGA	Multilateral Investment Guarantee Agency
MAI	Multilateral Agreement on Investment
MNE	Multinational Enterprise
MNC	Multinational Corporation
NAFTA	North American Free Trade Agreement
OECD	Organization for Economic Cooperation and Development
OLI	Ownership, Location, Internationalization Framework
OLS	Ordinary Least Squares
OPIC	Overseas Private Investment Corporation
RTB	Race to the Bottom
TRIMs	Trade Related Investment Measures
UNCTAD	United Nations Conference on Trade and Development
UNCTC	United Nations Centre on Transnational Corporations
VW	Volkswagen Corporation
WTO	World Trade Organization

NATION-STATES AND THE
MULTINATIONAL CORPORATION

1

Introduction

1.1 Introduction

Multinational corporations (MNCs) play a critical role in the global economy. By most estimates, production by multinational enterprises now accounts for over one-fourth of the world's output and one-third of world trade. Moreover, many scholars believe that the investments of multinationals, commonly known as foreign direct investment (FDI), have beneficial effects on economic growth, transferring technology and managerial expertise as well as providing capital.

A rich literature exists on firm-level decisions about FDI, but much less rigorous attention has been devoted to the national level. Why do certain countries attract multinational firms? Conventional wisdom holds that nations woo multinationals by lowering taxation levels. This act, in turn, results in invidious fiscal competition—the race to the bottom (RTB) thesis, as this phenomenon commonly appears in the literature.

In this study I show that the fiscal competition among governments to attract FDI has been grossly exaggerated. Fixation on the race to the bottom thesis has diverted attention from an even more important factor—the major political determinants of FDI flows. Foreign direct investment entails a substantial and lasting ownership stake in a venture in a host country. Activities of host governments affect the economic performance of the economy. Thus, perceptions about future conditions and future economic policies in the host inform investment decisions today. I assert that political factors have a marked influence on these decisions: governments that can commit to future economic policies conducive to multinationals' interests will achieve higher levels of FDI inflows.

In this book I argue that political institutions that provide commitments to these "market-friendly" policies for multinationals will systematically attract higher levels of foreign direct investment inflows. Which government policies prove beneficial to multinational operations? Which political institutions provide multinational corporations with credible commitments to these market-friendly policies? These emerge as the central questions of this book.

My overall theoretical perspective underscores that political institutions can provide credible commitments to sets of economic policies. In other words, political institutions can enhance the stability of economic policy, directed toward both multinationals (levels of taxation, for example) or more general economic policy that affects the domestic market. Institutions affect policies, and policies affect multinational operations.

My argument does not state that multinational corporations prefer static government policies. Strong economic performance necessitates policy change in a world of dynamic political and economic conditions. In the global economy, governments must make adjustments to economic policies according to the domestic economic situation (monetary and fiscal policy) and negotiate with other nation-states on the terms of international economic agreements (bilateral treaties, monetary cooperation, work within international organizations, etc.). For institutions to have value, they must allow for the policy flexibility required for changing economic conditions.

For example, in the realm of monetary policy few economists argue that governments should have fixed monetary policy (with the exception of some monetarists and their proposals on monetary constitutions). Instead, most scholars argue for the independence of central banks, institutions isolated from short-term political pressures, but not completely unaccountable to the country's citizens.[1] In short, independent central banks are institutions that limit policy autonomy and partisan control of monetary policy, but they also maintain some degree of policy flexibility. Elected politicians can no longer manipulate monetary policy, but monetary policy does remain responsive to changing economic conditions.

The main thesis of this book centers not only on the fact that political institutions that provide credibility are valuable to multinationals, but also that these institutions must be analyzed within a dynamic context. Political institutions that can make credible commitments to some level of policy stability and retain the necessary policy flexibility foster an environment multinational corporations desire. That is, political institutions must provide commitments to market-friendly policies both today and in the future. Those that can make this intertemporal commitment to multinational corporations will attract higher levels of FDI.

In this book I discuss and empirically test the the impact of three varieties of political institutions on flows of foreign direct investment in one hundred countries from 1970 to the present. I supplement my quantitative analysis with a series of interviews with representations of multinational corporations, investment promotion agencies, investment location consultants, and political risks analysts and insurers.

First, I argue that democratic political institutions can provide promises of market-friendly policies. The literature on the democratic peace points to a number of causal mechanisms linking democratic institutions to higher levels of credibility in the international system. Many of the same mechanisms also translate to higher levels of credibility when dealing with multinational firms. The institutional checks and balances associated with democratic systems decrease the likelihood of policy reversal, providing multinationals with a de facto commitment to policy stability. This policy stability allows multinationals to more accurately forecast budgeting needs according to future macroeconomic conditions and tax schedules, to hedge against currency risks, and to make managerial decisions in response to the predicted macroeconomic environment. In general, policy stability provides multinationals with greater assurances that the conditions that promoted entry into the market in the first place will persist.

Although multinationals value policy stability, democratic institutions also create incentives for governments to pursue policy changes that favor multinational corporations as well. I argue that the "audience costs" associated with democratic governance provide political leaders with the proper motivation to tailor policy toward multinationals.

In response to any negative policy change, multinationals can threaten political leaders that harm multinational operations by refusing further investment in the country, or by pulling out existing investments. This possibility exists in both types of political systems—authoritarian or democratic. Unlike authoritarian regimes, however, in democratic systems citizens have the ability to replace leaders with tarnished reputations through electoral mechanisms. Voters who want to reap the benefits of future FDI will choose candidates with the best reputations on election day. Therefore, political leaders must be wary of developing bad reputations, leading them to avoid policies that hamper multinationals' operations. While this system does not guarantee market-friendly policies, legislation that hinders multinationals in democratic societies nonetheless generates substantial political costs for leaders because the political position of multinationals proves even more "privileged" (in Lindblom's 1977 terms) than that of domestic businesses.

Second, I argue that veto players, defined as institutions that can block or stall policy change, can have a positive impact on multinational corporations. However, these veto players, like central banking arrangements, are complex, and simply providing a bias toward the status quo (make policy difficult to change) doesn't guarantee a more conducive environment for multinationals. I argue that one type of veto player demonstrates the important properties of credibility and flexibility: federal political institutions.

I define federal political institutions as institutions that allow regional units (states or provinces) representation at the national level. In the United States, states have both constitutionally guaranteed rights and institutionalized representation in the Senate (senators are selected from states). In other countries, such as Malaysia, subnational units have a formal veto over legislation. While the institutional structure of federal systems varies, I argue that one common theme exists. Federal political institutions increase the number of veto players in a political system and hence promote the kind of policy stability that multinationals like. Policy changes less readily as subnational governments become involved in national policy either through representation in one or both houses of a legislature or through the existence of formal veto authority.

Moreover, political federalism tends to produce market-friendly policies. Unlike Weingast's (1995) "market-promoting federalism" argument, I do not contend that competition among subnational units leads to market-friendly policies; rather, the differing incentives of subnational units from the central government regarding the treatment of multinational corporations holds the key to ensuring their enticement. That is, competition between states for multinationals holds little explanatory value. Instead, the complex relationship between the central government and subnational governments provides assurances of future economic policies that multinationals will prefer.

I argue that central governments have incentives to renegotiate policies with multinationals, such as taxation rates, after investment takes place, or to change macroeconomic policy without regard to the effects on multinationals. Indeed, a time inconsistency problem of government policy toward multinationals emerges. Governments often promise multinationals the world prior to investment, but once that commitment has been made, the central government has incentives to backtrack on these enticements. In centralized (nonfederal) systems, the national government must weigh the benefits of policy change against the negative reputation effects to the central government. In these systems, governments suffer constraints only when reneging on a contract with a multinational affects their reputation and thus their ability to attract other multinationals in the future.

In federal systems the incentive structure differs slightly. Although FDI benefits national economies in the aggregate, many of the specific goods are local, such as employment creation and spillovers on the local economy. I argue that these localized benefits depend on the productive operation of the multinational firm. Thus, subnational units possess both the incentive and the ability to veto legislation that would hamper the operations of the multinational, leading these corporations to prefer to invest in these types of systems.

One theme of this book centers on the effect of federal institutions on foreign direct investment inflows. I find that *politically* federal institutions, those that give regional units (states or provinces) representation at the national level, attract more FDI than unitary regimes. On the other hand, *fiscally* federal institutions, those that give regional units (states or provinces) the ability to tax and spend autonomously from the central government, have no impact on multinationals' investment decisions.

Third, I explore the impact of the International Monetary Fund (IMF) on foreign direct investment inflows. Countries in economic crisis sign agreements with the IMF that provide capital and conditions on future economic policies. IMF conditionality ties future loan disbursements to specific economic policies. One might think that IMF conditionality should help lock governments into a particular, market-friendly, policy equilibrium, spurring higher levels of policy stability and therefore leading governments under IMF programs to attract higher levels of FDI.

I argue, however, that while IMF agreements do promote policy stability, they also promote policies that do not attract multinationals. The IMF conditions loans on economic reforms, highlighting fiscal austerity among other things. These plans often lead to decreased spending on market-promoting public goods such as education and infrastructure—both of which are important to multinationals.[2] IMF conditions may actually increase political instability and social unrest by prescribing austerity policies in low-income and middle-income countries. These policies can create a societal backlash that may lead to escalating levels of protests and violence, along with electoral instability as incumbent governments fall from office. On balance, the IMF loans, and the conditionality associated with these funds, may increase levels of policy stability, but multinationals perceive them negatively due to the political and economic effects of these policies.

In an analysis of the impact of IMF programs I find that countries under IMF agreements tend to enjoy lower FDI inflows. These countries attract 28 percent less FDI, even when controlling for the macroeconomic factors that led these countries to seek IMF support in the first place. These results provide clear leverage over what has become a dense research thicket in recent years—the effects of political institutions on growth. No consensus exists, for example, on whether democracy, federalism, and IMF programs promote economic growth.[3] If FDI significantly drives growth, my results have powerful implications for the policy choices of national governments and for the behavior of international institutions such as the IMF.

1.2 The Conventional Wisdom: The Race to the Bottom Thesis

The myth of capital mobility hinders our ability to understand FDI flows. Much of the literature on the competition for FDI assumes that multinational corporations remain mobile in their investment decisions. According to this perspective, multinationals search the world for investment opportunities, playing governments against one another, entering and exiting domestic markets at will in an attempt to obtain higher returns. However, this view of high capital mobility—of frictionless investment across national borders—contravenes decades of research on FDI that has focused on *imperfect* market approaches in the study of multinational firms.

The race to the bottom thesis rests on this myth of high capital mobility. Scholars who argue this position assert that domestic governments must pander to multinational corporations, attracting them with the only viable tools at their disposal: regulation and fiscal policy.[4] Domestic governments, for example, loosen environmental protection, relax labor standards, and alter patterns of government fiscal policy. Governments must attract multinationals, the proponents of this thesis contend, by decreasing levels of capital taxation, leading either to lower levels of government spending or a shifting of the burden of taxation from capital to labor.

In reality, multinational investments, while relatively liquid ex ante, become much more illiquid ex post.[5] Once a multinational corporation commits resources to an investment location, it remains relatively immobile. Although multinationals may enjoy considerable bargaining power prior to investment, a large degree shifts to the host government once it secures the deal.[6]

This ex-post immobility of multinationals forces firms to try to predict the future policies of host governments. Politicians may attempt to make assurances on future policies, but governments have the incentive to change policy once a multinational has devoted substantial resources to the project.[7] Governments that can credibly commit to a specific policy equilibrium, ensuring policy stability, should attract higher levels of FDI by lowering political risks for multinationals. More importantly, governments that can offer market-friendly policies assure multinationals of a favorable policy environment for their operations. This ability to provide multinationals security on future policy proves central to attracting FDI.

By ignoring the complexity of investment decisions, the race to the bottom thesis overemphasizes the importance of fiscal competition for FDI and downplays the importance of the political factors that affect government policy. The following sections elaborate on the importance of political institutions on FDI inflows.

1.3 Democratic Institutions and FDI: Theory

The role of democratic political institutions on foreign direct investment remains seriously understudied. Many scholars and pundits argue that multinationals prefer to invest in dictatorships.[8] Dictators do not respond to an electorate, giving authoritarian leaders more room to maneuver and negotiate with multinationals. Although this argument seems persuasive, the view that multinational enterprises prefer authoritarian regimes is presumptuous. Indeed, few studies have actually examined the links between political regimes and multinational corporations. Given the tremendous literature on the effects of democracy on economic performance and international relations, these links between multinational corporations and political regimes remain glaringly underdeveloped. Even if one assumes the argument that multinationals prefer to bargain with authoritarian leaders, a number of other channels emerge through which democracy could affect FDI inflows.[9]

Profit-maximizing multinational enterprises will weigh the varying factors that impact operations in host countries. In this book I identify three mechanisms—information, representation, and credibility— through which these companies prefer democratic institutions over authoritarian regimes for their investments. These three mechanisms are:

Information. Democratic countries attract multinationals because of the better information available on government policy and current political and economic conditions. A large literature on the democratic peace in international relations highlights the role of information and democratic governance.[10] Democracies offer more transparency, both in their economic and political affairs. Moreover, domestic political processes produce commitments to external actors in democracies (Gaubatz 1996; Bennett 1997). These domestic political processes provide information to investors, allowing multinational firms to react to proposed changes in government policy before they are enacted.

Representation. Foreign investors may find avenues to pursue favorable policies, either directly or indirectly. Foreign investors can lobby government officials directly for their preferred legislative outcomes in democracies, but not in autocracies. Hansen and Mitchell (2000) find that foreign firms in the United States engage in lobbying activity just as frequently as domestic firms. As Hillman and Ursprung (1988) state, "Under representative democracy, foreign participation in domestic politics can take the form of campaign contributions, or other transfers directly aimed at influencing the trade-policy position taken by a political candidate."[11] The difficulties of influencing policy in authoritarian regimes negatively affect overall FDI inflows.

Even more importantly, MNCs may find vested interests in democratic systems already in place. A foreign MNC, once it sinks capital into a country, shares many of the same preferences as domestic producers.[12] If these democratic systems take the domestic producers' interests into account, the government will provide legislation favorable to the domestic producers and foreign investors.

Authoritarian regimes, however, may offer businesses the opportunity to influence policy decisions as well. Much of the nonacademic literature on multinationals assumes that firms prefer to bargain with authoritarian regimes, where authoritarian leaders appear willing to offer them substantial influence over government policy. According to this theory, authoritarian regimes would attract higher levels of investment.

Although this argument seems logically compelling, little empirical support exists that multinationals prefer to influence policy through these channels. For example, Wei (2000) finds that multinational corporations prove reluctant to invest in political systems with high levels of corruption. Multinationals may be more than willing to engage in corrupt deals with authoritarian leaders, but lobbying stands as the preferred mechanism for influencing policy.

Credibility. Although democracy's effect on information and representation remains important, in this book I stress its policy-enhancing nature. As highlighted earlier, multinationals face large political risks in their investments. Governments, or more specifically political institutions, that can help to decrease these political risks will attract higher levels of FDI, all else being equal.

Democratic governments make agreements with other nation-states credible (Cowhey 1993; Fearon 1994; Gaubatz 1996; McGillivray and Smith 1998; Leeds 1999). Explanations for this fact from previous scholarship range from the institutional checks and balances within democratic systems to the "audience costs" generated by elected leaders. Logically following from this large literature, democratic governments may also be more credible in their dealings directly with multinationals for these same reasons. These institutional features of democracies lead to higher levels of FDI inflows.

One mechanism that leads democratic governments to higher levels of credibility in terms of economic policy rests on the number of veto points in a democratic political system. These veto players can include chambers of the legislature, a supreme court, separation of the executive and legislative branches of government, or federal actors.[13] Democratic governments have these institutional constraints in place, making the possibility of policy reversal more difficult. As argued earlier, multinationals offering large illiquid projects may prefer to focus on countries where a lower probability of policy reversal exists once the investment has been made.

More importantly for multinationals, democratic institutions provide them benefits through the existence of audience costs. International relations theorists find democratic leaders accountable for their actions, including reneging on a promise or threat. These audience costs can also affect multinational investors. If governments make agreements with multinational firms and renege on the contracts after the investment has been made, democratic leaders may suffer electoral costs. The potential for these electoral backlashes may constrain these leaders.

Some scholars would be quick to point out that democracies experience higher levels of leadership turnover, which could have a negative impact on policy stability and ultimately country credibility. This theory was not supported by the qualitative evidence I collected for this project. Conversely, most interviews with multinational corporation representatives, investment promotion agencies, and location consulting firms supported the theory that democracies provided lower levels of political risks for multinationals. According to an interview with the deputy head of the Latin American Research Department for UBS Bank, democratic systems may lead to slightly more political volatility, but they provide less risky environments. This same theme ran through most interviews.

McGillivray and Smith (2000) point to a way in which leadership turnover could be associated with higher levels of credibility. They argue that political leaders play an "Agent Specific Grimm Trigger Strategy" where political leaders refuse to cooperate with other political leaders that have "defected" in the past. Multinationals can also play this strategy with governments that institute legislation or reverse policy in ways that negatively affect multinational corporations. Essentially, firms can hold individual leaders politically accountable for policy and refuse to cooperate (invest) in the future. In democracies, citizens who value the benefits of multinational production have the incentive and the opportunity to replace leaders with tarnished reputations through electoral mechanisms.

Given the influence of democracy on policy stability and content, I predict that the overall effect of democratic institutions should be positive. Democracies should be associated with higher inflows of FDI. Also, given the importance of these policies on the profitability of multinationals, the effects of these institutions should be comparatively large. The empirical results discussed later confirm both of these predictions.

1.4 Veto Players and FDI: Theory

Given the tremendous political risks of investments, multinationals want reasonable assurances on future policies. Multinational corporations may prefer to invest in countries with an institutional environment that biases policy toward the status quo. Dramatic policy change proves difficult, leading to a lessening of political risks. Henisz (2000) proposes this argument.

Two problems plague this logic. First, as Treisman (2000a) shows in the case of federalism and inflation, institutional structures that make policy change difficult can lead to either better or worse inflation performance. These status quo institutions, or veto players in the language of Tsebelis (1995, 2002), lock countries into an inflation equilibrium. Countries with policies conducive to low levels of inflation maintain future low levels of inflation. Countries with high levels of inflation become trapped, where current policies adversely affect inflation levels but resist change because of the institutional environment.

Using this reasoning, we would predict that countries with good or market-friendly policies toward multinationals benefit from a higher number of veto players. Countries with environments not conducive to multinational corporations (and attempting to attract FDI) struggle to implement necessary economic reforms because of the status quo bias of the institutional environment.

Second, a richer theory on the relationship between veto players and multinational corporations needs to be developed further. Veto players may exist within in the political system, but they need incentives to overrule policy change that would harm multinationals. A clear understanding of the institutional structure and preferences of the veto players remains necessary to understand their impact on FDI inflows.

I argue that while looking at the overall number of veto players reveals little about FDI inflows, certain types of veto players can grant market-friendly policies for multinationals. Politically federal institutions can provide these benefits to multinationals. Subnational actors can potentially offer "veto points" within the political system that enhance the credibility of host governments. The value of these veto points depends on the exact type of federal institutions.

An important theoretical distinction exists between political federalism and fiscal federalism that must be untangled to understand the independent effects of these institutions on multinational production. Before embarking on a discussion of *political* federalism and *political* decentralization, one must contrast these political arrangements with the growing literature on *fiscal* federalism and decentralization. Fiscal federalism and fiscal decentralization entail a degree of regional government autonomy from the central government in both taxing and spending. Although these works on fiscal decentralization provide important academic contributions, they miss an important institutional element of federal systems.

Weingast (1995) amends the literature on fiscal federalism, arguing that for states to be "market-preserving" federal countries, five conditions must be met:

1. A *hierarchy* of governments with a clear scope of authority must exist.
2. The *autonomy* of each government must be assured through some set of institutions.
3. The subnational governments are the primary agents responsible for *regulation* of the economy.
4. A *common market* of free trade between subnational units is guaranteed.
5. Subnational units face a *hard budget* constraint.

Weingast stresses that while the first two conditions may ensure a politically federal system as envisioned by Riker (1964), the final three conditions are necessary to give the subnational units enough autonomy to constrain the central government.

The definition of *politically* federal systems employed in this analysis is based on political relationships between the central government and local/regional governments. In contrast to Watts's (1999) conception of federalism as a combination of "shared-rule and regional self-rule," the working definition of political federalism in this study rests solely on the shared-rule dimension.[14] Specifically, political systems where regional actors affect *national* policies epitomize politically federal systems.

Political federalism differs from political decentralization, which encompasses the second part of Watts's definition, self-rule. Regional units often hold functional authority over certain policy areas, including autonomous regions within a polity that possess some degree of political autonomy but no real effect on the crafting of national policy.

The working definitions of these three concepts are:

1. *Fiscal Federalism*: Subnational units hold the primary responsibility of spending and raising revenue as well as regulating economic activity within their subnational territorial area.

2. *Political Federalism*: Subnational units do not tax and raise their own revenue but do help craft national policy. They also shape (in ways that will be described later) legislation at the national level.

3. *Political Decentralization*: Subnational units have autonomy over policy within their subnational territorial unit, short of taxing and spending their own revenue. They have no role in creating national policy.

These differing conceptions of federalism have potentially different effects on FDI inflows. Although most studies focus on the market-enhancing nature of fiscally federal systems, political federalism could provide substantial benefits to multinational investors. In politically federal systems, subnational units can provide a de facto veto on central government legislation.

This increase in the number of veto players provides higher levels of policy stability in a Tsebelis-style framework. More importantly, I argue that these veto players in federal systems have the incentives and the power to protect the operations of multinational firms. Multinational investments provide benefits to the nation as a whole (the central government) and benefits that are localized (concentrated in one or more subnational unit). Benefits include increased tax revenues, technology transfer, and foreign exchange at the national level and employment creation at the local level. These localized goods depend on the profitable operation of the multinational firm.

In a simple model constructed in chapter 4, I show that these differing incentives of the central and subnational governments can provide multinationals with a credible commitment to market-friendly policies. This market-preserving federalism only occurs within systems where the central government holds the power of taxation and subnational units have some degree of political power. Only *politically* federal systems provide commitments to market-promoting policies. These political systems attract higher levels of FDI.

1.5 International Monetary Fund Agreements and FDI: Theory

Although domestic political institutions can have major effects on government policy, and ultimately FDI, international institutions can also affect policy in ways that affect FDI inflows. In chapter 7 I explore the ramifications of signing agreements with the International Monetary Fund on FDI inflows. Countries in severe economic crisis turn to the

IMF for "lender of last resort" funds. These funds often come with explicit IMF conditionality, where disbursements of IMF funds hinge on specific macroeconomic reforms.

Signing a loan agreement with the IMF can provide international investors with a limited credible commitment to a specific package of future economic policies. Countries that sign IMF agreements face more than just reputation costs; they will incur actual fiscal costs in terms of lower levels of funding from the IMF for reversing policy. IMF packages should decrease the level of policy instability.

Unlike democratic institutions and federal institutions, IMF packages, while decreasing policy instability, do not ensure market-friendly policies. There are theoretical arguments for both positive and negative effects of IMF programs on domestic economies. Financial markets, in this case FDI flows, should provide the answer to whether or not foreign investors value these reforms. Economic reforms that will stabilize the economy and provide the foundation for robust future macroeconomic performance should be valuable to multinational corporations. Countries that sign IMF agreements should then be associated with higher FDI inflows.

At the same time a possibility exists that IMF programs could have a detrimental effect on multinational investors. Signing of IMF agreements could lock governments into an inefficient policy equilibrium. If the conditionality associated with IMF loans proves worse than the current economic policies, foreign investors will react negatively to IMF agreements.

Although on the surface this explanation may sound far-fetched, the negative impact of IMF policies is a distinct possibility. The IMF often prescribes austerity packages that may impose political and economic costs on domestic economies and multinational corporations.[15] For example, IMF conditionality may impose spending constraints on domestic governments. Governments must slash government spending to conform to agreed upon budget deficit levels. This decrease in spending can translate into a lower provision of public goods, such as education and physical infrastructure. If IMF conditionality forces governments to provide lower levels of market-enhancing public goods, multinationals may react negatively by refusing to invest in these countries.

Perhaps even more damaging, I argue in chapter 6 that the institutional structure of the IMF could lead to economic policies too "austere" to promote long-run macroeconomic recovery. Using a simple theory adapted from the literature on central bank independence, I argue that the system of weighted voting by relatively conservative actors leads to preference biases toward an overcontraction of the domestic economy.

Given this relationship, no a priori reasons exist why one should assume that the macroeconomic reforms prescribed by the IMF would attract foreign investors. They may provide credible commitments to a specific policy equilibrium, but the value of this equilibrium to foreign investors is unknown at best, and leads to an overcontraction of the domestic economy at worst. The overall effect of IMF agreements on FDI remains strictly an empirical question. The empirical results discussed below find a strong negative relationship between IMF programs and FDI inflows.

1.6 The Race to the Bottom and FDI: Empirical Results

In chapter 4 I study the effects of government fiscal policy decisions on FDI inflows. In an analysis of fifteen OECD countries from 1970 to 1993, I test the race to the bottom thesis by estimating the impact of taxation and spending on FDI inflows.[16] Contrary to the race to the bottom thesis, I find no support that levels of capital taxation, labor taxation, or social security transfers negatively affect FDI inflows. I also find no obvious relationship between partisan composition and the levels of FDI inflows.

The only support I find for the race to the bottom thesis rests on the fact that levels of government spending do affect FDI inflows, but not in the way that most scholars suggest. Indeed, I find that the overall level of government consumption across countries does not impact FDI inflows. On the other hand, some evidence exists that firms respond to levels of government spending. I conclude that firms respond to levels of government consumption, but no real pressure appears for the highest consumption (and tax) countries to conform to the policies of the lowest consumption (and tax) countries. In conclusion, I find very little overall support for the race to the bottom thesis.

1.7 Democratic Institutions and FDI: Empirical Results

In this book I examine the relationship between FDI and democratic institutions using a number of ordinary least squares (OLS) regressions. The first set of regressions relies on cross-sectional data for eighty countries on the determinants of FDI in the 1990s. These regressions reveal that democratic political institutions promote as much as 78 percent more FDI flows than authoritarian regimes. These robust results stand even when I control for other political factors.

A second set of regressions uses panel data to explore the effects of democratic institutions on FDI inflows from 1970 to 1998 for over one hundred countries. In this set of tests, I construct a number of Ordinary Least Squares regressions with robust standard errors using annual FDI inflows as a percentage of GDP for the dependent variable. As with the cross-sectional results, these regressions uncover that democratic institutions have a positive and statistically significant effect on FDI inflows. Moreover, these flows prove massive, with democratic institutions attracting almost 70 percent more FDI as a percentage of GDP. The cumulative effect of democratic institutions after ten years of continuous democracy amounts to an added stock of FDI of roughly 20 percent of GDP.

In the third set of empirical tests, I correct for the selection bias in democratic institutions by using a treatment effects selection model. As pointed out by Przeworski et al. (2000), the study of the economic effects of political regimes suffers from this selection bias. Democratic institutions in low-income countries seldom survive, collapsing into authoritarian regimes and leaving us with few observations of democracies in these low-income countries. Since these lower income countries often attract high levels of FDI as a percentage of GDP, the standard OLS regressions are biased against democratic institutions.

Using this selection model, I find the regressions biased and the effects of democratic institutions on FDI vastly underestimated. The selection-corrected estimates of the effects of democracy emerge roughly three times larger than the OLS results. Democratic institutions positively affect FDI inflows even more than originally estimated.

The final set of empirical tests explores the credibility-enhancing nature of democratic institutions by analyzing the effects of democracy on country sovereign debt ratings for eighty countries from 1980 to 1998. While not a direct test of the credibility-improving character of democratic institutions for multinational investors, it does help us more clearly examine the causal mechanism. The ex-post/ex-ante bargaining nature of FDI parallels the dilemma faced by political leaders attempting to obtain loans from foreign lenders. Governments make promises on the repayment of a loan, but once secured these conditions may not be met. Reputation costs come with defaulting, but often the short-run political and economic incentives outweigh this consequence.[17] Creditors must attempt to predict the potential of default by examining the country's economic conditions and political institutions along with future world macroeconomic conditions. My empirical results find a strong positive and statistically significant effect of democracy on sovereign debt ratings.

1.8 Veto Players, Federalism, and FDI: Empirical Results

To untangle the effects of political and fiscal federalism on FDI inflows, I employ a number of OLS time-series-cross-sectional regressions using net FDI inflows as the dependent variable. To test the independent effects of fiscal federalism and political federalism on foreign direct investment, I utilize three key independent variables. I operationalize fiscal federalism as the local government's share of revenue as a percentage of GDP from IMF sources.[18] For political federalism, I construct an ordinal measure of federalism from a number of sources for over one hundred countries from 1975 to 1995. To test the impact of veto players, I utilize a measure of veto players from the World Bank's Database of Political Institutions.

The estimated effects of political federalism on FDI prove positive and statistically significant. Politically federal countries attract higher levels of FDI, even when controlling for other political and economic factors. The effects on fiscal federalism and veto players are neither consistently positive nor are they statistically significant. These findings on the positive effects of political federalism and the null result on fiscal federalism and veto players have academic importance beyond the study of FDI flows. These results show that the economic effects of federalism hinge on the definition of federalism used. The lack of attention paid to these differing conceptions of federalism could help explain the lack of consensus on the overall effects of federalism on macroeconomic performance.

My final set of empirical tests explores the credibility-enhancing nature of subnational institutions by analyzing the effects of veto players, fiscal federalism, and political federalism on country sovereign debt ratings for eighty countries from 1980 to 1998. I find that both politically federal and fiscally federal systems have a positive impact on credibility for foreign lenders, while veto players have no impact.

1.9 International Monetary Fund Agreements and FDI: Empirical Results

To test the effects of International Monetary Fund agreements on FDI, I examine the effects of IMF programs on FDI inflows for one hundred countries from 1970 to 1997 using a number of time-series-cross-sectional regressions. Standard OLS analysis on this topic suffers from obvious selection bias; only countries in economic crisis sign IMF agreements. To correct for these effects I employ a treatment-effects selection model. This model relies on annual observations of FDI inflows and corrects for the selection bias of countries under IMF programs by predicting IMF participation through a number of economic control variables.

The empirical results establish the selection-corrected effects of IMF programs negative and statistically significant. Countries that sign IMF agreements attract lower levels of FDI—28 percent less than other countries. These results remain robust under a number of alternative specifications.

1.10 Qualitative Evidence

One criticism of quantitative work is the inability to test the causal mechanisms. In my empirical analysis I show that democratic institutions, federal political structures, and relations with the IMF affect FDI inflows. To explore the mechanisms linking political institutions and policies to FDI flows, I engaged in substantial fieldwork in 2004, interviewing representatives from country investment promotion agencies, multinational enterprise location consultants, political risk analysts and insurers, and decision makers at multinational corporations. A complete list of all interviews can be found at the end of the References section. In these interviews I asked open-ended questions on what factors were important in multinationals selecting investment locations, and I followed up these questions with specific questions on how they evaluated the importance of specific policies and institutions.

First, I selected a number of investment promotion agencies with variation on the key independent variables. These investment promotion agencies are generally government agencies engaged in the marketing and facilitating of multinational investments. For example, the Thailand Board of Investment, a government agency chaired by the prime minister and staffed with government and private-sector officials, markets Thailand as in investment location and administers financial incentives to facilitate FDI. Most of these investment promotion agencies are often the first contact for multinationals considering an investment in their representative country and all of them routinely interact with multinational corporation's decision makers.

Table 1.1 lists the democracy, political federalism, and IMF participation average scores from 1970 to 1998 for the eight investment promotion agencies I interviewed. I will discuss the construction of these measures in greater detail in the following chapters, but for simple presentation I will briefly introduce each variable. Democracy is a 0–20 measure of the level of democracy, where 0 is an authoritarian regime

TABLE 1.1.
Investment Promotion Agencies

Country	Democracy	Federalism	IMF Packages
Brazil	10.89	1.67	0.46
Bolivia	12.21	0	0.61
Canada	20	2	0
Costa Rica	20	0	0.64
Hungary	8.22	0	0.46
Ireland	20	0	0
Malaysia	14.79	2	0
Thailand	12.64	0	0.29
Dataset Average	9.87	0.24	0.30

and a 20 is a fully democratic regime. Federalism is a measure of sub-national actors (states, provinces, etc.) and their influence over national policy. Federal nations are scored a 2, mixed nations a 1, and unitary states a 0. The IMF measure is the percentage of the years in my sample (1970–1998) that the country was under an IMF program. To be clear, Canada was fully democratic throughout the time period (Democracy = 20), federal (Federalism = 2), and was not under any IMF agreements during this period (IMF = 0). Brazil, on the other hand, is more complex. For much of the time period it was an authoritarian regime (Democracy = 10.89), although it maintained political federalism during much of the time period (Federalism = 1.67), and was under IMF agreements 46 percent of the time (IMF = 0.46). Thailand shares a similar authoritarian past (Democracy = 12.64), but it was consistently unitary throughout the period (Federalism = 0) and was under IMF much less regularly than Brazil (IMF = 0.29). These investment promotion agencies have substantial variation in these key independent variables both across countries and over time.

Interviews with these agencies generally confirm the empirical results presented in this book. First, few investment promotion agencies considered tax rates or financial incentives as primary motivations for multinational investments. The exception was Ireland's investment promotion agency, which argued that financial incentives are a central aspect of FDI decisions. Most conceded that taxes were important, but these were generally secondary considerations for multinationals.

Second, there is overwhelming support that political institutions are an important determinant of FDI. For countries such as Hungary and Costa Rica, these were key determinants of FDI. For some nondemocratic countries such as Malaysia, the investment promotion agency explained the electoral process and Malaysia's political system and argued that it is democratic. Other authoritarian regimes in the sample did point out the level of political stability or contract law, but at no point did they highlight their political system as a positive for multinational investors. Democratic countries were quick to point out their political institutions; authoritarian countries either claimed they were democracies or simply argued that these specific political institutions were not of central importance. No investment promotion agency made any claims that nondemocratic institutions were conducive to FDI.

Third, there is limited support for the impact of federalism and subnational policies affecting FDI. Most agencies argued that multinationals preferred the "one-stop shop" model where multinationals only had to manage relations with the central government. Some agencies did highlight how subnational governments quite often would ally with multinationals to push for favorable national policies, although this evidence was less systematic than the importance of democracy for multinationals. No investment promotion agency made claims about the number of veto points in the political system as an important determinant of FDI.

Fourth, most of the countries in my sample are either currently under an IMF agreement or have been under an IMF agreement in recent years. These investment promotion agencies held nuanced views of the role of IMF policies on FDI inflows. No agency made the claim that IMF agreements, and the conditions imposed with these agreements, had a positive impact on FDI. Most agencies argued that these were not serious considerations for investors. The exceptions are two countries with recent financial crises, Brazil and Malaysia. Interviews with the Brazilian central bank and representatives from the Brazilian stock exchange confirm that access to IMF capital was an important consideration for multinationals, although the specific conditions were not important. The agency responsible for investment promotion in Malaysia argued that Malaysia's decision to not take an IMF package after the 1998 financial crisis actually was viewed as the correct strategy by multinationals. In both cases, the evidence suggests that IMF capital can be important, but IMF conditions have no impact (Brazil) or a potentially negative impact (Malaysia) on FDI inflows.

I also interviewed representatives at political risk assessment and insurance organizations.[19] These interviews also provided more evidence on the causal mechanism linking specific political institutions to higher FDI flows. These organizations, such as the World Bank's Multilateral Investment Guarantee Agency (MIGA), Canada's Export Promotion Canada (EPC), and the U.S. Overseas Private Investment Corporation (OPIC), both engage in political risk assessment and provide political risk insurance. In their political risk models, which predict government expropriations, political violence, and government restrictions on capital flows, political institutions are important. In most models, established democracies are predicted to have lower political risks than most other types of political systems.

These interviews were relatively silent in terms of subnational politics. All interviews confirmed that counting the number of veto players had no real impact on political risks, while the evidence was murky on the impact of federalism on FDI inflows. Generally these agencies either ignored subnational politics, arguing that they were not central to political risk, or argued that federalism was a complex institutional structure, in some cases decreasing political risks and in other cases increasing political risks.

None of these models have formal measures of the number of veto players, nor specific conditions on IMF loans. They do, however, consider good relations with the IMF as an important determinant; for example, EDC argues this is a possible predictor of exchange rate controls, but it is flows of capital for crisis-prone countries that is important, not conditions. None of the models specifically examined the details of IMF conditionality.

As a further exploration of the causal mechanisms in this book, I interviewed representatives from three companies that provide plant location consultation. These consultants specialize in helping multinationals select sites for foreign investments. In most cases, consultants highlight that tax rates and tax incentives are not decisive factors for multinational investments, while political risks can have an important impact on multinationals' decisions. Interviews with representatives of these location consultants further support the empirical evidence presented in this book and highlight the causal mechanisms linking democracy and federalism to higher FDI inflows, and how IMF programs are often associated with lower FDI inflows.

Finally, I interviewed representatives from a number of multinationals firms that engage in activities in both developed and developing countries. These multinationals are large and small firms, representing a number of industries. Table 1.2 provides a list of the multinationals contacted, their industry and main product line. Interviews with key decision makers, company presidents, and public relations staff both support the empirical findings in this book and provide detailed evidence on how political institutions affect FDI inflows. None of the multinationals interviewed highlighted tax rates or tax incentives as the primary motivation for investment decisions. In many cases, tax rates had essentially no role in their investment decisions.

Numerous representatives of multinationals highlighted the benefits of investing in democracies, and no multinational made any claim that nondemocratic regimes provide a more conducive investment environment. Many multinationals, such as Alcan, simply stated that demo-

TABLE 1.2.
Multinationals Interviewed

Company	Sector	Main Product
Alcan	Manufacturing	Aluminum Products
Citigroup	Service	Financial Services
Daimler Chrysler	Manufacturing	Automobiles
Inamed	Manufacturing	Medical Devices
Intel	Manufacturing	Semiconductors
L. L. Bean	Service	Textiles
Multi-mix	Manufacturing	Electronics
Weststar	Manufacturing	Contract Manufacturing
UBS	Service	Financial Services

Note: All interviews were conducted by the author with representatives of the national promotion agencies, with the exception of Brazil and Bolivia. For Brazil I interviewed an Investor Relations representative at the Central Bank of Brazil. For Bolivia I interviewed B-G Consulting, the company that facilitated a number of major investment promotions for Bolivia.

cratic governments provide lower risk environments. Other firms, such as Intel, articulated that their best insurance against adverse policy changes is to exert influence over the policy process. In systems where lobbying or other means of formal influence are most effective, usually in democratic systems, Intel is exposed to lower political risks.

Interview evidence on the role of veto players and federalism is a bit more mixed. No representative argued that the number of veto players in a system lowered political risks for the firm. Conversely, some multinationals did highlight the importance of local and regional governments in lobbying on behalf of the firm. This evidence was less systematic than the evidence linking democracy to lower political risks.

Finally, none of the multinationals argued that IMF conditionality helped reduce political risks or ensured a more favorable macroeconomic environment. Some firms, such as UBS, argued that IMF capital can be important, but IMF conditions are often aimed at performance targets and not appropriate policies. For many firms, IMF programs had little impact on perceptions of political risk. In chapter 7, I provide more details on these interviews.

1.11 Conclusions

The findings presented in this book, when incorporated with the existing work on FDI, provide an explanation of the distribution of foreign direct investment across countries. The empirical results point to the importance of political institutions on the political risks associated with foreign direct investment. These political institutions have massive effects on inflows of foreign direct investment. Understanding these political factors verifies comprehending the magnitude of the investments from multinationals. From a public policy perspective this book maps out the types of institutional arrangements most conducive to FDI.

These findings, while cumulatively adding to our general understanding of FDI flows, also debunks some myths of political institutions' effects on FDI. First, I show that government fiscal policy does not significantly determine FDI inflows. Government levels of spending and taxation affect FDI inflows in only marginal ways.

The relationship between multinationals and authoritarian regimes stands as another myth prevalent in public policy debates. Although the logic that multinationals prefer to bargain with dictators may have some conceptual appeal, a number of reasons exist why multinationals would prefer to invest in democratic regimes. Empirically the results prove rather conclusive—democracies attract more FDI.

A third myth relates to the market-preserving nature of federal institutions. As academic scholars debate the benefits of fiscal decentralization, and the World Bank pushes for fiscal decentralization in the developing world, the importance of more clearly understanding the effects of federalism on macroeconomic performance becomes even more important. This book stresses that the exact definition of federalism becomes central in more clearly understanding these effects. More specifically, the extensive focus on fiscal federalism and fiscal decentralization has overlooked the importance of political federalism.

Finally, and perhaps most timely in terms of public policy, the International Monetary Fund's role on macroeconomic performance needs examining. Recent debates have analyzed the effects of the IMF on long-run economic growth and short-term, portfolio capital flows. This study focuses on the nature of IMF programs on long-term, FDI inflows. These FDI inflows become important mechanisms for economic development and serve as an important barometer on the future of the economy. Essentially, by understanding how firms react to the signing of IMF agreements, we can examine how firms perceive the future of the economy. The empirical results in this book find that IMF programs lead to lower levels of FDI inflows.

2

Multinational Firms and Domestic Governments

2.1 Introduction

This book focuses on one of the most stable and economically important of the international capital flows, foreign direct investment (FDI).[1] These private capital flows are investments from a parent firm to a location outside of the parent firm's host nation; they consist of equity capital, intercompany debt, and reinvested earnings. An investment becomes a foreign *direct* investment, as opposed to portfolio investment, if it gives the parent firm some amount of control over the management of the enterprise, usually over 10 percent of the firm.[2] Companies use FDI, unlike portfolio investments, over long time horizons and generally not for speculative purposes, but rather to serve domestic markets, exploit natural resources, or provide platforms to serve world markets through exports.

A common form of FDI in developing countries is "greenfield investments" where multinational corporations construct subsidiaries in foreign markets from the ground up. These firms choose between locations across the globe, providing the financial capital and managerial know-how to establish a subsidiary. These greenfield investments can be made in virtually any industry, from manufacturing, to agriculture, to mining, to services.

Medical technology producer Medtronic's decision to construct a production facility in Tolochenaz, Switzerland, in 1995 is one example of manufacturing greenfield investment. Medtronic, the world's leading pacemaker producer, had established a presence in Europe since the mid-1960s and wanted to expand their production capacity beyond the existing production facilities. Fourteen months after Medtronic made the decision to invest in Switzerland, they had financed, designed, and completed the final production facility.[3]

"Brownfield investments" comprise a second form of FDI, very common in developed countries. These investments exist in established firms, through mergers and acquisitions, or through privatization programs. This form of FDI proves traditionally more common in developed nations, where large multinationals gain access to foreign markets by purchasing existing companies. More recently, a number of middle-income countries have attracted this form of FDI due to the privatization programs of former communist economies and Latin American nations.

In many locales, both types of multinational investments have been on the rise. In Eastern Europe, for example, multinational automotive producers have flocked to invest in existing state-run enterprises and to establish new production facilities. Auto giant Volkswagen (VW), for example, attempted both to expand auto production for Eastern European consumers and to take advantage of the potential to use Eastern European production to help supply world demand for autos. In the early 1990s, VW acquired the giant Czech auto firm Skoda and constructed a new Audi production facility in Hungary.

2.2 Multinationals and Multinational Investments

Multinational corporations play a major role in the world economy. Today over 63,000 multinational corporations own almost 700,000 foreign affiliates in virtually every nation in the world. Experts value the current stock of world FDI at well over $5 trillion and estimate annual trade of $3 trillion in goods and services. Taken together—both the parent firms and the foreign affiliates—multinationals account for one-quarter of the world's GDP (UNCTAD 2000). The importance of multinationals, and multinational investments (FDI), therefore, remains obvious.

The direct and growing significance of foreign direct investment on capital accumulation, the driver of economic growth in neoclassical economics, looms large and continues to grow. International capital flows have increasingly become dominated by flows of private capital. In 1990, 44 percent of all international capital flows were private; by 1996, 85 percent, and FDI stood as the largest single type of flow.[4]

Foreign direct investment has generally outpaced international trade, where FDI grew at an average rate of 13 percent per year from 1980 to 1997, as compared to an annual 7 percent growth rate for exports.[5] This trend of FDI outpacing exports continues to widen; in 1998 and 1999, FDI flows grew at an explosive rate of 25 percent and 28 percent respectively.

This comparison between multinational production and world trade may prove unfair. Most analysts estimate that a full 30 percent of world trade actually takes place within firms (Markusen 1995). When Ford imports components from a subsidiary in Germany, these statistics count as German exports and U.S. imports. FDI not only has been growing faster than international trade, it may even drive the growth of trade.

Even in all of its dynamic growth, FDI remains one of the most stable of all private capital flows. In the wake of the East Asian crisis, international capital flows plunged over 14 percent, decreasing the total to emerging markets from 11 percent of world capital flows in 1997 to 4.5 percent by 1999 (World Bank 2000, 21–22). During this same time period, FDI flows to developing countries remained relatively stable and showed some increases in 1999 and 2000. The total share of developing country FDI increased from 21 percent in 1991 to 36 percent in 1997, dipping back to 25 percent in 1998. This decline in the total share of FDI stemmed not from decreased FDI flows in developing countries, but from increased FDI flows between the developed countries in the merger mania of the late 1990s (World Bank 2000).

In 2001 and 2002, FDI flows declined as the advanced economies (mainly the United States, Japan, and the nations of the European Union) battled regressions and had large decreases in FDI outflows. This greatly reduced the global pool of FDI, leading to a decline in FDI inflows in most developing countries (UNCTAD 2003). Even with this global contraction, some countries, such as China and Ireland, continued to attract massive FDI inflows.

Even though FDI has ebbed and flowed over time, some interesting long-term trends are obvious. Figure 2.1 shows the average levels of FDI as a percentage of GDP for high-income countries, middle-income countries, low-income countries, and all countries averaged. For all sets of countries FDI showed solid growth since the early 1980s, only to explode in the early 1990s. The high-income countries, both the main recipients and the main suppliers of global FDI, have followed the world mean, averaging FDI inflows of roughly 0.5 percent of GDP in the early 1970s, surging to 1 percent in the 1980s, and topping off over 2 percent at the end of the 1990s.

Middle-income countries followed a similar trend, only with increased levels of FDI. These countries started attracting FDI flows more readily than the high-income countries (as a percentage of GDP) in the 1970s, and separated even further from the high-income countries by the 1990s. By the end of the 1990s, these middle-income countries attracted FDI flows at a magnitude of over 3 percent of GDP.

Most startling has been the growth of FDI inflows to the low-income countries of the world. Official FDI statistics did not even include many of these countries in the early 1970s, and they only really began attracting significant amounts since the 1980s.[6] In the early 1990s the importance of FDI flows exploded, increasing from considerably less than 1 percent of GDP in 1990 to around 3 percent of GDP by 1995.

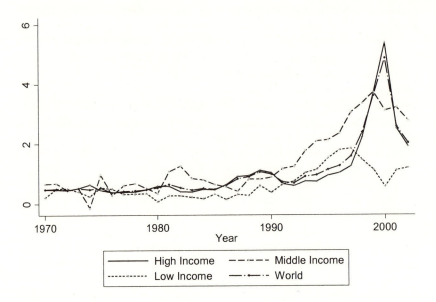

Figure 2.1. Net FDI inflows (% GDP)

These FDI figures are still small in currency value, but as a percentage of the domestic economies of these countries, FDI is a significant source of capital.

FDI flows have not only grown, they have outpaced domestic savings. By the end of the 1990s, FDI flows accounted for a full 7 percent of investment in most countries. For the low- and middle-income countries the sheer magnitude appears stunning. Investments from multinationals now account for roughly 10 percent of investment in low-income countries and almost 14 percent in middle-income countries. FDI has clearly made a tremendous impact on all countries.

Although FDI has become increasingly important for both developed and developing countries alike, large differences remain in the actual distribution of FDI between countries. For example, why did Malaysia succeed in enticing investments such as Korea's Wooribyul Telecommunications Company LTD in moving its headquarters from the Philippines, or Boeing its Southeast Asian headquarters? Why did Microsoft choose Brazil for a major game manufacturing facility, when traditionally it produced this software in the United States, Korea, and Taiwan? Why did General Electric and Hewlett-Packard choose India for call processing and accounting centers?

This empirical puzzle is best documented in the UNCTAD World Investment Report (UNCTAD 2003). As global FDI flows declined in

2001 and 2002, vast differences across regions became apparent. FDI flows to Africa, already very small compared to other regions of the world, declined 41 percent from $19 billion in 2001 to $11 billion in 2002, or from 2.3 percent of world FDI flows to 1.7 percent (UNCTAD 2003, 33). These regional figures mask the tremendous variation across countries in Africa, where the majority of countries, thirty of fifty-three Sub-Saharan African countries, actually attracted higher FDI inflows in 2002 than in 2001 (UNCTAD 2003, 34). Countries such as Angola, Chad, and Equatorial Guinea attracted massive oil investments; countries such as Botswana, Kenya, Lesotho, and Mauritius attracted FDI in export-oriented textiles; and South Africa attracted manufacturing investments. Other countries, specifically those plagued by civil conflict, attracted very little FDI.

In 2002, FDI flows also declined in Asia and the Pacific, but by much more modest amounts (a decline from $107 billion to $95 billion from 2001 to 2002). Once again, this minor decline hides the massive variation in FDI performance across countries. Of the fifty-seven countries in the region, the top ten attracted 93 percent of the region's FDI, led by massive FDI inflows into China and Singapore (UNCTAD 2003, 40). Some countries, such as Kazakhstan, attracted natural resource–seeking FDI; China continued to draw in market-seeking FDI, while India and Malaysia attracted export-oriented FDI.

These figures are slightly perplexing. Why did multinationals choose to increase export-oriented investments in Malaysia (FDI flows increased over 400 percent), while cutting back FDI investments in Bangladesh? Why does China's market of over one billion people attract market-seeking FDI while India's similarly massive market attracts little market-seeking FDI?

Similar issues arise in attempting to understand FDI patterns to Latin America. With decreases in world FDI flows, domestic financial crises, and political instability, Latin America saw FDI flows plummet to $56 billion, the lowest level since 1996 (UNCTAD 2003, 52). Some of the largest economies—Brazil, Argentina, and Chile—saw large decreases in FDI flows. Most of the countries in the region (29 of the 40 countries) saw decreases in FDI flows. Some of these decreases in FDI flows were due to a decline in service-based investments (Argentina, Brazil, and Chile), some due to decreases in natural resource investments (Venezuela), while some countries saw large decreases in manufacturing FDI (Mexico).

Some exceptions remain. Costa Rica, already a major recipient of a number of large FDI projects, increased FDI inflows by 41 percent (UNCTAD 2003, 53). Even in this scarce FDI environment, Costa Rica attracted major multinational projects in medical devices, services, and electronics manufacturing.[7] Many of these investments were expansions of existing FDI projects. For example, advanced manufacturing firms such as Intel and Multimix expanded production facilities with new capital investments in cutting-edge manufacturing and research and development facilities.[8]

In Central and Eastern Europe, FDI inflows are dominated by the top five performers—the Czech Republic, Poland, Slovakia, the Russian Federation, and Slovenia. These countries generally maintained their FDI position (Russia) or saw massive increases in FDI inflows (Czech Republic, Slovakia, and Slovenia) in 2002. Although over half of the nineteen countries in the region, such as Hungary and Croatia, saw FDI decreases, FDI flows into the region actually increased in 2002.

Although FDI flows into developing countries are important sources of finance, FDI flows remain dominated by the developed countries. Even with a 22 percent decline in FDI in 2002, FDI flows into the developed countries measured a massive $460 billion (UNCTAD 2003, 68). Tiny Luxembourg became the world's largest FDI recipient, propelled by a number of massive mergers and acquisitions. France and Germany attracted the second and third most FDI, while the United States slipped to fourth place after FDI into the United States fell 80 percent. Other important destination countries, such as the Netherlands and the United Kingdom, also saw massive drops in FDI inflows.

Explanations for this distribution of FDI flows are either nonexistent or generally ad hoc. This study explores how political institutions help explain these cross-country variations in FDI inflows. Before we examine these political institutions, we should have a better understanding of the significance of foreign direct investment.

2.3 The Positive Effects of Multinationals

Scholars studying the impact of multinational corporations argue that foreign direct investment can have the following positive impacts on domestic economies:

2.3.1 Productivity and Technology Spillovers

The figures cited previously on the magnitude of FDI flows obscure a more important element of FDI flows—the role of multinational production in transferring technology. The potential for technological transfer readily appears if one examines the characteristics of most multinational firms. "Multinationals tend to be important in industries and firms with four characteristics," according to Markusen (1995), "high levels of R&D relative to sales; a large share of professional and technical workers in their workforce; products that are new and/or technically complex; and high levels of product differentiation and advertising. These characteristics appear in many studies, and I have never seen any of them contradicted in any study."[9] Investments by these technologically advanced firms may translate directly into growth-promoting technical advances for the host nation.[10]

In a literature review on effects of FDI on host countries, Blomstrom and Kokko argue that multinational corporations transfer technology through formal (either passive or active) mechanisms. Formal active mechanisms, such as joint ventures or licensing agreements, often have explicit technology-sharing agreements, or at least entail the multinational introducing new technologies used in joint production. Formal passive mechanisms, such as the establishment of linkages between firms and individuals with technological expertise, remain less obvious. Blomstrom and Kokko explain:

> For instance, linkage effects can take place between firms in different countries, like when exporters learn from the feedback they receive from their multinational customers abroad, but perhaps even stronger when they arise between local firms and MNC affiliates operating in the same country (as will be seen in the ensuing discussion of spillovers). Similarly, many informal transfers where MNCs have a passive role—those that come about as a result of any kind of personal contact with people who know about MNC's technologies—are obviously facilitated by the presence of foreign affiliates (1997, 4).

Empirical studies attempt to examine the actual role of FDI in technology transfer. Scholarship by Barrel and Pain (1999) finds that for four industrialized European countries, a 1 percent increase in FDI, boosted technological progress by 0.18 percent. In another study, De Mello (1999) uses time-series-cross-sectional data for fifteen OECD countries and seventeen non-OECD countries from the period 1970–1990 and finds that FDI does increase growth, but the growth-enhancing effects depend on the level of technological backwardness. For the less advanced countries, FDI proves more productive than domestic investment.

These are just a few examples of the extensive literature available on the topic. A number of studies find little evidence for the productivity-enhancing impact of FDI, while some find large impacts on domestic productivity.[11] This thicket of competing results becomes more clear when one differentiates between horizontal, forward, and backward spillovers. Horizontal spillovers are technological spillovers from the multinationals to other firms in the same industry. Forward spillovers are spillovers to industries or firms consuming the products made by

the multinational. Backward spillovers occur when multinationals induce higher productivity or share technology with suppliers.

In an important recent contribution, Javorcik (2004) argues that multinationals have strong incentives to protect trade secrets and technology, limiting technological spillovers to rivals in the same industry. Javorcik argues that technological spillovers are most likely to be found
in backward and forward linkages. In an empirical study of FDI to
Lithuania, Javorcik finds strong evidence for increases in productivity
through backward linkages.

2.3.2 Exports

Although the direct effects of FDI on capital accumulation and technological transfers remain the most important economically, other economic and political effects of FDI should not be overlooked. FDI con-
centrates most often in export sectors, generating foreign exchange for
the host nation.

This link between trade and FDI deserves closer examination. A pil-
lar of the theory of international trade, the Heckscher-Olin-Samuelson
model, predicts that international trade and capital will serve as perfect substitutes.[12] Numerous authors have attacked the assumptions of
this model, generating substantially different results. In many of these
new models, a positive link exists between the level of international
investment and trade (Kemp 1966; Jones 1967; Purvis 1972; Markusen
1983; Svensson 1984; Markusen and Svensson 1985). A number of empirical tests validate the link, however complex, between higher levels
of investment and trade (Goldberg and Klein 1998, 1999).

Recent models described as "new trade theory" made the largest advances in this field. These models increasingly abandon the simplistic
assumptions of the earlier models, allowing for a more rich analysis of
international trade. Contributions, such as Ethier and Markusen (1996),
examine more generally the mode of entry of multinationals, whether
through international trade, FDI, or licensing agreements. As Ethier
and Markusen (1996, 2) state: "the new trade theory emphasizes just
those features that appear to be central to multinationals: economies
of scale, imperfect competition, strategic considerations, and technological change and diffusion."

Along with these theoretical and empirical studies, casual observation also leads us to a mixed and complex view of FDI's role in increasing exports. In a recent study on FDI in Latin America, multinationals
had very different effects on the export position of Mexico, Argentina,
Chile, and Colombia.[13] In Mexico, FDI concentrated in manufacturing
industries designed for export, such as the automotive industry, and

local firms supplied them. Although FDI had a major impact on the export position of Mexico, the impact was more modest in Argentina. A large quantity of FDI investment in Argentina served the domestic market, having no impact on the export position of the country. In Chile and Colombia, FDI flooded into natural resources: mining in Chile and oil and mining in Colombia. Although these industries generate exports, there is little evidence to indicate that the purchase of these resources by multinationals has greatly increased the volume of exports beyond that of what local owners would have done.

In most of these studies multinational production seldom serves as a substitute for international trade.[14] At the same time, FDI does not always coincide with higher levels of country exports. Multinationals attempting to serve the domestic market often do not impact country exports, while multinational production in the natural resource sector remains mixed. Multinationals can often just take over existing operations of firms already using natural resources or may be associated with large capital investments in natural resource industries, leading to booms in natural resource production and natural resource exports.[15] In any case, multinationals have the ability, in many circumstances, to greatly increase exports for the host country.

2.3.3 Employment

FDI provides jobs for host countries. Multinational enterprises employ some 70 million workers, with 22 million of these jobs in foreign subsidiaries (OECD 1995, 10). In the OECD, FDI accounts for roughly 2 percent of total employment (OECD 1995, 12). FDI also generates employment through the indirect effects on the economy, such as domestic industries emerging to complement the new foreign firms (OECD 1995, Markusen and Venables 1999).

This employment creation component is often concentrated regionally. Multinationals invest in production facilities in specific locations, generating employment in the surrounding community. National governments recognize this and attempt to use incentives to channel multinational investment into areas that enjoy less economic development.

The importance of employment generation is both obvious to the casual observer and an issue mentioned by most investment promotion agencies. Most investment promotion agencies articulate the importance of targeting multinationals for capital and specific types of job creation. For Canada and Hungary, investment promotion agencies attempted to maximize the high-technology jobs used to serve the NAFTA and EU market respectively. All investment promotion agencies listed job creation as a primary concern.

2.3.4 *Economic Growth*

These individual positive effects of FDI all translate into higher levels of economic growth, especially when combined with other domestic conditions. The most obvious mechanism emerges through the expansion and deepening of a nation's capital stock, leading to economic growth based on neoclassical growth models.[16] In these models, the value of FDI hinges on decreasing returns to capital. In capital-abundant countries, FDI should have only a small impact on economic growth.

Romer (1986) proposes a deeper model of the role of capital on economic growth, arguing that capital should not be viewed simply as a factor of production, but as "knowledge." In Romer's theory, firms invest in private capital (knowledge), inadvertently leading to an increase in the public pool of knowledge. Under this theory, capital could lead to increasing returns to scale, where rich, technologically advanced countries can continue to sustain high levels of economic growth.

The most promising research explores how FDI interacts with existing domestic conditions and institutions. Balasubramanyam, Salisu, and Sapsford (1996) find that FDI contributes most effectively to growth in countries following export promotion strategies. Balasubramanyam, Salisu, and Sapsford (1999) discovered that FDI has a large positive effect on growth, especially strong in countries with a minimum level of human capital. Many of these studies have appeared very recently and leave many questions unanswered, but they do point to the need for a closer examination of the effects of foreign capital flows on domestic political and economic factors.

Balasubramanyam et al. (1999) summarize this vast literature on FDI and economic growth, noting:

> Although there is no consensus, the following appear to be the factors identified in the literature on FDI.
>
> (a) FDI is a composite bundle of capital, know-how, and technology.
>
> (b) Its main contribution to growth is through technology transfer and technology and skill diffusion in the countries importing FDI.
>
> (c) The effectiveness of FDI in promoting growth is, among other things, a function of the type of trade regime in place in the host country. FDI in the presence of a protectionist regime is likely to immizerize growth, whereas a liberal trade regime is likely to promote growth.
>
> (d) Most empirical studies suggest that foreign-owned firms in comparable industry groups exhibit superior productive efficiency relative to that of locally owned firms, on most criteria of efficiency. But whether or not the social rate of return to FDI is on par with the private rate of return is a matter of dispute.[17]

Intel's investment in a microchip processing facility in Costa Rica in the mid-1990s exemplifies the potential impact of FDI projects on national economies. Intel, a company that boasted sales in 1996 three times larger than Costa Rica's GDP, originally pledged a $300 million investment that grew to an estimated $500 million by 1998.[18] At full capacity, this plant promised to produce microchip exports that would equal or exceed total exports from Costa Rica. By 1999, production from Intel's plant accounted for over half of the total growth of the Costa Rican economy.[19] Today, Intel remains an important part of the Costa Rican economy, expanding production from microprocessors to "chipsets" for handheld devices and research and development facilities.[20]

2.4 The Critics' View of FDI

Although a growing consensus suggests that FDI flows have positive effects on the national economy, multinationals and their investments often suffer negative portrayals regarding their roles in the global economy. The criticisms can be placed in two camps, one on the direct negative effects of FDI and the other on the negative effects of the competition between countries for FDI.

Dependency theorists have long argued that FDI holds serious negative political and economic consequences. Early versions of dependency theory originally focused exclusively on the lack of bargaining power of developing countries vis-à-vis multinational corporations. Later considered overly simplistic, these early views forced a recasting of dependency theory to account for the variations in success of developing countries in economic development.

Peter Evans's (1979) contribution focused on the potential alliances between local political and economic elites and foreign capital. This "triple alliance" mixed cooperation and conflict, as each set of actors leveraged their power to gain the most from the alliance. The citizens in developing countries stayed outside this alliance and suffered greatly from the distorted policies created by this system.

Other scholars within the dependency theory literature focus on the process of "denationalization," where foreign capital absorbs local assets. Foreign firms exploit profit-making opportunities in developing countries but expatriate the profits to the wealthy host countries. Some scholars such as Gereffi (1983) argue that, even worse, these multinationals also preempt the development of indigenous industries and firms, although this claim remains difficult to test in reality.

Economists and political scientists have harshly criticized the dependency literature. Casual observation shows that multinational corporations have been used in East Asian countries' development strategies, producing dramatic levels of economic growth. Some countries may have fared so poorly because of a failure of development strategies, not the negatives of FDI. As Haggard (1989) states: "Virtually all of the major works in the vein have been drawn from import-substituting manufacturing." Although some of the arguments of dependency do have their merits, these works do not lead us to the conclusion that FDI, in all cases, creates negative political and economic consequences.[21]

More recently, scholars have focused on the effects of the competition for international capital and domestic governance. They now generally recognize that the existence of multinational corporations can have positive effects on the economy (for the reasons stated above) but that the process of attracting FDI can produce a number of substantial costs on governments and their populations.

One example of this is in the United States, where state and local politicians have engaged in bidding wars to attract multinationals, in some cases at a tremendous cost. A recent, glaring example of this was a bidding war between U.S. states to attract a Mercedes-Benz assembly plant, through which Alabama outbid other states, providing a $250 million incentive package that amounted to $168,000 per job created (Mutti 2003, 11).

Academics have highlighted the tensions between government macroeconomic policy and capital mobility.[22] One strand of the literature focuses on governments that want to attract multinationals in today's global economy by slashing government spending and taxation in a race for the neoliberal bottom.[23] In chapter 4 I examine this race to the bottom (RTB) perspective. The central theoretical point made in this chapter asserts that the race to the bottom thesis assumes a degree of capital mobility completely unrealistic when applied to FDI. The study of FDI focuses on the study of imperfect markets (as highlighted below), while the race to the bottom thesis relies on an analogy based on perfect markets. Empirically little support exists for the race to the bottom thesis. As chapter 4 reveals, I find practically no relationship between government spending and taxation and FDI.

2.5 Invitations to Multinationals

In this study I do not explore the positive and negative impacts of FDI for developed or developing countries. Rather, my focus is on the public policy aspect of attracting multinationals. FDI promotion, in any form, has become an important economic development strategy for countries of all economic levels of economic development. The enthusiasm to attract investment seems evident in the rise of government-sponsored marketing campaigns to attract multinationals. In the period between 1991 and 1998 alone, over fifty-eight countries initiated investment promotion programs, joining the forty-eight already using these tactics (Moran 1998, 37).

The Invest in Sweden Agency (ISA) provides one example. This agency answers directly to the Swedish Ministry of Foreign Affairs and is responsible for attracting international investors to Sweden. The agency focuses on special marketing opportunities in the sectors it believes Sweden can best offer to foreign investors. Currently the automotive, call center, direct marketing, food, health care, information technology, microelectronics/software, mineral exploration, and wood processing sectors fit that description. Although the agency's primary responsibility remains disseminating information on business opportunities in Sweden, it also provides free legal assistance and even introduces executives to government officials and business associations.

Some of these investment promotion programs, such as the Austrian Business Agency, have moved from passively attempting to contact interested investors to actively recruiting companies. These recruitment tactics stem from advertising in magazines such as the *Economist* to more targeted individual contact between investment agencies and multinationals that could potentially provide FDI.

One interesting and immensely effective investment promotion agency is the Costa Rican Investment Board (CINDE). This autonomous agency started with a small contribution from the Inter-American Bank to help promote FDI inflows into Costa Rica. This agency remains independent of the central government, drawing resources from this original endowment and private contributions. CINDE serves as a one-stop shop for interested investors, providing executives with tours of existing multinational facilities, arranging meetings with lawyers and government officials, and addressing customs concerns.

Beyond investment promotion, countries have also taken bold steps in the liberalization of the investment regimes, allowing for further penetration of multinationals into domestic markets. The United Nations documented 1,035 worldwide changes in laws governing FDI from 1991 to 1999, where 94 percent of these created a more favorable environment for multinationals. The annual number of positive changes seems staggering, as exhibited in figure 2.2 (UNCTAD 2000). Many of these changes have been in response to international agreements on FDI liberalization as mandated in the EU, NAFTA, WTO and other regional agreements. Whatever the impetus for these

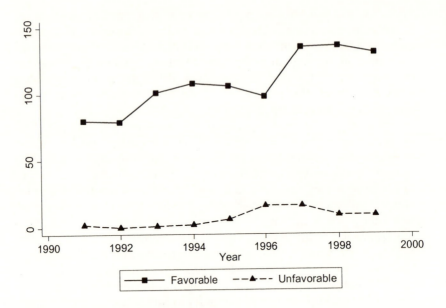

Figure 2.2. Changes in FDI Restrictions

changes, scholars and experts agree that an economy open to FDI remains necessary in the twenty-first century.

The forms of FDI liberalization vary across countries. Different countries have decreased the use of capital controls on FDI inflows, increasingly allowed multinationals into sectors often reserved for domestic firms, opened up privatization programs to foreign firms, and generally enacted laws allowing multinationals treatment that is more similar to that of domestic firms.

The importance of liberal entry conditions has become the most important change in FDI laws. The increasing trend in allowing multinationals greater participation in foreign markets can be seen through the decreased use of capital controls on FDI inflows. Figure 2.3 shows the increasing capital account openness of countries around the globe over time. Since 1973, the average number of countries with a completely open capital account has more than doubled, only decreasing slightly in the wake of the East Asian financial crisis.

This focus on attracting multinational corporations has spread to countries around the world. In Sub-Saharan Africa, an area known for nationalization of multinationals in the 1960s and 1970s, the mood toward FDI shifted from hostility to accommodation. According to one scholar:

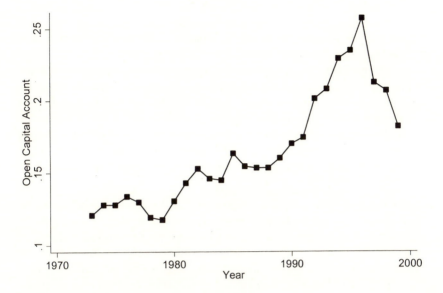

Figure 2.3. Decreasing Restrictions on Capital

During the last decade, most SSA governments have made concerted attempts to improve the investment climate for transnational corporations and other foreign investors. New investment codes have been promulgated that have swept aside many of the restrictions and impediments that had limited FDI in the past, replacing them with a variety of investment incentives and guarantees. These include the freedom to remit profits, the removal of limits on the level of foreign equity, and the granting of work permits for all necessary expatriate personnel. Foreign investors are now actively wooed by senior politicians and government officials. High-profile investment conferences are regularly held both in-country and overseas.[24]

In Argentina, the path toward accommodating multinationals has been a smoother one:

Regulations on FDI were established as early as 1976 to provide equality of rights and obligations with local investors. The regulations permitted incorporation of used capital goods, capitalization of intangibles, profit remittance, and unlimited capital repatriation. Beginning in 1989, prior official approval was no longer required for FDI in the computer industry, telecommunications and electronics. But authorization was still required for FDI in the defense and national security sectors, energy, the communications media, education, insurance, and finance except banks. Meanwhile, the state reform law established the legal framework for the process of privatization of public enterprises through external debt conversion, and it authorized the entry of foreign capital into the program of privatization of sanitation, electricity, gas, telecommunications and postal services.

In September 1993, a new text was approved for the Foreign Investment Law incorporating all these modifications. The new law established no requirement or conditions for profit remittance (and also exempted profit from any specific tax) or capital repatriation. It deregulated various activities still under the prior authorization regimen, authorizing grants of licenses for the exploration of mines and gas and oil fields (without changing the regimen of government ownership), and deregulated the domestic and foreign marketing of crude oils and fuels.[25]

In Hungary, the socialist government in the 1980s partially opened the doors for multinational production. The limiting condition required that the central government attempt to control their balance of payments by ordering firms to acquire "export credits" in order to import raw materials. Essentially, the government forced multinationals to offset the value of any imported goods with exports of final products.[26] For Ford in Hungary, in the early 1980s, this policy meant establishing one plant that provided electronic components for export to other Eastern European markets and another that would import semi-finished goods to produce automobiles for the domestic market. Hungary dropped these policies in the early 1990s, paving the way for even more multinational investment.

Although the forms of policy change toward multinational corporations vary, the direction remains the same. Most countries have increasingly opened their doors to multinationals, attempting to establish policies and institutions conducive to their growth. Many countries in the developed and developing world have begun using investment incentives, such as Ireland providing grants toward start-up costs and research and development. The promotion and targeting of multinational investments has become an important economic development strategy.

2.6 Conclusion

In this chapter I argue that multinational corporations, and their investments (FDI), provide important contributions to the global economy. Although many scholars remain critical of the impact of FDI on domestic economies and societies, a growing consensus exists on the net positive impact of FDI on the macroeconomy. This consensus has led to increased activity by domestic governments to attract multinational corporations. In the following chapter, I argue that domestic political institutions and government policies significantly contribute in attracting these important investments of multinationals.

3

Theory

3.1 Introduction

Ireland, the Celtic Tiger, has harnessed massive amounts of foreign direct investment in recent years. By providing generous tax rates and substantial tax incentives, Ireland has propelled itself from one of the least developed nations in the European Union to one of the most dynamic economies in the world. At the same time, Finland, an example of a social democratic government with strong environmental regulations, strong unions, and less generous tax policies, has consistently ranked as one of the best environments for multinational corporations. Two countries with very different types of policies toward multinationals are perceived as hospitable environments for FDI.

Other sets of countries, similar in very important ways, have vastly differed in their success in attracting FDI. For example, most scholars cite China as attracting many of the world's leading multinationals. These firms want to tap China's vast consumer market. Yet, India, the second largest market in the world, hasn't been nearly as successful in attracting FDI. The Czech Republic and Slovakia, sharing a similar recent political history, have differed quite dramatically in their ability to attract FDI. What explains these differences?

In this chapter I provide a brief overview of the existing literature on the determinants of foreign direct investment. What explains patterns of foreign direct investment flows across the globe? Why do some countries succeed in attracting FDI while other countries struggle to obtain commitments or capital from multinationals?

For example, what explains the recent surge in foreign investment in Russia, a transition economy that holds tremendous political risks for foreign investors? The oil industry comprises much of the FDI flowing into Russia, lending support to economic theories that explain investment patterns by natural resource endowments. Ford and General Motors' recent investments in auto facilities, candy maker Mars's in a Moscow factory, and Frito-Lay's in Russian potato fields remain unexplained, however. What accounts for this recent interest by multinational investors?[1] Do changes in economic conditions spur interest, or do politics and political institutions provide important explanations as well?

The existing literature on the determinants of FDI, mostly in the economics school, has overlooked an important dimension of these determinants. Specifically, this literature underestimates, or fails to estimate, the value of political institutions that can commit to market-friendly policies. I argue that political institutions can be an important component in limiting the "political risks" of investment for multinationals. That is, multinationals investing in large, illiquid projects obtain reasonable assurances about the future policies and performance of the host economy.

Political institutions that exhibit both policy credibility and flexibility provide these assurances to multinationals. These corporations prefer institutions that limit the discretion of the executive to change or reverse decisions, those that have either a direct or an indirect impact on multinationals, and at the same time allow for some degree of policy flexibility.

How do these political institutions work? This chapter, along with the rest of the book, answers this question. In the next section I review the existing literature on the determinants of FDI and argue that previous works have not given adequate attention to FDI's political determinants.

3.2 Existing Theories on the Determinants of FDI Inflows

The growth in the magnitude and importance of FDI flows (either positive or negative) has not been matched with an increased understanding of the actual impetus behind these flows. Although a few broad, systematic studies on this phenomenon exist, the OECD's simple distinction between the "push" and the "pull" factors provides an excellent starting point (OECD 1998). Push factors motivate foreign firms to invest capital abroad. These factors help explain the surges in FDI flows, such as the role of decreasing communication and transportation costs that make international multistage production feasible or recessions in OECD countries decreasing FDI flows in recent years.

Hymer (1976) became one of the first scholars to separate FDI from portfolio investment, sparking a new literature on the determinants of FDI. Investment theory in the neoclassical tradition focused on the behavior of investments in perfect markets, positing that firms invest abroad simply in search of higher returns. Hymer noted that investment flows did not conform to the predictions of the neoclassical models and argued that firms' investments that sought control (FDI) should be separated from other investments (portfolio capital flows).

Contrary to neoclassical theory, he argued that FDI responded to "imperfect markets."

The ensuing boom in academic scholarship on FDI in response to imperfect markets is far too extensive to review in its entirety here; thus, I will only focus on a few of the pinnacle works. Kindleberger (1969) discusses the forms of market imperfections that make FDI possible. These include:

> **1**. Departures from perfect competition in goods markets, including product differentiation, special market skills, retail price maintenance, and administered pricing.
>
> **2**. Departures from perfect competition in factor markets, including the existence of patented or unavailable technology, of discrimination in access to capital, and of difference in skills of managers organized into firms rather than hired in competitive markets.
>
> **3**. Internal and external economies of scale, the latter being taken advantage of by vertical integration.
>
> **4**. Government limitations on output and entry. (Kindberger 1969, 14)

Although a considerable debate flourishes within the literature, the works of Caves (1971), Aliber (1971), and Dunning (1971) all focused on this general imperfect markets approach.[2]

John Dunning's OLI framework offers the paradigmatic theory of the multinational firm's investment decisions, where MNEs invest internationally for reasons of ownership, location, and internalization.[3] Firms have *ownership advantages* when they have access to some asset or process that provides leverage over existing firms in the foreign market. These can be physical in the sense of patented products or production processes as in the case of pharmaceuticals, or more intangible, such as Nike and Coca-Cola's global brand name recognition. Multinational firms invest abroad to exploit these firm-specific advantages in foreign markets to secure higher returns.

Firms may also be motivated to look abroad because of *locational advantages*. They may invest in production facilities or service in foreign markets because transportation costs restrict serving these markets through exports. This result could either be directly related to the actual nature of the good or service—being a high bulk item or a service that needs to be provided on site—or due to policy factors such as tariff rates, import restrictions, or issues of market access that make physical investment advantageous over serving the market through exports. For example, multinational banks such as Citigroup enter foreign markets by establishing physical bank locations in foreign markets. Auto manufacturers, such as Toyota, established production facilities in the

U.S. to avoid U.S. tariffs, quotas, and voluntary export restraint on Japanese automobiles.

Locational advantage can also be related to the actual endowments of the host location, either a rich source of natural resources or a high-quality, low-cost labor force. Oil company investments in Nigeria and Kazakhstan are the most obvious examples. Less obvious are companies that require energy-intensive manufacturing processes, such as aluminum manufacturer Alcan; such firms make location decisions based on access to inexpensive power either directly through local power distributors or through the construction of hydroelectric power generators.

An *internalization advantage* provides the third and most complex factor, according to Dunning. While the other two OLI factors highlight reasons why firms would move production to a foreign location, they do not point to why a firm would forgo licensing a foreign producer to make the item. A multinational could simply provide the technology needed for the production process and the blueprints for the product to a local firm. This concept of internalization advantage captures the specific motivations for a firm manufacturing the product within the organization itself in a foreign location.

Closely related to Dunning's work, other scholars have developed a number of theoretical models to explain firms' decisions to invest abroad. These models can be roughly classified as theories based on "vertical" firms, "horizontal" firms, and the "knowledge capital model" of multinational firms.[4] Vertical firms separate activities by the level of capital intensity, producing different goods and services at different physical locations (Helpman 1984). Although an important contribution to the understanding of multinationals' investment decisions, theories based on vertical multinationals fail to account for the existence of firms replicating the production of the same goods and services in different physical locations.

Markusen (1984) explains this pattern of replicating production by creating a model of "horizontal firms" with firm-level economies of scale that integrate horizontally across national borders.[5] Markusen's (1997) knowledge-capital model weaves these horizontal models into the existing vertical models of multinational firms. In this framework, multinational firms can produce the same product or service in multiple locations (horizontal) or geographically separate their firm's headquarters from the production location (vertical).

Although the OLI framework and the horizontal/vertical/knowledge-capital models of multinationals all remain strong tools to understand the motivations for MNE foreign investment, they still doesn't provide answers for one of the more important questions of international development: which *countries* attract foreign direct investment? Foreign direct investment remains a firm-level decision, but countries have differed in their abilities to attract it. The question remains, what characteristics do these countries exhibit that affect FDI inflows?

Although most of the attention on FDI determinants focuses on economic decisions at the firm level, economic and political analysis at a macro level enjoys some attention as well.[6] Some theoretical and empirical work exists on the relationship between economic policy and foreign direct investment, especially in terms of trade and tariff policy (Bhagawati et al. 1992; Blonigen and Fennstra 1996; Ellingsen and Wärneryd 1999).[7] Henisz (2000, 2002) argues that multinational corporations choose their entrance strategy in order to minimize political risks. In countries with a high number of veto players, firms have more confidence in the stability of government policy. In systems with fewer veto players, firms remain open to government actions targeted at expropriating the firms' assets or income streams. To minimize these political risks, firms choose to enter these markets via joint ventures.

Tax rates and international capital provide another area of research that has received more attention lately. The argument assumes that capital mobility forces governments to lower capital taxation rates in order to attract foreign investors.[8] The empirical literature on this topic remains divided, with some theorists arguing that corporations are now more sensitive to tax rates in their investment decisions (Altshuler 2001) while others find that tax rates have no significant effect on international investment.[9]

One recent study conducted by the Multilateral Investment Guarantee Agency and Deloitte & Touche directly surveys multinationals on the most critical location decision factors. The top five factors, in order of the number of respondents claiming these are "very influential" in site selection, are: access to customers (77 percent of respondents), a stable social and political environment (64 percent), ease of doing business (54 percent), reliability and quality of infrastructure and utilities (50 percent), and the ability to hire technical professionals (39 percent) (MIGA 2002, 19). National tax rates ranked eleventh (29 percent of respondents) and local taxes tied for fourteenth (24 percent).

In the transition economics of Eastern/Central Europe and the former Soviet Union, Jensen (2002) finds that the level of economic reform (as measured by economic transition indexes by the European Bank for Reconstruction and Development) and the level of administrative corruption (as measured by an extensive World Bank survey on "state capture") significantly determine FDI inflows. In a related article, Jensen (2003b) argues that the population's socioeconomic conditions, specifically its susceptibility to poverty, predict the level of economic reform achieved by transition countries. Taken together, this body of research stresses how socioeconomic factors, and social forces, affect flows of foreign direct investment.

Other studies have highlighted the effects of direct labor costs,[10] political stability,[11] and host country legislation that affect FDI.[12] Even with this body of literature on the determinants of FDI, the literature remains relatively disjointed and fail to explore how political risks affect FDI inflows. This chapter attempts to link the empirical and theoretical scholarship on the determinants of FDI and incorporate the role of democratic governance into this body of work. In the empirical chapters of the book I use a core baseline model of FDI inflows.[13] This model includes:

- Past FDI inflows
- Size of the domestic market
- Economic growth
- Level of trade
- Level of economic development

Past FDI inflows are important in that they both can provide important networks of suppliers and distributors in developing countries, and they can serve as signals to multinationals about the business environment. For example, representatives of the Thailand investment promotion agency assure multinationals about the low level of political risk in Thailand by citing the number of other multinationals that are both present and still investing in Thailand. Past FDI serves as a signal to potential investors on the investment climate in Thailand.

The size of the domestic market and the economic growth rates are both important considerations for market-seeking multinationals. Large and growing consumer markets should be preferred for multinationals. The level of trade can also be an important determinant of multinationals' investment decisions. As trade complements FDI, countries that are open to the world economy should be more inviting to export-seeking multinationals.

Finally, the level of economic development can be an important determinant of FDI inflows. The Solow (1956) growth model assumes that capital exhibits decreasing returns. Thus, capital should flow from capital-rich countries to capital-poor countries. Empirically, most FDI flows between rich countries, while very little capital flows to the poorest economies of the world. In the empirical section I explore how the level of economic development affects FDI inflows, after I control for other economic and political factors.

3.3 The Importance of Political Risk and Policy Change

Vernon (1971) identified the "obsolescing bargaining" nature of FDI, where multinational investment remains mobile ex ante, yet relative immobile ex post. It behooves governments to make promises to multinationals, but once the multinationals have sunk their investment, governments have the incentive to renege on the contracts. Governments may attempt to renegotiate contracts with multinationals (Gatignon and Anderson 1988; Williamson 1996) or to expropriate assets or income streams unilaterally (Kobrin 1984). These political risks color multinationals' investment decisions.

Much of the literature on the determinants of FDI flows focuses on the actual decisions of individual firms. Unfortunately, this literature has not been incorporated into the political risk literature, which has a long, rich history in business and economics.[14] Understanding political risk proves central to understanding foreign direct investment.

Definitions of political risk vary greatly, but the simplest version focuses on how social or political factors affect the profitability of a multinational investment. In common usage, political risk refers to when government policy, political institutions, or any other political factor negatively impacts multinational ownership or operations.

These political risks should not be confused with political instability or government policy change. Political risk contains a probabilistic element, where countries with high levels of risk have greater expectations of political factors adversely affecting the profitability of an investment. Countries with high levels of political instability can have low levels of political risk if this instability does not threaten the operations of foreign firms. Conversely, nations with little or no political instability may have high political risks if there is high probability of political events or government policies that could harm multinationals.

What political factors exist that could negatively affect multinationals? While nationalization and expropriation characterize political risk, it encompasses much more. Kobrin (1982) notes that political risk can be a result of major power shifts (such as in Iran in 1979), but also can stem from ordinary policy making. Robock (1971) classifies these risks as either macro or micro. Macro risks are common to all firms operating in a country; foreign firms tend to attract macro risks, while micro risks plague specific firms or industries.

One example of macro risks are the threats to multinational operations in countries with large-scale political violence. Any multinational operating in this environment, such as Iraq, is at risk. An example of a micro risk is the July 18, 2004, referendum in Bolivia to determine whether the government should reassert its control over the largely foreign-operated oil and gas industries.

Within these sets of micro and macro risks, differentiations exist between risks that affect ownership and those that affect operations (Kobrin 1982). The threat of mass expropriation of all foreign firms exemplifies a macro ownership risk, whereas the possibility of a firm expropriation is a micro ownership risk. Examples of operations risks, such as imposing capital controls (macro) and enacting legislation that affects an industry (micro), also prove important.

While the nationalizations of the 1960s and 1970s often conjure up images of the risks of international investment, these are far from the most common risks. Kobrin (1985) argues that expropriation only commonly occurred in the period from 1968 to 1975.[15] Similarly, MIGA (2004b) analyzed political risk insurance claims from 1971 to 2000 and found that the period 1971–1980 was dominated by transfer risk and expropriation risk, 1981–1990 saw an even larger increase in transfer risks, and 1996–2000 saw modest increases in political violence and war risks.

Most political risks today do not change ownership dramatically, from foreign firms to host governments. Instead, they comprise policy changes that affect operations of a multinational firm.[16] These changes in the policy environment that adversely affect multinationals are commonly referred to as "creeping expropriation."[17] Governments today seldom directly nationalize industries, but often they make attempts to wrestle control or capture income streams from the corporation. Part of this creeping expropriation includes the difficulty of specifying complete contracts. In technology joint ventures, for example, multinationals remain wary of how technological leaks or inadequate enforcement of property rights could threaten an investment. These contracts, even if they are fully enforced, prove difficult to specify given the complexity of writing a contract about assets that have yet to be created and the uncertainty of the pace and scope of technological innovation (Freeman 1982; Mowery and Rosenberg 1989; Oxley 1997). Not only do multinationals have to predict contract enforcement, but they must also handle resolution of disputes over the unspecified elements of the contract itself.

Not all scholars argue that political instability and political risks always have negative consequences on multinational corporations. Kobrin argues that political instability may actually lessen the probability of political risk. For example:

> After the Peronist regime was overthrown in Argentina, the government's attitude toward foreign direct investment became more positive; in fact, pre-

viously expropriated firms were returned to their owners. Similar policy shifts occurred after the demise of Sukarno in Indonesia and the violent overthrow of Allende in Chile. (Kobrin 1982, 37)

In an interesting study, Frynas (1998) finds that Shell Oil Corporation adapted to high levels of political risk in Nigeria, providing high returns on their investment, stemming from an increased entry barrier for other multinationals. Perhaps even more striking, Frynas finds that political turmoil benefits Shell by both deterring new entrants into the Nigerian oil industry and using political instability, specifically terrorist attacks, to limit its liabilities for a number of oil spills in Nigeria.

Although these instances of political risks having a positive impact on multinationals seem to have some validity, the general consensus concludes that political risks have serious negative effects on multinational investments. Numerous studies have found that higher political risks lead to lower returns on equity investments.[18] Higher political risks also affect the types of entry decisions of multinational firms, whether wholly owned subsidiaries, licensing agreements, or joint ventures (Gatignon and Anderson 1988; Murtha 1991; Oxley 1997; Henisz 2000). For example, Colorado-based Teton Petroleum entered the Russian oil industry via joint venture with a Russian company to "avoid the bureaucratic pitfalls" of investing in Russia.[19] Why would Teton Oil invest in the Russian oil industry, rather than Venezuela or Colombia? The answer given by Howard Cooper, CEO of Teton Oil, suggested that investment in Russia actually proves less of a risk than in Venezuela or Colombia.[20]

One extreme contemporary example of political risk can be found in the oil industry's investments in Iraqi oil. On August 21, 2002, Russian government officials held talks with the Iraqi National Congress (INC), the U.S.-backed opposition group to Saddam Hussein, in order to negotiate potential oil investments in the event of the collapse of Hussein's government following a U.S.-led invasion of Iraq. These negotiations focused on future oil investments and concerns of the potential renegotiation of existing oil contracts after the fall of Saddam Hussein's regime. According to Faisal Qaragholi, an official with the INC, "If the deal [oil contract] helps the Iraqi people then it will be carried on, if it does not, it will be renegotiated."[21]

The importance of political risks emerged in numerous interviews with representatives of multinational corporations. For example, Canadian aluminum producer Alcan stressed that their time horizon for investments was upwards of sixty years. Investment site selection includes a long series of studies, starting with preliminary feasibility studies, then more detailed business and engineering studies, then to the executive committee, and finally the decision goes to the board of directors. Although economic factors are important determinants of FDI decisions, the macroeconomic policy framework and political risks are significant determinants as well.

A number of private and multinational political risk analysts and insurers have emerged in recent years. These companies attempt to systematically predict political risks and provide insurance for multinationals. These companies generally break political risks into four components:

1. War and Political Violence
2. Expropriation
3. Breach of Contract
4. Transfers Risk/Inconvertibility.[22]

War and political violence risks are the direct or indirect impacts of political violence, such as civil war, uprisings, or some types of terrorist attacks. The second type of risk, expropriation risk, covers direct nationalization and expropriation of assets. Breach of contract covers a government's failure to fulfill the terms of a contract and some other types of government policy changes that affect income streams and profitability. Finally, transfer risk encompasses the risk of governments restricting capital flows in ways that harm multinational corporations. Usually these risks emerge when developing countries impose capital controls to stem a financial crisis.

Organizations such as the World Bank's Multilateral Investment Guarantee Agency (MIGA), Canada's Export Development Canada (EDC), and the U.S. Overseas Private Investment Corporation (OPIC) all provide political risk insurance for these types of risks in some of the most difficult environments. Unfortunately for multinationals, risk coverage does not cover all types of political risks, and it is expensive.[23] For example, "MIGA prices to risk, and premium rates are decided on a per project basis, usually ranging between 30 and 100 basis points per risk (up to 150 in some cases) per year" (MIGA 2004a, 5). Also, many of these coverages require the multinational to "walk away" from their investment. For example, the EDC requires that for a country to claim their coverage, they must turn over control of the assets to the EDC. In cases where multinationals are severely damaged by a government policy change, they are often forced to either accept the situation as it is or to write off the whole investment. Finally, most organizations require investors bear at least some of the risk, where OPIC, for example, covers a maximum of 90 percent of the investment.

These insurance markets have provided investor protections in some of the highest risk markets, but obviously even with political risk insurance, multinationals are exposed to tremendous risks. Insurance can help minimize these risks, but it is often expensive and incomplete. Countries that can lower these political risks for multinationals, ceteris paribus, will attract more FDI.

In a recent survey of 191 multinationals, MIGA found that many multinationals were very concerned with all of the mentioned aspects of political risk. Most companies were especially concerned with physical security and staff (85 percent of respondents claimed they were "somewhat concerned" about this risk) followed by the concern of war or civil disturbances (78 percent). Reponses varied by the type of FDI. Multinationals invested in manufacturing facilities cited war and civil disturbance as the great perceived risk, followed by physical security, currency inconvertibility, and government refusal or inability to enforce laws. Service sector multinationals were less concerned with civil war and cited physical security and staff as the greatest perceived risks (MIGA 2002, 27). Whatever the particular form of political risk, this survey supports the view that political risks have a large impact on multinationals' operations and investment decisions. The following section explores how political institutions can lower these risks.[24]

3.4 Credible Policy Makers, Dynamic Policy, and Multinational Enterprises

I assert that political institutions that can credibly commit to market-friendly policies will attract higher levels of FDI. This response includes fostering hospitable environments for multinationals and providing a venue for dynamic policy change in response to changing world conditions. Governments and political leaders that can credibly commit to the policy preferences of multinationals will more likely attract higher levels of FDI inflows.

This is not a bold prediction. The literature on political institutions and property rights (North and Weingast 1989; North 1990) offers an interesting and influential body of work related to this theme. Their main line of reasoning is the same. Political institutions that can constrain the predatory nature of rulers will lead to higher levels of economic growth and long-run economic development, and according to Sobel (1999), political institutions stabilize the expectations of foreign investors (in debt markets).

Before testing the relationship between political institutions and FDI, I first explore how public policy affects FDI. In chapter 4, I provide an examination of the effects of government policy on multinational corporations in the OECD. Speaking to two audiences in particular, first, its main purpose demonstrates overemphasis in the literature on the effects of fiscal policy on FDI inflows. Second, I engaged in a public policy debate that directly challenges the existing "race to the bottom" theories on the competition for multinational investments in both developed and developing countries. Scholars argue that the increased competition for multinational corporations drives levels of corporate taxation, environmental standards, and ultimately the benefits to countries, to rock bottom levels.

My argument counters this position, at least in terms of multinational corporations and fiscal policy. Not only has this thesis been overemphasized, it proves simply wrong. Very little evidence emerges that competition for multinational investments leads to a fiscal race to the bottom in the OECD.

In the following three chapters, I examine the impact of three types of political institutions. First, in chapter 5 I make the case that democratic political institutions can provide both the commitment and the credibility to a market-friendly environment. I argue that democratic governments, unlike authoritarian governments, offer mechanisms for multinationals to influence policy and "punish" policy makers for taking positions that would harm multinationals.

Second, in chapter 6 I explore how political institutions that introduce "veto players" in the political system influence the decision of multinational corporations to invest in countries in either the developed or less developed world. I find that the number of veto players has no significant role on FDI inflows. Even though veto players stabilize policies, this stability has two sides. On one hand, it reduces the possibility of major policy changes, allowing multinationals to enter foreign markets and have reasonable expectations on future policies. On the other hand, the political institutions can lock governments into "unfriendly" policy positions for multinationals. Governments may be locked into specific policy positions, when flexibility in policy responses to changing macroeconomic environments could help promote the interests and investments of multinationals. I argue, on the other hand, that certain political institutions may be valuable for multinational investors. As one example of these market-promoting institutions, I focus on the impact of federalism on FDI inflows.

I also examine how international institutions can provide credible commitments to specific reform packages. In particular I focus on the IMF's role in promoting economic reform that would stimulate long-run macroeconomic growth and higher levels of foreign direct investment flows. I argue that IMF programs place conditions on rescue packages, leading governments to recommend macroeconomic reforms and to link future disbursements of loans to enacting policies that make these reforms possible.

On the surface, the IMF and its conditions seem like another example of market-promoting economic reform. This organization "encourages" countries in crisis to enact market reforms. Multinationals, ceteris paribus, would prefer to invest in countries that turn to the IMF for support, rather than to weather the crisis through other means.

In chapter 7 I argue that the institutional structure of the IMF leads the institutions to promote policies not conducive to multinationals (or long-run economic growth). The IMF maintains an important hand in encouraging countries to make deep macroeconomic reforms. These reforms may entail more policy stability for a country in crisis than if the country attempted to deal with the crisis without the help of IMF loans and IMF conditionality. The impact of these policy positions and reforms on a country's macroeconomic performance, however, remains less clear.

I argue that considerable evidence exists that IMF programs, while providing some of the policy stability that veto players offer force countries to take policy positions that actually harm them in the long run. Indeed, the overly contractionary policies promoted by the IMF may have a deleterious effect on the economy. In chapter 7 I show that IMF programs result in lower FDI inflows.

In short, part of the message of this book is simple. Institutions matter. Political institutions can provide guarantees, or at least mitigate political risks for foreign investors. This message becomes more complicated when we examine how they matter, in what cases, and in what way. Specifically, this project examines how democratic institutions, federalism and decentralization, and agreements with the International Monetary Fund affect a government's ability to attract multinational investments. Chapters 5, 6, and 7 more closely explain the effects of these three political institutions on FDI inflows.

4

The Race to the Bottom Thesis and FDI

4.1 Introduction

Tax policy is at the forefront of debates on attracting mobile capital. For example, Finland, long considered one of the most hospitable environments for FDI, recently proposed cutting its corporate tax rates from 29 percent to 26 percent in response to the perceived losses of FDI to lower tax Estonia.[1] Other Western European countries have simultaneously proposed domestic tax and labor market reforms and called for an end to "harmful tax competition," whereas low tax countries such as Ireland have attracted massive FDI inflows, at the expense of other European Union members.

In the United States, the issue of outward FDI flows, sometimes labeled outsourcing, was a hot-button issue in the 2004 presidential election.[2] The Republican Party, including the incumbent Bush administration, has historically been supportive of lower taxes both on capital and labor. Ironically, at the time of this writing, it was democratic nominee John Kerry who proposed the most comprehensive corporate tax reform that would end U.S. companies' ability to defer taxes, eliminate a number of tax loopholes, lower the corporate tax rate 5 percent, and offer a one-time tax holiday for profits repatriated to the United States. The net impact of this proposal is to lower taxes for over 99 percent of taxpaying companies in order to encourage U.S. firms to remain in the United States and to increase the competitiveness of U.S. firms by lowering the U.S. tax rate relative to other countries.[3] The reason for the Democratic Party's convergence to lower tax rates on capital was what John Kerry called "Benedict Arnold" corporations that moved American jobs offshore in response to lower wages and tax rates. In the United States, both the left and the right were rallying for lower corporate income taxes.

These fiscal wars go beyond simply lowering corporate tax rates. Countries are increasingly using financial incentives to attract multinational corporations. According to the United Nations Conference on Trade and Development's World Investment Report, "The use of locational incentives to attract FDI considerably expanded in frequency and value." It goes on to argue that "developed countries and economies in transition frequently employ financial incentives, while developing countries (which cannot afford a direct drain on the government budget) prefer fiscal measures" (UNCTAD 2003, 124). In other words, developed countries give immediate cash grants or credits and developing countries provide exemptions from future tax liabilities.[4]

These examples show that most of the attention on the political determinants of FDI has focused on government fiscal policy. Scholars have long debated the reactions of footloose capital to the level and growth of government taxation and spending. The now almost cliché view of the race to the bottom thesis posits that multinational firms force governments into tax competition, lowering levels of corporate taxation and spending to attract mobile factors of production.

Although a number of scholars examine the relationship between capital account openness and spending, few studies to date have actually analyzed the causation of international capital flows in terms of government spending and taxation patterns.[5] Does international capital flow to countries with lower levels of government spending and taxation?

This chapter attempts to answer at least part of that question. I utilize an existing data set to examine the FDI flows to fifteen OECD countries from 1960 to 1993, illuminating the link between government fiscal policy and multinational investments and contributing to an underdeveloped literature by answering the question: Do multinationals prefer to invest in countries with low levels of spending and taxation? At the end of the chapter I generate a few conjectures on how these findings relate to non-OECD countries.[6]

The empirical results in this analysis confirm that the pessimism about the role of government fiscal policy in attracting foreign direct investment suffers from over-exaggeration, directing our attention away from the institutional determinants of FDI. Little evidence exists that government spending or taxation levels have a negative effect on FDI inflows. Government devotion to social security, often characterized as economically unproductive market intervention, does not deter multinational investments. More generally, left-wing governments do not suffer from lower levels of FDI inflows. In sum, multinational corporations' investment decisions do not seriously challenge government fiscal policy autonomy. The focus on fiscal policy determinants of FDI inflows directs our attention away from the other important determinants of FDI.

This chapter proceeds as follows. Section 4.2 examines the recent growth in FDI flows into the OECD. Section 4.3 discusses the political ramifications of these flows and reviews the existing theory on the links between government fiscal policy and FDI. Sections 4.4 and 4.5 flesh out the empirical methodology, the data, and the empirical results of the effects of fiscal policy on FDI flows. In section 4.6 I present qualitative evidence on the relationship between government fiscal policy and FDI, and section 4.7 concludes.

4.2 Foreign Direct Investment: Importance and Trends Within the OECD

Virtually every OECD country has lowered barriers to multinational entry, either unilaterally or through negotiated agreements. Moreover, most OECD countries now have at least one agency wooing FDI, providing information, contacts, and legal support for foreign corporations.[7]

Simple economic reasoning provides one explanation for this increased interest in attracting multinational investments. A growing consensus asserts that FDI has positive effects on macroeconomic performance.[8] An increase in the domestic capital stock through multinational investments provides the most obvious mechanism. Capital accumulation drives economic growth in the neoclassical model; thus, FDI should directly and positively impact economic growth.[9]

As argued in chapter 3, although the impact of FDI on a nation's capital stock in the OECD proves economically important, its largest economic benefit comes from the diffusion of technology. The potential for technological transfer appears readily if one examines most multinational firms' characteristics. Multinationals tend to produce technologically complex products that require large R&D investments and employ large numbers of professional and technical workers.[10]

The growing interest in FDI also stems from the increase in the sheer magnitude of multinational investments over time, as highlighted in chapter 2. Figure 4.1 shows the growth of FDI as a percentage of GDP since the 1970s. In the 1970s, FDI flows stood at roughly 2 percent of GDP, jumping to over 4 percent in the late 1980s and early 1990s. With the merger mania of the late 1980s fading, FDI slipped back to roughly 3 percent of GDP in 1992 and has grown steadily to over 6 percent of GDP by 1998. This increase in the global importance of FDI flows has government officials scrambling to attract multinationals' attention and ultimately their investments.

4.3 Foreign Direct Investment and Domestic Politics

Scholars have highlighted the tensions between government macroeconomic policy and capital mobility.[11] Governments that want to attract multinationals in today's global economy must slash spending and taxation in a race for the neoliberal bottom.[12] These theories has migrated

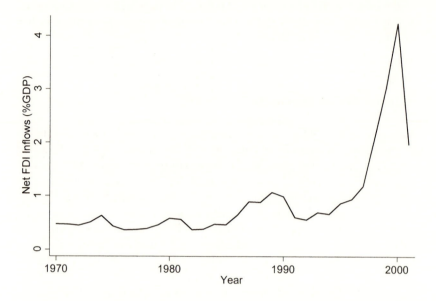

Figure 4.1. Net FDI Inflows (% GDP)

from academic debates to public policy circles to mass-market books. In the words of a popular best seller on globalization, "In a world in which capital is mobile, you cannot adopt rates of taxation that are far from the rates that prevail in other countries and when labor is mobile you can't also be out of line with others wages" (Friedman 1999, 108). The race to the bottom theory has become almost cliché.

The second strand of this literature focuses on the domestic political pressures for "compensation" from the losers of globalization.[13] Governments under conditions of high levels of trade and capital mobility feel pressured by their citizens to provide increased levels of protection in the face of growing economic insecurity in a dynamic global economy.[14] Even if markets prefer small government, citizens may respond to globalization by demanding more from their governments. These works remind us that politicians respond to electoral pressures, not just market pressures.[15]

Although the compensation hypothesis seems to have some strong empirical and theoretical validity, my work takes one step back and focuses on the actual market pressures on patterns of government policy. Before we ask the question of whether governments choose to listen to markets over voters or vice versa, we must first understand what the markets actually want. Does systematic evidence exist that multinationals actually prefer low levels of government spending and taxation? To answer this question we must understand the details for the "efficiency hypothesis."

The efficiency hypothesis actually contains two interrelated theories. One, often called the race to the bottom thesis, argues that governments constantly compete for international investment. Governments must act and react to the world policy environment, bidding against other countries by lowering levels of spending and taxation, loosening labor and environmental legislation, and generally providing a more hospitable environment for foreign investors.

In the strongest form, capital remains mobile and governments are little more than commodities.[16] Global corporations search the world for countries willing to offer the most attractive environments for their investments. Potential host governments can do little more than bend to the whims of multinationals, providing these firms extremely lucrative investment opportunities and policy environments. Governments throw out domestic environmental legislation, lower levels of corporate taxation, and eventually alter their patterns of spending. Democratic decision making diminishes while footloose capital makes its voice heard as firms "vote with their feet."[17] In essence, domestic governments must give up the ability to control their taxing and spending decisions.

Theoretically, serious flaws plague this race to the bottom perspective. This theory assumes a degree of capital mobility and perfect markets that are not supported by economic theory or casual observation. As Goodman (1976, 68) clearly states: "The perfect competition model fails to take into account the complexity of the firm's environment." In one of the most comprehensive studies of multinationals responses to tax policy, Mutti (2003) argues that specific factors such as economic rents, natural resources, or location advantages are key determinants of FDI decisions. As I argued in chapter 3, decades of research on foreign direct investment have been centered on the study of *imperfect* markets (Hymer 1976; Dunning 1977, 1981).

These imperfect market approaches cast serious doubt on the race to the bottom thesis. If multinational investment decisions hinge on grounds much more complex than government taxation and spending levels, then the competition between governments for investment through taxation and spending may be much more muted than generally acknowledged. Multinationals do care about levels of taxation, but a number of other important decision factors emerge as well. The race to the bottom thesis rests on an analogy of capital mobility that proves questionable when applied to FDI.

Empirically, the race to the bottom thesis has also been harshly criticized. Little evidence exists to support any convergence toward the neoliberal bottom in terms of government spending. Most recently, Garrett (2001) finds that capital mobility has no effect on government spending patterns in over one hundred countries from 1970 to 1995. Drezner (2001, 75) summarizes the vast literature on the race to the bottom, concluding:

> The lack of support for the RTB (race to the bottom) argument is striking. This absence of supporting evidence continues if one looks at other issue areas. Most economic studies show that increased capital mobility has not constrained the ability of states to tax capital. One comes to a similar conclusion with regard to the regulation of consumer health and safety. Even in macroeconomic policy, an area commonly thought to provide the strongest support for the RTB hypothesis, the empirical evidence is debatable. Repeated studies have showed that domestic institutions, interests, and political parties have a significant effect on fiscal and monetary policies. This sort of variation is inconsistent with a race to the bottom.

With such weak theoretical and empirical support the race to the bottom thesis rests on very shaky ground. Furthermore, the empirical section of my analysis finds no support for the race to the bottom thesis in relation to flows of foreign direct investment.

A second, and more realistic, subtheory within the efficiency hypothesis does not relate directly to policy competition between countries. Rather, firms opt for "lean government" regardless of the level of policy competition. In this theory, multinationals obviously prefer to pay less tax than more tax, but they do not jump from country to country solely based on taxation and spending decisions. Multinationals choose production locations based on a number of criteria, one of these being the level of government spending and taxation.[18]

Governments can lower their taxation levels to attract more multinationals, but no direct competition erupts between all countries for multinational investment on this one dimension of public policy. Countries offer multinationals different bundles of costs and benefits relate not only to the level of government spending, but also to the uses of government spending.[19] Countries always feel pressure to find new ways to make government "leaner," but no pressure arises for the Scandinavian countries to follow the Anglo-Saxon model. Countries can lower government spending and taxation rates to attract higher levels of FDI.

These two variants of the efficiency hypothesis make very different predictions on the effects of government activity on FDI inflows. The race to the bottom thesis would create a systematic relationship between high levels of FDI and low levels of spending and taxation *across* countries. Alternatively, the lean government thesis would argue that we should see a systematically negative relationship between high levels of FDI and low levels of spending and taxation *within* countries over time.[20] The empirical results presented in the next section reveal that neither theory adequately explains FDI patterns over time.

4.4 Methodology

The empirical technique used to examine this relationship relies on a series of ordinary least squares regressions (OLS) for a panel of fifteen OECD countries from 1960 to 1993; annual observations and all independent variables lagged one year. I also employ the Beck and Katz (1995) recommended panel-corrected standard errors to control for the possible bias in the standard errors generated by OLS.[21] The regression equation is:

$$\text{Net FDI Inflows}_t = \alpha + \beta_1(\text{FDI}_{t-1}) + \beta_i(\text{Independent Variables}_{t-1}) + \varepsilon_i$$

All regressions include a lagged dependent variable as recommended by Beck and Katz (1995). The lagged dependent variable also serves as an important control for the "self-perpetuating" nature of FDI. Countries that attracted higher levels of FDI in the past should lure more investment through multinationals reinvesting earnings, further investments in existing facilities, and the "learning" about the market that the multinational has experienced.[22] All regressions also include a trend variable to capture the increasing values of FDI over time.

For each set of regressions I estimate the same model both with and without country dummy variables. The models with no country dummies ascertain the relationship between the independent variables and FDI across countries. I pool all country years to examine the effects of government spending and taxation levels on FDI flows. This set of tests determines if countries with lower levels of spending and taxation attract higher levels of FDI.

Next I include models with dummies for all fifteen OECD countries. For these regressions all nations have a unique intercept, allowing each country to have its own baseline level of FDI. These regressions reveal how variations within countries over time relate to FDI inflows. This set of regressions also captures country-specific factors that do not vary over time, such as natural resource endowments or geographic location. Once I control for these factors, the relationship between government spending and taxation within countries can be more closely examined.

The data used for this analysis come from Garrett and Mitchell (2001). To reiterate, I define foreign direct investments as private capital flows from a parent firm to a location outside of the parent firm's host nation. These investments consist of equity capital, intercompany debt, and reinvested earnings. An investment becomes foreign direct investment, as opposed to portfolio investment, if the investment proves large enough to give the parent firm some amount of control over the management of the enterprise, usually over 10 percent of the firm.[23] Net FDI inflows as a percentage of GDP from the IMF's balance-of-payments statistics is the dependent variable.

I use control variables from the baseline FDI model constructed in chapter 3, including the level of trade (exports + imports/GDP), market size (log of GDP), the level of economic development (GDP per capita in constant dollars), and economic growth (GDP per capita growth). Higher values for all of these control variables correspond with higher levels of FDI flows.[24] I also include a measure of the level of budget deficits (overall budget deficit/GDP). The original sources and descriptive statistics for all of these variables can be found in the appendix to this chapter.

4.5 Results

4.5.1 Government Consumption

Many scholars point out that the effects of capital mobility directly influence a government's ability to tax and spend. Short-term borrowing often finances high levels of government spending, which leads to higher interest rates and eventually leads to higher levels of taxation. This dynamic can create an appreciation in the exchange rate, making investments by multinationals more costly. Proponents of the race to the bottom thesis argue that the need to attract capital forces governments into a competition for foreign investors. Governments must cut spending and taxation in order to provide environments conducive for multinationals.[25]

The lean government hypothesis proposes that governments feel pressured to provide an environment conducive to multinationals. Similar to the race to the bottom thesis, this theory asserts that each government has the incentive to reduce government spending and taxation to induce more multinational investment. Contrary to the race to the bottom thesis, however, governments do not converge to the lowest levels of consumption and taxation. Countries such as Finland, for example, should not mirror spending patterns in low consumption/ tax countries such as Ireland.

TABLE 4.1.
Government Spending and FDI Inflows

	Model 1	Model 2	Model 3	Model 4
Lagged FDI	0.781***	0.583***	0.782***	0.525***
	(12.10)	(6.42)	(12.21)	(5.68)
Trade	0.004**	0.003	0.005**	−0.000
	(2.43)	(0.46)	(2.53)	(−0.05)
Market Size	0.031	−1.640	0.037	−1.756
	(0.95)	(−1.28)	(1.26)	(−1.38)
Development	−0.284	−0.412	−0.307	0.101
	(−1.09)	(−0.27)	(−1.17)	(0.06)
Growth	0.009	0.026	0.011	0.011
	(0.60)	(1.52)	(0.66)	(0.64)
Deficit	0.000	0.011	0.000	−0.019
	(0.01)	(0.65)	(0.00)	(−0.99)
Government Spending			0.004	−0.112***
			(0.39)	(−2.87)
Constant	−33.181**	−90.844**	−33.58**	−90.680**
	(−2.03)	(−2.23)	(−2.05)	(−2.19)
Trend Variable	Yes	Yes	Yes	Yes
Country Dummy	No	Yes	No	Yes
Observations	284	284	284	284
Countries	15	15	15	15
R-sq	0.68	0.72	0.68	0.73

*** = 99% confidence level, ** = 95% confidence level, * = 90% confidence level

Table 4.1 presents an empirical examination of the determinants of foreign direct investment in the OECD. Models 1 and 2 estimate the baseline FDI models constructed in chapter 3. In Models 3 and 4 I include the independent variable, Government Spending, which represents general government consumption as a percentage of GDP from the OECD. Model 3 reveals the relationship between government spending and FDI inflows by using an OLS without country-specific dummies. Levels of government spending have no statistically significant relationship with the levels of FDI inflows. This result agrees with previous work that found no systematic relationship between capital mobility (measured in terms of capital account openness) and government consumption (Garrett 2001). Taken with the existing studies that find a positive relationship between capital mobility and government spending (Quinn 1997; Swank 1998), these results generate serious doubts about the validity of the race to the bottom thesis.

Model 4 presents the same regressions using country dummies. These regressions generate a separate constant for each country, allowing us to examine how changes in the levels of government spending affect FDI inflows. Unlike the earlier regressions, the coefficient on government spending emerges as negative and is statistically significant, lending limited support to the efficiency hypothesis. A one standard deviation increase in government consumption (an increase of 4.15 percent of GDP) leads to a 0.54 standard deviation decrease in FDI flows (a decrease of 0.47 percent of GDP).

These aggregate figures mask the differentiation in types of government consumption. In one study, Gilady and Jensen (2002) found that military spending has a large negative impact on FDI inflows. Other types of government spending, such as spending on market-promoting public goods like education and infrastructure, may have a positive impact. My empirical results show that the net impact of government spending on FDI inflows is only significant in regressions with country dummies and is relatively modest in magnitude.

4.5.2 Social Security

The growing strain on national social security systems pose one of the most important future challenges to governments in the OECD. The graying of the "baby boomer" segment of the population and the advances of medical technology increased the percentage of the population nearing or at retirement age. This demographic reality has the potential for an economic crisis, as social security systems, already strained in many countries, will be forced to fund more retirees with less people paying contributions.

Some scholars argue that the globalization of multinational production compounds this demographic crisis. Even if one accepts the tenets of new growth theory—that market failures leave room for government intervention—few scholars would argue that social security contributions provide many direct benefits to multinationals. As countries look for ways to trim government spending to attract multinationals, the future of social security seems even less promising.

Politicians may be tempted to slash government spending, or curb its growth, to attract more multinational corporations. At the same time these politicians may be under intense pressure to "compensate" the losers from economic globalization and to provide adequate benefits to those living in retirement. Do politicians face a no-win situation?

These doomsday predictions could be real, but to date there are no direct tests of the effects of social security transfers on multinational investments. Are social security transfers a drag on the economy, providing multinationals with few benefits and high costs? Conversely, do these social security expenditures exist as part of the social fabric,

TABLE 4.2.
Social Security, Capital Taxation, and FDI Inflows

	Model 5	Model 6	Model 7	Model 8
Lagged FDI	0.773***	0.600***	0.752***	0.500***
	(11.93)	(6.63)	(8.76)	(4.51)
Trade	0.007***	0.003	0.006***	0.005
	(2.65)	(0.46)	(2.72)	(0.63)
Market Size	0.038	−1.695	0.048	−0.794
	(1.16)	(−1.40)	(1.40)	(−0.56)
Development	−0.313	−0.365	−0.281	−2.06
	(−1.27)	(−0.25)	(−1.07)	(−1.20)
Growth	0.004	0.024	0.010	0.028
	(0.28)	(1.43)	(0.66)	(1.45)
Deficit	−0.001	0.010	0.007	0.031*
	(−0.14)	(0.48)	(0.64)	(1.79)
Social Security	−0.014	−0.006		
	(−1.62)	(−0.22)		
Capital Taxation			0.006*	−0.002
			(1.67)	(−0.27)
Constant				
Trend Variable	Yes	Yes	Yes	Yes
Country Dummy	No	Yes	No	Yes
Observations	284	284	284	284
Countries	15	15	15	15
R-sq	0.70	0.73	0.69	0.74

*** = 99% confidence level, ** = 95% confidence level, * = 90% confidence level

allowing for low levels of political unrest, union cooperation, and perhaps even higher levels of worker productivity?

This analysis makes no claim at independently sorting out the answers to these questions; rather, I focus on the overall empirical relationship between social security transfers and FDI inflows. In table 4.2, Models 5 and 6, I present this relationship using social security transfers as a percentage of GDP from the OECD as the key independent variable and examine the effects of these transfers on FDI inflows. In all models, no evidence suggests that the cutting of social security transfers affects the level of foreign direct investment flowing into the economy. The doomsday predictions may be plausible, but the empirical evidence to date does not support it.

4.5.3 Capital Taxation

An examination of multinationals' reactions to capital taxation levels provides a more direct test of the constraints posed by capital mobility.

The race to the bottom thesis often cites the tax wars between countries as evidence of the dire straits of host governments (Oman 2000). Gropp and Kostial state:

> Tax competition for foreign direct investment (FDI) can have adverse effects on corporate tax revenue. In fact, these effects may have already become evident in the sharp decline in corporate tax revenue in some member countries of the Organization for Economic Cooperation and Development (OECD). It is interesting that the countries experiencing revenue declines also offer the least attractive corporate tax regimes within the OECD. Although part of the decline can be attributed to business-cycle variations or changes in tax codes, its extent and persistence suggest that additional factors may be at work, including the direction and size of FDI flows. (2001, 2)

For a country to attract high levels of multinational investment, it must provide a tax environment competitive with other nation-states.

In table 4.2, Models 7 and 8, I present the links between multinational investment and the effective capital taxation levels from Mendoza et al. (1997). Model 7 finds a *positive* and weakly statistically significant relationship between high levels of capital taxation and FDI. Higher taxes are associated with higher FDI inflows. One conjecture could lend support to the recent contributions to new growth theory, where countries can tax corporations and provide market-enhancing public goods, goods that lead to higher levels of multinational investment. In any case, this evidence allows us to reject the race to the bottom thesis.

Model 8 examines the same regression with country dummy variables. As predicted by the lean government hypothesis, the coefficient on capital taxation becomes negative, but not statistically significant. Essentially, no real evidence emerges that capital mobility forces governments to slash levels of taxation to attract more multinationals.

On the surface these results may be startling. One of the central arguments of many of the doomsday predictions on the effects of capital mobility makes the assumption that firms prefer low tax environments. This assumption simply enjoys no empirical validation. In the abstract, firms obviously prefer lower taxation to high taxation, all else being equal. In reality, the 200 plus countries of the world experience a tremendous amount of variation in their geographic locations, market characteristics, levels of economic and social development, and government policies relating to monetary and fiscal policy. Countries provide unique bundles of benefits and costs to multinationals. The level of taxation offers only one of many of the elements.

In a survey of the literature on multinational production in the global economy, James Markusen summarizes these links between taxation and FDI: "There is little support for the idea that risk diversification or tax avoidance are important motives for direct foreign investment (Morck and Yeung 1991; Wheeler and Mody 1992). Apparently, most firms first choose foreign production locations, and then instruct their tax departments to minimize taxes" (Markusen 1995, 171). The negative relationship between capital taxation and FDI has, at the very least, been overemphasized. At the most, scholars and experts have figured it completely wrong.

4.5.4 Taxation of Labor

A second related test examines the links between FDI and the labor taxation level. Many scholars highlight that the burdens of taxation fall onto the shoulders of labor.[26] Firms may choose to invest in countries with high levels of public good provision, but they surely would prefer not to pay for these goods.[27] Footloose capital will pressure governments to shift taxation from capital to labor.

In table 4.3, Models 9 and 10, I present the empirical results of the relationship between labor taxation levels and FDI inflows.[28] Neither Model 9 nor Model 10 finds a statistically significant relationship between labor taxation and FDI inflows. Once again, the predictions of the race to the bottom and the lean government hypothesis do not stand up to the empirical tests. No empirical support suggests that shifting taxation to labor has any significant impact on attracting multinational corporations.

4.5.5 Social Democratic Governments

The race to the bottom thesis and the lean government thesis make pessimistic predictions for social democratic governments. Social democracy rests on the foundation of market intervention and economic protection for the citizenry. Has capital mobility destroyed the "left" alternative offered by social democratic governments?

Table 4.3 provides a crude test of this question. If social democracy really offers an economically inefficient political arrangement, market forces should punish these governments with lower levels of capital inflows. A leftist government would signal a commitment to costly market intervention, decreasing the country's attractiveness to multinational corporations. The percentage of left cabinet portfolios from Swank (1998) is the independent variable, Left Government.

The empirical results presented in table 4.3 clearly do not support this pessimism. In both Model 11 and Model 12, left governments have no statistically significant effect on patterns of foreign direct invest-

TABLE 4.3.
Labor Taxation, Left Government, and FDI Inflows

	Model 9	Model 10	Model 11	Model 12
Lagged FDI	0.743***	0.509***	0.783***	0.570***
	(9.04)	(4.58)	(12.18)	(6.21)
Trade	0.008**	0.004	0.004**	0.003
	(2.45)	(0.58)	(2.41)	(0.42)
Market Size	0.051	−0.890	0.026	−2.235
	(1.36)	(−0.63)	(0.79)	(−1.48)
Development	−0.341	−2.005	−0.283	−0.088
	(−1.27)	(−1.20)	(−1.09)	(−0.05)
Growth	0.002	0.030*	0.010	0.026
	(0.879)	(1.74)	(0.63)	(1.53)
Deficit	0.011	0.031*	0.000	0.013
	(0.93)	(1.72)	(0.03)	(0.77)
Labor Tax	−0.008	0.014		
	(−1.51)	(0.66)		
Left Government			−0.000	0.001
			(−0.33)	(0.89)
Constant	−43.80***	−125.87***	−32.77**	−94.978
	(−2.28)	(−2.61)	(−2.02)	(−2.33)
Trend Variable	Yes	Yes	Yes	Yes
Country Dummy	No	Yes	No	Yes
Observations	284	284	284	284
Countries	15	15	15	15
R-sq	0.69	0.74	0.68	0.72

*** = 99% confidence level, ** = 95% confidence level, * = 90% confidence level

ment over time. No systematic relationship emerges between partisanship and FDI inflows.

This null result should not surprise us, given the results on spending and taxation. Table 4.4 summarizes the general findings on the relationship between government fiscal policy and FDI inflows. No systematic evidence lends credence to the race to the bottom thesis. Simply no relationship exists between countries with low taxation and spending levels and higher FDI inflows. Similarly, little support appears for the "lean government hypothesis." Only the level of government consumption holds a negative effect over FDI inflows. For both the race to the bottom thesis and the lean government thesis, then, little empirical support exists.

One potential criticism of these empirical tests is that all models include a lagged dependent variable. This lagged variable is meant to capture the impact of past FDI on future FDI, but it may be simply proxying for other variables. For example, if a country like Ireland at-

TABLE 4.4.
Summary of Government Fiscal Policy and FDI

	Support for Race to the Bottom Thesis	Support for Lean Government Thesis
Government Spending	Mixed	Yes
Social Security Transfers	Mixed	Mixed
Capital Taxation	No	No
Labor Taxation	No	No
Left Governments	No	No

tracted vast amounts of FDI because of low tax rates, my empirical test includes both levels of capital taxation and a measure of past FDI flows. In my results, I may be underestimating the impact of capital taxation because of the inclusion of the lagged dependent variable.

As a robustness check, I ran Models 1 through Model 10 without the lagged dependent variable. In these models, the only new supporting evidence for the race to the bottom thesis was that social security transfers became negative and statistically significant and government spending also remained negative and statistically significant. In the other models, a number of key independent variables became statistically significant and *positive*. For example, higher corporate taxation and social democratic governments were all associated with more FDI inflows, while high levels of labor taxations lead to lower FDI inflows.

To summarize, those empirical results without the lagged dependent variable generally conform to the results presented in tables 4.1, 4.2, and 4.3. There is some evidence for lower FDI inflows on the consumption side, but no evidence that high levels of taxation or social democratic governments deter FDI inflows. Government fiscal policy seems to have little impact on FDI inflows.

Do these empirical results extend to non-OECD countries? Although comparative data on government tax and fiscal policy are not available in similar time-series for non-OECD countries, data do exist on maximum marginal corporate tax rates in 2002 and FDI flows. Although these maximum tax rates are an imperfect measure of multinationals' tax rates, and inferior to the data just used in the preceding analysis, these tax rates do provide some insight into the responses of multinationals to cross-national tax differences.[29] As a simple check, I explored the correlation between rates of capital taxation and FDI inflows for ninety-five countries. The correlation is only -0.11.[30]

These results are echoed in a recent survey of multinational firms conducted by the World Bank's Multilateral Investment Guarantee Agency and Deloitte and Touche. In this survey of 191 multinational firms, decision makers were asked which factors were "very influential" in selecting an investment location. Access to customers emerged as the most important factor (77 percent of respondents), followed by a stable social and political environment (54 percent), ease of doing business (54 percent), and reliability and quality of infrastructure (50 percent). National taxes ranked 11, with only 29 percent of respondents claiming that this was a "very influential" factor, while local taxes tied for 14 with only 24 percent of respondents. Taxes matter, but other factors are more influential (MIGA 2002, 19).

4.6 Qualitative Evidence

Can tax policy really have such a small impact on multinationals' investment decisions? Do government officials, location consultants, and multinational corporations consider tax policy to be so unimportant? To answer this, I interviewed country investment promotion officials, multinational location and tax consultants, and a number of major multinational corporations.

First, interviews with eight country investment promotion agencies confirmed that fiscal policy is not generally a major determinant of FDI inflows. Only Ireland and Canada stressed taxes as a major determinant, but this was coupled with a high-quality labor force, access to the U.S. or European markets, and a host of other factors. For other countries such as Costa Rica, Hungary, and Malaysia, taxes were not primary factors for attracting FDI.

Interviews with investment location consultants also confirm the results presented here. For example, in an interview with B-G Consulting, the level of tax rates was seldom a primary determinant for FDI decisions; rather, systems with complicated and nontransparent tax systems could serve as a deterrent to FDI. An interview with a representative of IBM Plant Location International provides a slightly different perspective. For some high-margin industries, such as pharmaceuticals, tax rates can have a strong influence over location decisions. For other industries, tax rates are of marginal importance. Generally, lower tax rates were always preferred to high tax rates, but the sensitivity of firms to taxes varied dramatically.

How do firms respond to tax rates? Do they place tax rates and tax incentives as primary determinants of FDI decisions? Few multinational corporations actually listed taxes or tax incentives as primary concerns. Of those that listed tax rates as important, these were always coupled with numerous other important location factors. For example Alcan listed taxation as a primary concern, along with distance from export markets, raw material availability, electricity, labor costs, currency stability, the economic environment, and political stability.[31] For Daimler Chrysler, workforce availability, workforce competence, cost of labor, investment requirements, infrastructure, and intangibles all rank as important factors along with tax rates.[32]

Field research in Costa Rica also supports this conclusion on the importance of taxation and tax incentives. Costa Rica offers a very generous set of tax incentives for multinationals, including an eight-year exemption from corporate taxes and a 50 percent exemption for four additional years if companies qualify as a Free Zone Company.[33] Of the five firms interviewed in Costa Rica, four argued that these tax incentives were not a major factor and that they most likely would have continued with their investment even without incentives. Only one firm, Intel, the largest investor in Costa Rica, argued that incentives were a major factor for their investment decisions, along with issues of political stability, labor costs, level of education, and infrastructure. An unfavorable tax regime may have deterred Intel from investment, but a number of other conditions were also necessary.

This qualitative evidence is striking when coupled with the quantitative analysis. Although my empirical analysis only included OECD countries, there is little reason to believe that the relationship between taxation and FDI is any stronger in non-OECD countries. According to the investment promotion agencies, it is the OECD countries that stress tax rates as marginally important for FDI, and the non-OECD countries claim it is secondary at best. Although I leave an empirical analysis of the relationship between taxation and FDI in non-OECD countries to future research, there is little support to indicate that taxes are a major determinant of FDI to developing countries.

4.7 Conclusion

This chapter attempts to contribute to the debate on the effects of capital mobility on government policy by isolating the relationship between government fiscal policy and foreign direct investment inflows. Do multinationals prefer to invest in countries with lower levels of government spending and taxation?

Based on the analogy of country competition for international investment, the answer may seem obvious. Multinationals search the globe for investment opportunities, pitting governments against one another, forcing political leaders to decide between fiscal policy autonomy and attracting foreign direct investment.

The theoretical literature highlighted in this chapter argues that this pessimism may be overemphasized. The existing literature in business and economics stresses that imperfect markets drive multinationals' decisions to invest abroad. An analogy based on perfect markets, such as employed in the race to the bottom thesis, does not correspond to the study of FDI. Only through careful empirical analysis can we examine the real relationship between government fiscal policy and multinationals' investment choices.

Contrary to the pessimistic views on governments' ability to spend and tax in a world of capital mobility, the empirical results presented in this chapter highlight the weak relationships between these variables. Only in government consumption do I find any negative relationship between government intervention and lower levels of FDI inflows. In the following chapters I will explore how political institutions, rather than government fiscal policy, provide the central determinants of FDI inflows.

APPENDIX

TABLE A4.1.
Data Sources

Variable	Definition	Original Source
FDI Flows	FDI inflows/GDP (%)	IMF BOP
Trade	X + M/GDP (%)	OECD 6094
Level of Development	GDP per capita in constant $	OECD 6094
Economic Growth	GDP per capita growth	OECD 6094
Government Spending	Government consumption/GDP	OECD 6094
Social Security Transfers	Social Security Transfers/GDP (%)	OECD 6094
Capital Taxation	Effective capital tax rate	Mendoza 1997
Labor Taxation	Effective labor tax rate	Mendoza 1997
Left Governments	Left cabinet portfolios (%)	Swank 1998
Budget Deficits	Overall budget deficit	WDI 2002

TABLE A4.2.
Descriptive Statistics

Variable	Obs	Mean	SD	Min	Max
FDI	464	0.655	0.835	0	5.3
Trade	612	57.10	27.446	9.4	156.3
GDPPC	476	11309.68	2531.804	4491	18095
Growth	612	2.593	2.477	−7.9	11.6
Government Consumption	612	16.906	4.147	7.3	29.6
Social Security	654	13.692	5.429	3.7	28.9
Capital Taxation	372	35.719	11.721	13.942	74.332
Labor Taxation	372	31.767	10.091	10.96	53.581
Left Government	612	30.428	37.307	0	100

5

Democracy and FDI

5.1 Introduction

Canadian-based Alcan Corporation is arguably the largest aluminum manufacturer in the world, with 2002 revenues topping $12.5 billion and business operations in more than forty-one countries.[1] Many of these operations entail a massive fixed investment, such as their bauxite and alumina facilities in West Africa and Australia, and aluminum smelting facilities in Canada, the United Kingdom, Iceland, and Brazil with time horizons of fifty to sixty years.[2] Many of these production processes are extremely energy intensive, where the company often invests in power facilities, generating over 60 percent of their own power for their smelting operations. In countries where it is not economically feasible to generate their own power, the company is dependent on third-party or government power providers.

Alcan has extensive operations in Brazil, including energy-intensive smelting operations. Alcan's operation is not mobile; the company has invested millions in high-fixed-cost smelting operations with essentially no other use than aluminum manufacturing. Unfortunately for Alcan, the Brazilian central government has recently proposed increased energy transmission surcharges for Alcan and other businesses. A modest increase in the price of power can turn a profitable facility into a multimillion-dollar loss-making enterprise.

This is just one example of the political risks multinationals face when doing business abroad. Unlike the outright nationalizations, many political risks are not obvious, but extremely important for firms. In the previous two chapters I argue that scholars overemphasize the impact of government fiscal policy on FDI, and that political institutions affect multinationals' perceptions of political risk. Political risk is a central concern for multinationals such as Alcan. In this chapter I explore how democratic political institutions can lower political risks for multinationals.

Scholars argue that the need to attract FDI pressures governments to provide a climate more hospitable to foreign corporations, potentially altering patterns of domestic economic policy, possibly even challenging the de facto sovereignty of the nation-state and the capacity for democratic governance.[3] Some scholars also see democracy as an inefficient institutional structure in the global economy.[4]

In this chapter I empirically assess these predictions about the political preconditions for attracting FDI using both cross-sectional and time-series-cross-sectional regression analysis for up to 114 countries. The cross-sectional regressions estimate the effects of economic conditions, policy decisions, and democratic political institutions in the 1980s on the level of FDI inflows in the 1990s. The time-series-cross-sectional regressions explore how alterations in economic policies and political institutions affect changes in FDI inflows in the period from 1970 to 1997. Next, I use a treatment effects selection model to explore the robustness of the relationship between democratic governance and FDI. Finally, I explore the causal link between democracy and FDI by determining the effects of democratic governance on country credibility. In this final section, I test the effects of democratic institutions on country sovereign debt ratings for seventy-nine countries from 1980 to 1998.

My results show the importance of democratic institutions as a determinant of FDI inflows, but prove inconsistent with the dire predictions on the effects of the competition for FDI on domestic politics. Democratic political institutions correspond to higher levels of FDI inflows. Democratic governments, even when controlling for other political and economic factors, attract as much as 78 percent more FDI as a percentage of GDP than their authoritarian counterparts. This result is robust under different model specifications and types of empirical tests.

The remainder of this chapter flows as follows. In section 5.2 I explore the link between economic development, international conflict, and democratic institutions. In section 5.3 I discuss the causal links between democracy and higher levels of FDI inflows. In section 5.4 I provide a brief overview of the empirical tests. In the following two sections I construct empirical tests of the determinants of FDI flows, examining levels of FDI relying on cross-sectional data (section 5.5) and using panel data including a treatment effects selection model (section 5.6). Section 5.7 explores the link between democracy and credibility by empirically examining the effects of democratic institutions on country sovereign debt ratings. In section 5.8 I present qualitative evidence. Section 5.9 concludes.

5.2 Development, Growth, Conflict, and Democracy

The debate over the relationship between political institutions and economic performance generally hinges on the theories of democracy and economic development. Econometric studies, and casual observation, find a positive association between democratic institutions and higher levels of economic development. Almost all of the economically developed nations exist as democratic regimes, while few democracies exist in less developed countries. Although most scholars recognize this relationship, a considerable amount of controversy remains on the causal direction between democracy and economic development.

Modernization theory, usually attributed to Lipset (1959), argues that democratic institutions stand at the end of a long process of economic and political development. Most recently, Przeworski, Alvarez, Cheibub, and Limongi (2000) assert that this process of modernization does not explain the correlations between economic development and democracy. The "endogenous" theory forwarded by modernization theorists assumes that higher levels of economic development create democratic institutions. But Therborn (1977) argues that many European countries democratized following wars. Moreover, the democratic waves felt in Africa and Eastern Europe, often associated with the end of the cold war, lie far from the causal mechanism of modernization theory.

The ground-breaking work of Przeworski et al. (2000) advances a theory of regime dynamics contrary to modernization theory. They argue that regime transition theories must examine patterns of democratization and breakdowns of democratic rule. Only by understanding these regime transitions can scholars make any meaningful link between democratic governance and economic development. To understand the relationship between development and democracy, we must have theories on the transitions from authoritarian rule to democracy and democracy to authoritarian rule.

Using a number of advanced statistical models, Przeworski et al. (2000) find that democratic governments, although fragile in developing countries, prove intractable in the most developed countries. The richest democratic regime ever to collapse, Argentina, had a level of GDP per capita of $6,055 at its downfall in 1975 (p. 98). No country with a higher level of GDP per capita has experienced a democratic breakdown. Their final conclusion, a compelling one, argues that the correlations between economic development and democratic institutions center on the "survival" of democracies. Democracy does not "cause" development, nor does development "cause" democracy. Democratization emerges in both rich and poor countries, but only in the wealthy countries does democracy endure.

The literature on the link between democracy and economic growth remains equally divided. Early theorists speculated that democratic institutions may spark popular demands for government consumption, lowering economic growth (Huntington 1968). More recently, theorists have argued that some degree of democracy can spur growth (Barro 1990, 1996).

Przeworski et al. (2000) argue that no difference exists in the economic growth level between democracies and dictatorships. In poor countries, no variation emerges in the rates of investment, growth of the labor force, or returns on capital or labor. In richer countries, democracies tend to pay higher wages, have lower levels of investment, but they have higher returns to capital. The dictatorships exploit low-wage labor, obtain higher levels of investment, but have lower returns on capital and labor. In the end, both political regimes grow at roughly the same rate. Although this contribution provides a rich analysis of the relationship between political institutions and economic growth, there exists no strong consensus on the relationship between democracy and economic growth.

This lack of consensus stands in stark contrast with the generally accepted link between democracy and lack of international conflict. Dating back to Kant, international relations scholars have long theorized on the effects of democratic institutions on conflict between nations. In empirical literature, pioneered by the works of Bruce Russett, theorists have examined the link between democratic institutions and the lack of military conflict between nations. Prima facie, the case seems rather compelling: no two democratic nations have ever fought each other. Like the link between democracy and development, this relationship has generated a tremendous amount of controversy in international relations.

In an early work, Small and Singer (1976) found that democratic states move toward military conflict just as readily as authoritarian states. However, a number of more recent studies (Bremer 1992; Russett and Oneal 2001) refute this finding. Even more powerful, a number of statistical analyses find that when two nations live under democracy, this provides "virtually a sufficient condition for peace between countries" (Russett and Oneal 2001, 48). Democratic states also remain less likely to initiate conflict against any type of states, authoritarian or democratic (Rousseau 1996; Rosseau et al. 1996; Rioux 1998).

Challenging this empirical finding, some scholars argue that common interests, not democratic institutions explain the lack of conflict between nations. Farber and Gowa (1995, 1997) argue that the empirical link between democratic institutions and the lessened probability of conflict proves spurious. Historically, democratic states showed common interests, for example Britain, the United States, and France all confronted Germany in the World Wars. These collective concerns, in line with realist international relations theory, explain these patterns of conflict.

Other scholars examine how changes in democratization affect the prospects for peace, perhaps in ways contrary to the "democratic peace."[5] Mansfield and Snyder (1995) argue that although established democracies enjoy relative peace, democratizing states prove more war prone than either democratic or authoritarian states. Ward and Gleditsch (1998) conclude that while large increases in democracy significantly decrease the probability of conflict, small moves of liberalization can increase this probability. Gleditsch and Ward (2000) also assert that large swings between democracy and authoritarianism raise the risk of conflict. Finally, a number of more recent studies (Oneal and Russett 1997; Russett and Oneal 2001) suggest that democratization does not affect the probability of conflict at all.

Although considerable controversy remains within this democratic peace literature, the general finding—that democratic states do not fight each other—proves compelling and approaches general acceptance in the discipline. The realist critiques of the democratic peace argue that common interests, not common institutions, explain the period of peace between democracies. As Russett and Oneal (2001) point out, the larger question becomes why democratic states perceive their interests to be common. To explain this finding, democratic peace scholars have focused on cultural and structural explanations.

Cultural arguments, dating back to Kant, focus on "shared democratic principles, perceptions, and expectations of behavior."[6] Democratic states therefore tend to settle disputes through peaceful means and abhor war with groups of individuals sharing similar values. Structural arguments focus on the unique institutional structures of democratic systems, highlighting the institutional constraints imposed on policy makers. As asserted originally by Kant and then most recently by Russett and Oneal (2001), these sets of explanations complement each other and may involve a "virtuous circle" where democratic institutions foster democratic norms and democratic norms strengthen democratic institutions.

Russett and Oneal (2001) carefully argue that this link remains "overidentified." The debates on the structural or cultural aspects of the democratic peace prove difficult to test. More importantly, Russett and Oneal argue that these two explanations complement each other, that both of these factors have independent and mutually reinforcing effects on the prospects for peace.[7]

This well-developed literature on the democratic peace helps us understand the potential benefits of democratic governance structures for foreign investors. Beyond the obvious attraction of democratic states avoiding conflict with other democracies (often other large, economically developed countries) and winning the conflicts in which they engage authoritarian states, multinationals may have preferences for investing in democracies. If democratic political institutions engender higher levels of cooperation between states, they may also allow for more cooperation between states and multinational corporations.

5.3 Three Theories on Democracy and FDI

Few empirical studies examine the relationship between democratic political institutions and FDI flows. The little work that directly explores this issue finds that FDI flows either do not respond to political regimes (Oneal 1994; Alesina and Dollar 1998) or that democratic political institutions are correlated with lower levels of FDI inflows (Jessup 1999; Li and Resnick 2003). Given these recent findings, little support exists in the literature for linking democratic political regimes to higher FDI flows. I argue that three mechanisms link democracy to higher FDI inflows.

The first reason centers on *information*. Much of the literature on the democratic peace in international relations highlights the role of information and democratic governance.[8] Democracies prove more transparent, both in their economic and political affairs. In order for politicians to be held accountable to voters, democratic systems must provide information on the decisions and actions taken by the ruling elite, including a general openness of the decision-making processes and support for a free press.

In democracies, commitments to external actors still arise through these same domestic political processes (Gaubatz 1996). One example of the difficulties of investing in authoritarian governments in terms of market information comes from a recent volume from Rosen (2001) on the experiences of foreign executives in China. Rosen cites four areas of concerns regarding obtaining information in China.

> First, Chinese statistical data at all levels—local, provincial, and central—are subject to both intentional and unintentional biases. For example, production might be overstated to attract investors, or understated to avoid taxes: because the inaccuracies have so many causes, it is difficult to adjust for them.
>
> Second, until recently private reporting on economic matters—which can help fill the gaps left by uncertain state statistics—was discouraged, and even prohibited. Seemingly mundane statistics were treated as state secrets, and reporters were threatened or occasionally imprisoned for violating national security when they provided basic economic information to main-

stream media. Obviously, in such an environment good sources of market and economic analysis were hard to come by.

Third, in response to the growing demand for better economic information, the central government proposed to loosen its tight hold—but only to the extent of giving the state-run Xinhua New Service a monopoly to disseminate official data. This idea did not go over well with the foreign community or with domestic businesses, long accustomed as they were to Chinese media that lied about even the weather. . . .

Fourth, the interviews for this study suggest that much of the information that firms depend on—to get approvals, learn about contracts, resolve disputes, appeal a customs duty rate and the like—is gleaned from inside or "informal sources." (Rosen 2001, 31)

Given the importance of information in international economic relations, specifical long-term investments, this advantage of democratic systems could attract higher levels of investment. Foreign firms hold more knowledge about the workings of the political system and the available information to make predictions on future policy. In a simple statistically study, PriceWaterhouseCoopers (2001) found that higher levels of transparency were associated with more FDI inflows.

Also, the free press often associated with democratic systems can provide spillovers for foreign investors, including critical analysis of government policy and unbiased (or less biased) information on both economic and political affairs. In a famous work, Drèze and Sen (1989) find that no democratic nation has ever experienced a major famine; they attribute this phenomenon to the information provided by the press and the political opposition. They cite Mao after the Chinese famine of 1962, that a "free press and an active political opposition constitute the best early warning system that a country threatened by famine can possess" (from Przeworski et al. 2000, 144). Democracies clearly provide better information.

A second possible reason for democratic systems attracting higher levels of FDI, *representation*, stems from democratic theory. Foreign investors may find avenues to pursue favorable policies either directly or indirectly. They can directly lobby government officials for their preferred legislative outcomes in democracies, an action not possible in autocracies. While some form of lobbying activity remains possible in authoritarian regimes, it often isn't institutionalized or as transparent in these systems.

Considerable evidence exists that foreign firms do in fact lobby national governments. According to a study by Hansen and Mitchell (2000), foreign firms in the U.S. just as readily engage in lobbying activity as domestic firms. Moreover, Hillman and Ursprung (1988) state, "under representative democracy, foreign participation in domestic politics can take the form of campaign contributions, or other transfers directly at influencing the trade-policy position taken by a political candidate."[9]

The difficulty of lobbying a government for preferred policy proves obvious in authoritarian countries. For example, a recent article in the *Economist* documented the multinationals' difficulties in lobbying the Chinese government. Unlike most democratic nations, lobbyists in China have no formal mechanisms for influencing policy (such as campaign contributions) and have difficulty in even identifying which decision makers the firms should target. Even the threat of disinvesting large FDI projects has little effect: "The lobbyists sigh that China is still an authoritarian government, and economic clout (of multinationals) remains limited."[10] The difficulty of influencing policy in authoritarian regimes negatively affects FDI inflows.

Even more important, MNCs may find vested interests in democratic systems already in place. A foreign MNC, once it has sunk capital into a country, shares many of the same preferences as domestic producers.[11] If these democratic systems take domestic producers into account, the government will be providing legislation favorable to domestic producers and foreign investors.[12]

One possible criticism of this representation theory suggests that firms may simply find other mechanisms in which to manipulate government policy in authoritarian regimes—for example, the use of bribery or other forms of corruption to influence central or local governments. Multinational investors may prefer to invest in dictatorships where they endure less media scrutiny and authoritarian decision makers do not answer to the citizenry in the deals they can strike with multinational corporations.

But the empirical evidence strongly points to the contrary. In a comprehensive study of a large sample of countries, Wei (2000) finds that higher levels of corruption correspond to lower levels of FDI inflows. Even if means of influencing policy in authoritarian regimes exist, corruption seems to stand far from the preferred form of policy influence for multinational corporations.

Even with the informational and representational elements of democratic institutions, the conventional wisdom concludes that multinationals prefer to invest in authoritarian regimes. Authoritarian leaders can provide multinational firms with better entry deals, due to the lack of popular pressure from below and their repression of labor unions to drive down wages. This relationship leads to higher levels of FDI inflows to authoritarian countries.

   The second of these arguments, on the role of authoritarian regimes in providing a lower cost workforce, does have some support in the literature (Rodrik 1999). The real question becomes, does this policy translate into higher levels of FDI inflows? Most FDI scholars argue that the impact of low wages has been overemphasized as a determinant of FDI and that the wage rate forms just one of many decision factors for multinational firms (Markusen 1995).[13] I will argue later that the positive impact of democracy institutions offsets the influence of lower wages for multinationals.

   The other argument, on the role of authoritarian regimes in bargaining with firms, also has been greatly exaggerated. Most scholars assume that the lack of checks and balances for authoritarian regimes leads to a more generous situation for multinationals. As Putnam (1988) shows, the logic of a two-level game provides both constraints and leverage to political leaders. Although the democratic constraints imposed on leaders may limit the amount of discretion in offering multinationals deals, they can also provide benefits to multinational firms. Indeed, I argue that these constraints lead to lower levels of political risk.

   In this chapter I assert that credibility provides the main advantage of democratic institutions to multinational investors. As pointed out in chapter 3, foreign direct investment, while mobile ex ante, remains relatively illiquid ex post (Vernon 1971). Once foreign capital is invested in a country, firms could suffer from policy change or reversal by the central government. Once multinationals make investments, considerable political risks emerge.

   Democratic institutions can provide a mechanism to decrease these political risks. Democratic governments ensure more credibility in making agreements in the international arena (Cowhey 1993; Fearon 1994; Gaubatz 1996; McGillivray and Smith 1998; Leeds 1999). These explanations range from the institutional checks and balances within democratic systems, to the "audience costs" generated by elected leaders. Logically following from this large literature, democratic governments may create more credibility in their dealings directly with multinationals.

   One specific mechanism that leads democratic governments to higher levels of credibility hinges on the number of *veto points* in a democratic political system. Tsebelis (1995, 2002) argues that the existence of these veto points, including chambers of the legislature, a supreme court, separation of the executive and legislative branches of government, or federal actors, can increase policy stability. Henisz (2000) asserts that foreign firms change their entrance strategies into domestic markets conditioned on the number of veto players. Democratic governments have these institutional constraints in place, making the pos-

sibility of policy reversal more difficult. Multinationals that enter foreign markets can be reasonably confident that the government policies
in place when the firm entered the country will continue over time.

A second potential reason for the credibility of democratic systems,
perhaps even stronger than the veto point argument, appears in the *audience cost* literature. While the veto points in a political system generate
higher levels of policy stability, an even more important component of
credibility centers on a government's commitment to market-friendly
policies in the future. International relations theories find that democratic leaders undergo scrutiny for their actions, including reneging on
a promise or threat. These audience costs can also prove important for
multinational investors. If governments make agreements with multinational firms and renege on the contracts after the investment has been
made, democratic leaders may suffer electoral costs. The potential for
these electoral backlashes may constrain democratic leaders.

McGillivray and Smith (2000) argue that political leaders play an
"Agent Specific Grimm Trigger Strategy" where political leaders in one
country refuse to cooperate with other political leaders in another country that have "defected" in the past. Multinationals can also play this
strategy with governments that institute legislation or reverse policy in
ways that negatively affect multinational corporations. Essentially,
firms can hold individual leaders politically accountable for policies
and refuse to cooperate (invest) in the future. In democracies, citizens
have the incentive and the opportunity to replace leaders with tarnished reputations through electoral mechanisms. Thus, the leadership
turnover in democratic systems (or the potential for leadership turnover) can provide more market-friendly policies for multinationals.[14]

This argument on the role of leadership turnover in ensuring more
market-friendly policies obviously ignores the potential political benefits of expropriation for leaders. In both democratic and authoritarian
countries, there may be some immediate benefits to expropriation.[15] Political leaders may use the assets or income streams from policy changes
to essentially buy off key support groups. My argument maintains that
in both types of regimes, political leaders enjoy a key support group,
the "selectorate," which must be appeased for political survival.[16]
In both systems, politicians may have some demands for expropriation. I argue that in democratic systems, expropriation is both more
difficult and more costly for the politician.

All three of these links between democratic institutions and FDI inflows point to one conclusion: democratic institutions help countries
attract higher levels of FDI inflows. This analysis makes no further attempt to disentangle the causal link between democratic institutions

and FDI inflows, rather focusing on establishing the general relationship between democracy and FDI inflows. The central question that the empirical analysis attempts to answer considers whether a significant positive link between democracy and FDI inflows exists.

5.4 Empirical Tests: Overview

I now explore the relationship between foreign direct investment and democracy in four sets of empirical tests. The first set of tests will estimate the effects of democratic institutions on FDI inflows in a cross-section of countries in the 1990s. These tests will examine the general relationship and the robustness of the findings on the effects of democracy on FDI inflows. The second set of empirical tests explores this relationship by using times-series-cross-sectional regressions both with and without country dummy variables. The third set of empirical tests will employ a selection model to further analyze the robustness of the relationship. The final set of empirical tests establishes the causal mechanism linking democracy and FDI by assessing the effects of democratic institutions on sovereign debt ratings. The first three sets of tests confirm the hypothesis that democratic institutions correspond to higher levels of FDI inflows and the final test highlights the link between democracy and credibility.

5.4.1 Empirical Analysis: Cross-Sectional Results

Although many studies provide either a theoretical motivation for investment or limited empirical tests, they leave us unable to understand fully the political determinants of FDI inflows. The first analysis uses cross-sectional ordinary least squares regressions for seventy-four to eight-one countries, employing White's correction for heteroscedasticity.[17] In order to mitigate problems of reverse causality, I lag all independent variables, using either 1980s averages for most of the economic variables or a 1990 measure for most of the political variables.

I test the following cross-sectional regression equation:

$$\text{NET FDI INFLOWS}_{1990-97} = \alpha + \beta_i \, (\text{INDEPENDENT VARIABLES}_{1980-89}) + \varepsilon_i$$

The dependent variable, the average net foreign direct investment inflows as a percentage of GDP from 1990 to 1997, comes from the World Bank's World Development Indicators 1999. To control for economic factors that affect FDI inflows, I utilize the baseline FDI model constructed in chapter 3. In all FDI regressions I control for the size of the domestic market, GDP growth, the level of trade, the level of development, government consumption, and overall budget deficit.

To test the influence of political regime type on FDI performance, I use a standard measure of democracy. The variable democracy measures political regime averages for 1990 from the Polity IV data set by Marshall and Jaggers (1998).[18] This variable provides an ordinal ranking of political regimes on a scale of 10 to −10 (democracy to authoritarian regimes) that I have rescaled to a 0 to 20 scale for easier interpretation. A 20 constitutes the highest democracy score.[19]

I also tested for the impact of natural resource endowments on FDI inflows using a Sachs and Warner (1995) measure of primary exports as a percentage of GDP. This natural resource variable is an important control variable because of resource-seeking FDI and because high natural resource endowments are often associated with authoritarian regimes.[20]

The results are given in table 5.1. The baseline model (Model 1) supports much of the theoretical work done on foreign direct investment and on economic growth more generally. Trade is a complement to FDI, where countries that tend to be more open to trade, attract higher levels of foreign direct investment. This could be a direct causation, or there is a possibility that some other latent factors that increase a country's ability to export products overseas and its ability to attract foreign direct investment are present, for example, a country's policy toward trade and FDI could be linked.

Government consumption has a small negative effect on a country's ability to attract FDI, consistent with other works that find government consumption having a negative effect on economic growth (Barro 1990). This result is only statistically significant in the first two models. The empirical result on the effects of budget deficits on FDI performance confirms the prior hypothesis. Countries with higher budget deficits (large negative numbers in the data) attract higher levels of FDI. The variable for market size is also statistically insignificant. Large markets tend to attract high levels of FDI, but not more FDI as a percentage of GDP.

Surprisingly, the level of economic development seems to have no statistically significant effect, which can be interpreted as finding that international capital, even when other domestic factors are controlled for, does not flow from the rich countries to the poorer countries of the world. Much of the work on economic growth done by Robert Barro argues for "conditional convergence" where when other domestic factors are controlled for, the less developed countries grow at faster rates than more developed countries.[21] This empirical finding produces one microfoundational flaw in this argument where growth-promoting

TABLE 5.1.
Democracy and FDI (Cross-Section)

	Model 1	Model 2	Model 3
Trade	0.058***	0.060***	0.059***
	(8.11)	(7.09)	(6.69)
Market Size	0.165	0.208	0.177
	(1.31)	(1.59)	(1.07)
Level of Development	0.26	−0.020	−0.246
	(1.34)	(−0.07)	(−0.66)
Economic Growth	−0.232**	−0.268***	−0.306**
	(−2.60)	(−2.94)	(−2.61)
Budget Deficits	−0.151**	−0.121**	−0.135***
	(−2.37)	(−2.13)	(−2.66)
Government Consumption	−0.077**	−0.059**	−0.052
	(−2.53)	(−2.05)	(−1.62)
Natural Resources	3.372	5.983***	6.393***
	(1.34)	(2.92)	(3.09)
Democracy		0.055**	0.077***
		(2.34)	(2.89)
Government Reputation			0.182
			(1.08)
Expropriation			−0.127
			(−0.64)
Corruption			−0.341**
			(−2.06)
Rule of Law			0.212
			(1.11)
Bureaucratic Quality			0.150
			(0.81)
Constant	−6.801***	−6.122**	−4.170
	(−2.95)	(−2.44)	(−1.34)
N	81	80	74
R-sq	0.60	0.69	0.73

*** = 99% confidence level, ** = 95% confidence level, * = 90% confidence level

FDI flows are not attracted at any higher rate to the developing countries than the developed countries.

The result for economic growth is the opposite of what most economic literature would expect. Countries with higher levels of economic growth generally attract lower levels of FDI. A number of potential theories could explain this result, but the most obvious would be the "scaling effect," where countries that have growth rates that exceed the growth in FDI have a decrease in FDI as a percentage of GDP. Another alternative explanation would be the result of business cycles, specifically given that during the 1980s (the period of the independent variables) a number of the industrialized countries were in recession. This business cycle explanation is confirmed in section 5.7.

In Model 2 I include the Polity measure of democracy. This provided solid evidence of the positive effect of democracy on foreign direct investment inflows. There is an obvious linear positive relationship between democracy and a country's ability to attract foreign direct investment. This result is robust under different model specifications and even using a different measure of democracy.[22]

The substantive effects of different levels of democracy on FDI inflows are large. Countries that move from one standard deviation below the mean to the mean level of democracy, a change in the democracy score from 3.03 to 10.9, increases FDI inflows an added 0.43 percent of GDP. A move to full democracy would increase FDI as a percentage of GDP by 1.1 percent. The magnitude of these swings is quite remarkable, where the average level of FDI for the sample is 1.96 percent of GDP. A move from an authoritarian regime to a democratic regime increases FDI inflows by 56 percent.

These positive results on the effects of democracy on FDI inflows remain extremely robust under multiple specifications. To test the robustness of the democracy I have included a number of variables from the William Easterly Data Set, including Government Reputation, Expropriation, Corruption, Rule of Law, and Bureaucratic Quality.[23] These are subjective evaluations of political institutions that are all highly correlated with democracy, with correlations ranging from 0.46 to 0.59. First, I tested whether any of these individual variables were significant in regressions where I include one of the five variables into Model 1. None of these variables were statistically significant. Next, I ran five regressions where I included the polity variable and each of the five institutional variables. Democracy was positive and statistically significant. Finally, I included all five variables into the Model 3. Only the variable on corruption was statistically significant, while the result on the impact of democracy on FDI inflows remained robust. In this final model, fully democratic regimes attract over 78 percent more FDI than authoritarian regimes.

My empirical results remain robust with the inclusion of other control variables. In Jensen (2003a), I show that the impact of formal controls on inflows and outflows of FDI from Brune, Garrett, Guisinger, and Sorens (2001), and a measure of human capital from Barro and Lee (1993), have little impact on the significance or substantive impact of democracy on FDI inflows. The results I present in table 5.1 are robust. Democratic institutions are associated with much higher FDI inflows than authoritarian regimes.

5.5 Time-Series-Cross-Sectional Results

To explore how domestic variables affect FDI inflows over time, I have constructed a time-series-cross-sectional data set for 114 countries from 1970 to 1997. I employ an OLS regression with panel-corrected standard errors as recommended by Beck and Katz (1995). I run all regressions both with and without country dummy variables. As defined earlier, annual FDI inflows as a percentage of GDP serves as the dependent variable. The independent variables economic growth, level of development, market size, trade, government consumption, budget deficits, and democracy remain the same as one used in earlier regressions. The variable FDI inflows stays the same as the one I used in earlier regressions. I lag all independent variables one year and include a lagged dependent variable as well.[24] The time-series-cross-sectional econometric equation becomes:

$$\text{Net FDI Inflows}_t = \alpha + \beta_1(\text{Net FDI}_{t-1}) + \beta_i(\text{Independent Variables}_{t-1}) + \varepsilon_i$$

I present the results in table 5.2. The results of baseline FDI models with and without country dummies are given in Models 4 and 5. All models show positive and statistically significant effects of trade and past foreign direct investment flows on current FDI inflows. Not surprisingly, trade is statistically significant and positive in models without country dummy variables (4 and 6), and in the models with country dummies (Models 5 and 7) it is no longer statistically significant. This is because in many countries the level of trade is relatively consistent over time. The countries with high levels of trade exposure, such as the Netherlands, also have high inflows of FDI, but when a country dummy is included the coefficient on the dummy captures this.

Conversely, the level of development is only significant in Model 5 and weakly significant in Model 7 (with country dummies). There is limited support that FDI flows to rich countries, rather than to poorer countries. This results turns out to be unstable in the regressions in the following chapters. My overall conclusion is that there is no conclusive evidence on the relationship between economic development and FDI inflows.

Interestingly, the findings on the level of government consumption are similar to the findings in chapter 4. Government consumption does not have a strong impact in the regressions without country dummies, but it is negative and weakly significant in the models with country dummies. This provides evidence that firms prefer lower levels of government spending, but only after other fixed country factors are controlled for. Thus, there is little support that FDI flows to countries with

TABLE 5.2
Time-Series-Cross-Sectional Analysis

	Model 4	Model 5	Model 6	Model 7
Past FDI	0.598***	0.379***	0.574***	0.364***
	(7.49)	(4.63)	(8.62)	(5.06)
Market Size	−0.54	−0.689	0.008	−0.554
	(−1.29)	(−1.51)	(0.33)	(−1.24)
Growth	0.022***	0.021***	0.025***	0.024***
	(2.86)	(2.69)	(3.15)	(2.96)
Trade	0.007***	0.002	0.009***	0.006
	(3.51)	(0.37)	(4.71)	(1.25)
Level of Development	0.075	1.151**	0.007	0.834*
	(1.11)	(2.54)	(0.14)	(1.87)
Budget Deficits	0.005	−0.033***	0.004	−0.023**
	(0.50)	(−3.02)	(0.39)	(−2.19)
Government Consumption	−0.001	−0.061***	−0.013*	−0.039**
	(−0.12)	(−3.01)	(−1.69)	(−2.36)
Democracy			0.012**	0.021***
			(2.41)	(2.61)
Constant	0.643	5.727	−0.124	12.428
	(0.80)	(0.98)	(−0.19)	(1.24)
Time Dummies	Yes	Yes	Yes	Yes
Country Dummies	No	Yes	No	Yes
Observations	1823	1823	1630	1630
Countries	128	128	114	114
R-sq	0.52	0.63	0.54	0.61

*** = 99% confidence level, ** = 95% confidence level, * = 90% confidence level

low levels of government spending, but a given country can increase FDI inflows if they can maintain the same quality of infrastructure and level of workforce quality and at the same time decrease levels of government spending. Efficient governments can attract FDI, but this is different from arguing that small government attracts FDI.

The picture on economic growth also changes dramatically from the cross-sectional regressions. Growth proves rather significant and positively associated with higher levels of FDI as a percentage of GDP for both sets of models. The difference in this result and the cross-sectional results obtained earlier most likely hinges on business cycles. When I include a longer timer period, it becomes obvious that countries with higher growth rates attract more FDI. The level of budget deficits is negative and statistically significant in models with country dummies but insignificant without these dummy variables.

Democracy is positive and statistically significant in all models. This result proves especially interesting given the regressions with country dummies, where even when I control all time-constant country attributes, nations that increase their level of democracy will boost their FDI inflows. Fully democratic governments (scores of 20) attracted and added 0.24 percent to 0.42 percent more FDI flows as a percentage of GDP than fully autocratic countries (scores of 0). Considering that countries over this time period have an average FDI flow level of 1.3 percent of GDP, democratic political regimes enormously affect FDI inflows.

This effect appears even larger considering the cumulative influence of democratic institutions on FDI. The empirical framework of this chapter analyzes the effects of democratic political institutions on FDI *flows*. These flows contribute to the *stock* of foreign capital in the country, where democratic political systems accumulate a larger capital stock over time than their authoritarian counterparts. The most conservative long-run estimate of democracy's effect on FDI inflows (the lowest coefficient on democracy in Model 6) predicts that a democratic country will attract an added 0.56 percent as a percentage of GDP, which amounts to an increase of over 43 percent of FDI inflows. Using the coefficients from Model 7, this estimate jumps to an added 0.66 percent of GDP, or an increase of over 50 percent.[25]

These empirical results remain robust under a number of different model specifications. In Jensen (2003a) I explored whether the advanced democratic countries in the OECD may drive the positive link between democracy and FDI. A second potential objective is that the independent variables like market size and level of development may correlate highly and may bias the empirical results.[26] The finding on the positive relationship remains positive and statistically significant in all models. This relationship on the impact of democracy on FDI inflows is the strongest finding in this book.

Another potentially serious criticism is that these results may be driven by a particular measurement of the democracy. Although the Polity measure of political regimes remains largely the standard measure of democracy employed in most empirical studies, it is essentially a subjective measure. Unfortunately, all measures of democracy contain some degree of subjectivity.

Theoretically, the strongest measure of political regimes comes from Alvarez, Cheibub, Limongi, and Przeworski (1996). This variable codes a democracy as a 0 and an authoritarian regime a 1. This measure, referred to henceforth as ACLP remains in many ways less subjective than the Polity III variable since it uses a stricter, more minimalist definition of democracy, and it relies solely on observables.[27] Countries

are only considered democratic if they fulfill a very specific set of criteria. Any country that fails to fulfill any of these criteria is coded as
authoritarian. Thus, a fully democratic regime is coded in the Polity
data set as a 20 and a 0 in the ACLP data set, while the most authoritarian systems are coded as a 0 in the Polity data set and a 1 in the ACLP
data set. Although the ACLP measure correlates highly with the Polity
variable in my sample (-0.87), it remains at a minimum an important
robustness test of the link between democracy and FDI.

In table 5.3, Model 8, I present empirical estimates using the ACLP
measure of political regimes in the most conservative regressions—a
lagged dependent variable OLS panel corrected standard errors with
country dummies. The empirical results remain unaffected by this
change in measures of democracy. Dictatorships attract less FDI.

The final set of empirical tests on the determinants of FDI examines
the potential selection effects of democracy on FDI inflows. Przeworski
et al. (2000) find that very few poor democracies survive adverse economic conditions, leading to fewer observations of democratic governments in poor countries. Empirical tests that do not account for this
dynamic may suffer from a potential selection bias, in my case biasing
the results on the effects of democratic governance on FDI inflows.

To control for these effects, I use a treatment effects selection model.
To estimate the selection corrected effects of democracy, I use the level
of GDP per capita and the number of past democratic breakdowns to
generate probit estimates of the existence of democratic regimes. I then
use this predicted result in a standard OLS regression with country
and time dummies.[28]

I present the results as Model 9 in table 5.3. For this regression, all
variables remain the same as those employed earlier, except that I sub-
stituted the Polity III measure of democracy with a dichotomous measure of dictatorship from Alvarez et al. (1996), because of the need for
a dichotomous measure of democracy to employ this empirical technique. This ACLP measure finds a similar impact of democracy on FDI
inflows. Democratic regimes attract roughly 0.38 percent more FDI as
a percentage of GDP than their authoritarian counterparts. When I employ the selection model, I find that a significant selection bias in the
OLS results.[29] I vastly *underestimated* the effects of democratic governance on FDI inflows. When I take these selection effects into account,
democratic governments attract 0.95 percent more FDI as a percentage
of GDP per year. Democratic countries attract 73 percent more FDI
than their authoritarian counterparts.

These selection effects hinge on the size of FDI inflows to developing
countries. Although the majority of FDI occurs between developed
countries, when measured as a percentage of GDP, developing coun-

TABLE 5.3.
Selection Models of Democracy and FDI

	Model 8	Model 9
Past FDI	0.309***	0.311***
	(3.98)	(14.65)
Market Size	0.614	−0.631
	(−1.33)	(−1.44)
Growth	0.023***	0.022***
	(2.71)	(3.10)
Trade	0.007	0.007**
	(1.55)	(2.35)
Development Level	0.947**	0.810
	(2.14)	(1.57)
Budget Deficits	−0.024**	−0.024***
	(−2.16)	(−2.95)
Government Consumption	−0.045**	−0.045***
	(−2.45)	(−3.30)
Dictatorship	−0.380***	−0.952***
	(−3.99)	(−2.90)
Constant	8.594	10.169
	(1.14)	(1.59)
Time Dummies	Yes	Yes
Country Dummies	Yes	Yes
Observations	1584	1584
Countries	104	104
R-sq	0.60	
Rho	—	0.261
		(0.130)
Sigma	—	1.260
		(0.031)
Lamda	—	0.329
		(0.170)
LR Test, Chi-sq (Probability)	—	0.138

*** = 99% confidence level, ** = 95% confidence level, * = 90% confidence level

tries attract the highest amount of FDI in the sample. These developing countries also tend to be authoritarian, or at least more authoritarian than the developed countries in this sample. This result can lead us to a spurious correlation between authoritarian regimes and high levels of FDI inflows. In actuality, lower levels of economic development explain the high levels of FDI as a percentage of GDP.

Essentially, the standard OLS regressions understate the effects of democracy on FDI. The OLS regressions ignore the fact that poor countries attract more FDI as a percentage of GDP, and that poor countries also tend to be authoritarian. When I control these effects using a standard treatment effects selection model, I find that the true positive effects of democratic institutions on FDI inflows are even more significant than reported in the OLS estimates.

5.6 Democracy and Sovereign Debt Risk

Although this chapter argues that the informational and representational characteristics of democratic systems positively affect FDI inflows, the greatest benefit remains that democratic systems increase the credibility of political leaders. This section attempts to examine the effects of democratic institutions on levels of political risk. According to my theory, democratic institutions should decrease the potential risks of government leaders choosing policies that negatively affect multinational operations.

To address this relationship empirically, I examine the link between democracy and government credibility by how democratic institutions affect the sovereign debt ratings of governments. Granted, this measure does not directly test the credibility-improving character of democratic institutions for multinational investors, but it does help us to examine more clearly the causal mechanism. The ex-post/ex-ante bargaining nature of FDI proves similar to the dilemma faced by political leaders attempting to obtain loans from foreign lenders. As I argued earlier, governments make promises on the repayment of loans, but once disbursed, these conditions may not be met. Reputation costs emerge for default, but often the short-run political and economic incentives outweigh this downside.[30] Creditors must attempt to predict the potential of default by examining the country's economic conditions and political institutions along with future world macroeconomic conditions.

Do democratic governments less frequently renege on foreign debtors? More specifically, are democratic governments less risky in terms of sovereign debt? To answer this question I have constructed a number of empirical tests of the effects of democratic institutions on country risk ratings. A number of empirical studies examine the economic determinants of country risk ratings.[31] These works have found that the level of economic development, the government current account balance, and the level of country debt all associate with country risk. I build a model of the economic determinants of country risk using data on the level of development (GDP per capita), debt (central gov-

TABLE 5.4.
Democracy and Sovereign Debt Ratings

Variable	Institutional Investor	Institutional Investor	Euromoney	Euromoney
Development Level	0.809***	0.149*	0.874***	0.250*
	(29.317)	(1.898)	(16.296)	(1.821)
Democracy	0.031***	0.011***	0.027***	−0.000
	(9.173)	(3.772)	(6.974)	(−0.006)
Current Account	0.014***	−0.003	0.008	0.005
	(−8.014)	(−1.074)	(1.215)	(1.040)
Debt	−0.004***	−0.003***	−0.002***	−0.004***
	(−8.014)	(−7.467)	(−3.732)	(−5.821)
GDP Growth	0.024***	0.009***	0.026***	0.020***
	(3.304)	(2.735)	(3.071)	(4.187)
Time Dummies	Yes	Yes	Yes	Yes
Cntry Dummies	No	Yes	No	Yes
No. Countries	73	73	79	79
No. Obs	695	695	705	705
R-sq	0.70	0.96	0.63	0.90

*** = 99% confidence level, ** = 95% confidence level, * = 90% confidence level

ernment debt/GDP), and current account balance (current account/ GDP), all from the World Bank's World Development Indicators.

For these regressions, I use both the Institutional Investor credit ratings and Euromoney as the dependent variables. The Euromoney credit rating scores are constructed by a panel of experts who assign values to countries in a number of economic and political categories and generate an aggregate measure of country risk using weighted averages. The Euromoney credit risk ratings come from a survey of roughly one hundred international banks on the probability of default. Sticking to convention, I use the logistic transformation of both ratings.[32]

In table 5.4 I present the results of a series of OLS regressions with panel-corrected standard errors that examine the determinants of sovereign risk ratings. As expected, in all models, the level of economic development has a positive and statistically significant effect on country risk ratings, while the level of country debt has a negative effect. The current account deficit does not statistically affect country risk, while GDP growth was positive, although not statistically significant. All models are robust, also controlling for levels of inflation or exchange rate variations.[33]

In both sets of models, democratic institutions correspond to higher country sovereign debt ratings. In the first set of models without country dummies, the one with the Institutional Investor scores as the dependent variable, democracy emerges as positive and highly statistically significant. In the final model, the Euromoney regression with country dummies, I find no relationship between Euromoney ratings and political regimes—not a surprising finding given the stability of Euromoney ratings over time. Essentially, the country dummies do most of the work in this regression. Other important controls that do not vary much over time, such as the level of economic development, remain only weakly statistically significant.

In summary, when I control for all other economic factors, democratic institutions correlate with lower levels of political risk in terms of sovereign default. This result sheds some light on the earlier finding that democratic governments attract higher levels of FDI. As stated earlier, the political risks involved with multinationals' investment decisions appear similar to those faced by multinational corporations investing in foreign markets. Although this measure does not directly test the causal mechanism, it does provide a foundation for the credibility-enhancing nature of democratic institutions.

5.7 Qualitative Evidence

To further test the relationship between political institutions and FDI inflows, I interviewed representatives of investment promotion agencies, location consultants, political risk insurers/analysts, and multinational corporations. These interviews unequivocally support the view that democratic institutions lower political risks for multinationals. Below I highlight some of the details from these interviews.

One preliminary way to test the relationship between democratic institutions and FDI inflows is to examine how investment promotion agencies attempt to attract FDI inflows. As mentioned in earlier chapters, although these agencies have the incentive to engage in "cheap talk," making the claim that their country is a fantastic environment for multinationals, the way in which these agencies discuss political institutions is indicative of the types of environments they are attempting to convey to multinationals. What factors do investment promotion agencies pitch to interested multinationals?

I performed a content analysis of the Web sites of 115 investment promotion agencies to explore this question.[34] Of these 115 agencies, 66 agencies either highlighted their country as "democratic," or gave specific details on the democratic process, such as describing the electoral system. This set of countries that listed themselves as democratic is largely made up of developing countries such as Belize and India, and middle-income countries such as Poland. Simply counting the number of countries that list democracy as an important factor may not be fully representative of the importance of democracy for multinational investors. Many of the wealthiest, long-standing democracies, such as Canada, Sweden, Switzerland, and Japan, did not formally mention their democratic institutions. Does this mean that democracy isn't important for multinationals? One possibility is that every investor in the world knows that Canada is a democratic country with strong property-rights protection, but for developing countries, investment promotion agencies are attempting to convey their political environment as conducive to FDI inflows.

These poorer developing countries are a different story. For the less developed democratic countries, such as Belize, the investment promotion agencies clearly pointed out democracy as an important factor for investment.[35] For the nondemocratic systems, some countries made claims of being democratic or transitioning to democracy, for example China's claims of a transition to "socialist democracy."[36] Other countries simply did not mention their political system in any way, such as Singapore's stressing of mostly economic factors and no specific mention of political institutions.[37] No investment promotion agency made the case that nondemocratic institutions were beneficial for interested investors.

To further explore this relationship I interviewed representatives of investment promotion agencies. The democratic regimes, such as Costa Rica and Hungary, carefully highlighted their political institutions as an important selling point for multinational investors. For example, in an open-ended interview a representative of the Office of the Hungarian Trade Commission highlighted all three causal mechanisms linking democratic regimes to higher FDI flows. Democratic institutions in Hungary provided investors with better information, avenues for representation, and higher levels of credibility. Interestingly, the representative also argued that admission into the European Union, beyond opening a larger export market for multinationals, provided a credible signal to multinationals about Hungary's political institutions. Prior to EU admission, investors often asked detailed questions about Hungary's political institutions. Now, EU admission provides investors information on the quality of Hungary's political institutions, including their level of democracy.

Malaysia, a political regime coded as authoritarian in most data sets, provides a different example. Representatives of the Malaysian Industrial Development Authority stated that most investors inquired about Malaysia's political institutions. The representative would usually discuss the specific features of Malaysia's electoral process and make the case that Malaysia is in fact democratic. Whether Malaysia is authoritarian, as coded in most political science regime variables, or a legitimate democratic regime, I leave to the reader. The key point is that democratic institutions are a selling point for investment promotion agencies.

In an interview with a representative of B-G Consulting, a consulting company that helped provide support for the Bolivian Investment Promotion Agency, political risks emerged as an important topic of discussion. High political risks are a major concern for multinationals considering investments in Bolivia. How does this relate to democracy? According to the president of B-G Consulting, democracies simply have lower political risks than nondemocracies.

This same argument was made by investment location and public relations consultants. A representative of Baker, Donelson, Bearman, Caldwell & Berkowitz P.C., a firm that provides a number of business consulting services, argued that the link between political risks and democracy was fairly straightforward. Democratic systems entail lower political risks.

I also discussed the impact of democratic institutions on political risks with the World Bank's Multilateral Investment Guarantee Agency (MIGA) and Export Development Canada (EDC). Both of these agencies provide both political risk assessment and political risk insurance to multinationals investing in risky environments.

EDC employs both qualitative and quantitative analysis for Canadian multinationals considering investments abroad. First, they subjectively examine political risks through "country filters" where they have an expert on the country or region generate a benchmark political risk score. After this initial country filter, EDC uses quantitative variables to rate the country in terms of transaction risks (currency controls, etc.), expropriation and breach of contract, and political violence.

Although measures of transaction risks (currency risks) don't use any specific regime variable, both political violence and expropriation specifically include measures of democracy. In terms of political violence, the countries with high probabilities of political violence include those with existing violent conflicts, those with high socioeconomic tensions or ethnic and religious tensions, and those lacking "legitimacy." Nondemocratic countries are coded as having higher political violence risks.

In the EDC model of expropriation and breach of contract rating, one of the variables considered is category of regimes. The most stable of these regimes are stable democracies with limited party fractionalization, and monarchies with successors. The medium-risk category comprises monarchies without successors, democracies with highly fractionalized parties, and authoritarian regimes. Finally, the highest risk category is authoritarian regimes with "strong-man" style rule and "immature democracies." These immature democracies are undergoing their first election and there is a reasonable probability that major political conflict will occur after the election.[38] Although they find that some types of monarchies can be just as stable as established democracies, these monarchies are fairly rare in the world. In most cases, democratic regimes lead to lower levels of expropriation risks.

The World Bank Groups Multilateral Investment Guarantee Agency (MIGA) has recently implemented a program that predicts the probability of expropriation and breach of contract claims. In their model, their best predictor is a subject measure of risk by Political Risk Services. This measure, ICRG Political Stability, is a composite measure of twelve factors, including a component for "democratic accountability.[39] Beyond the inclusion of democracy within this political risk composite score, MIGA found that "institutionalized democracy" alone predicted 22 percent of the expropriation claims in their sample. This single variable had a higher predictive power than GNP per capita and a host of other socioeconomic variables. In their model, democratic institutions are associated with lower risks.

Finally, interviews with a number of decision makers and public relations officers representing multinational corporations provide further tests on the impact of democracy on FDI decisions. For example, Alcan, the story highlighted at the introduction of this chapter, engaged in a major contract dispute with a democratic government. What was Alcan's response? They have actively engaged in lobbying the government with other international and domestic firms through the Brazilian aluminum producers groups. Democratic Brazil hasn't erased political risks for Alcan, but it has given the firm an avenue to influence government policy.

A similar story comes from Intel Corporation. Intel has massive production and R&D facilities around the world. Interviews with Intel representatives highlight the importance of both economic and political factors for their investment decisions. Political factors such as political and economic stability, along with macroeconomic management, are important. How does Intel minimize political risks once they establish a presence in a country?

One of Intel's largest and most sophisticated production and R&D facilities is located just outside of San Jose, Costa Rica. The Costa Rican government is proposing sweeping changes in their individual and corporate tax rates. How does Intel minimize the political risks of negative tax changes? They count on their influence with the central government, specifically through lobbying both individually and with groups of likeminded foreign and domestic firms.

This story on Intel and Costa Rica is not an isolated one. In interview with six multinational firms that have invested in Costa Rica, most argued that political factors had some influence over their investment decisions. Many of these firms had explored other investment locations, such as L. L. Bean comparing Costa Rica and Peru and Weststar exploring the possibility of production facilities in Indonesia. In both cases the firms ruled out the other country because of political risks.

A number of multinational representatives directly argued that the policy stability and credibility of promises made by governments are important factors for investment in democracies. For example, the deputy head of the Latin American Research Department at UBS plainly stated that democracies may have some policy volatility, but they are less risky for multinationals. Dictators are more likely to dramatically change policies that may directly or indirectly harm multinationals.

Most multinationals interviewed highlighted the advantages of investment in democracies. No firm interviewed made any claim that other regime types provided a more favorable investment environment. Firms stressed different causal mechanisms for preference for democracies, but a general consensus found that democracies provided less political risks for multinationals.

5.8 Conclusion

I began this chapter with Alcan's power dispute in Brazil. Interestingly, Brazil is a democratic country that seemingly is engaging in "creeping expropriation" of Alcan's future income streams. Isn't this a counterexample of the relationship between democracy and political risks? Not exactly. Although at the time of this writing, the dispute was still ongoing, Alcan was rallying other multinationals and domestic firms to protest the change in power prices. Alcan found natural allies in the Brazilian Aluminum Association and has pressed the government on this issue. I take no normative position on whether the final outcome will be good or bad for the Brazilian economy or people, but clearly Brazil's democratic institutions provide avenues for influence.

The empirical analysis in this chapter develops a number of models of FDI inflows, checking the robustness of the link between democratic governance and FDI by changing the model specifications and empirical tests. The evidence on political regimes proves relatively conclusive; democratic governments attract higher levels of FDI. These results remain robust across empirical tests and model specifications. Democratic institutions have a large positive effect on FDI inflows. These results become even stronger when I control for the selection effects of the lack of democracies in developing countries. In sum, all of these empirical tests find that democracies attract higher levels of FDI.

The results on sovereign debt risk point to one possible link between democracy and higher levels of FDI. Democratic governments, when I account for all other economic conditions, correspond to lower country risk. These risks associated with debt risk parallel those faced by multinationals investing in foreign locations. One logical conjecture stemming from this result becomes that democracy lowers country risk, for both lenders and multinational investors.

The qualitative analysis in this chapter highlights the importance of democratic institutions. In essentially every interview, the qualitative evidence supports the qualitative evidence provided in this chapter: Democratic institutions are preferred for multinationals investors.

Taken as a whole, these empirical results cast serious doubt on the doomsday prediction about the link between democratic political institutions and FDI. Democratic institutions do not prove inefficient in terms of attracting multinational corporations. Simply no empirical evidence exists that multinationals prefer to invest in dictatorships over democratic regimes. On the contrary, the empirical evidence in this chapter suggests that democratic regimes attract as much as 73 percent more FDI than authoritarian regimes.

APPENDIX: DESCRIPTIVE STATISTICS

TABLE A5.1.
Descriptive Statistics: Cross-Section Variables

Variable	Obs	Mean	SD	Min	Max
FDI inflows	165	1.96	2.68	−11.03	13.59
Wealth	111	7.95	1.07	5.99	9.8
Exports	156	33.72	24.48	3.38	189.07
Taxes on Trade	130	21.05	17.29	0	68.29
Natural Resources	120	0.24	0.4	0	3.74
Growth	105	0.201	2.33	−6.35	6.6
Government Consumption	163	16.9	7.71	2.36	58.31
Budget Deficit	126	−4.4	6.1	−39.61	24.51
Human Capital	102	4.86	2.88	0.54	12.039
Income Inequality	102	39.2	9.99	21.19	60.95
FDI Laws	93	2.6	0.87	1	5
Democracy	130	10.9	7.87	0	20
Effective Party Control	118	1.49	0.97	0	4.885
Reputation	123	5.81	2.34	1	10
Expropriation	123	6.55	2.22	1	10
Corruption	123	3.3	1.48	0	6
Rule of Law	123	2.98	1.63	0	6
Bureaucratic Quality	123	3.19	1.55	1	6

TABLE A5.2.
Descriptive Statistics: Time-Series-Cross-Sectional Variables

Variable	Obs	Mean	SD	Min	Max
FDI inflows	3519	1.34	2.93	−30.33	39.21
Wealth	3141	7.99	1.08	5.44	10.32
Exports	3808	34.21	24.65	0.89	215.38
Taxes on Trade	2639	18.9	17	0	76.51
Growth	3833	3.37	7.46	−52.3	181.15
Government Consumption	3772	16.02	7.22	0.9	76.22
Budget Deficit	2521	−3.64	5.96	−61.14	58.71
Democracy	3727	9.69	7.78	0	20
Capital Controls	4247	0.19	0.39	0	1
Exchange Rates	1420	116.58	66	37.1	921.42

6

Veto Players and FDI

6.1 Introduction

In 1997, Alabama won a bidding war among thirty other U.S. states for a $300 million Mercedes-Benz production facility in Tuscaloosa. The negotiated entry deal included a $250 million incentive package that amounted to a transfer of $168,000 per job created. While it is unclear what impact this production facility has had on the Alabama economy, the production facility has been a success for the firm and the company has invested in a $600 million expansion that will add an additional two thousand jobs.[1]

A similar situation arose in Brazil, where Ford and General Motors (GM) chose Rio Grande do Sul as their location for automotive production facilities. Both companies were granted generous tax breaks and financial incentives for their investment. In 1998, the new mayor of Rio Grande do Sul, Olivio Dutra, argued that the tax incentives offered to the auto companies were excessive and they would be renegotiated. GM had completed construction of their $600 million auto production facility, while Ford had only prepared its site for the plant but had not begun construction.

Ford began negotiating with other states on similar incentive packages, and made an agreement with the state of Bahia.[2] Bahia matched the original incentive package, while Ford was also offered additional incentives from the central government that provided support to firms investing in poor regions of the country, including a low-interest rate $300 million loan. Ford abandoned its plans in Rio Grande do Sul and built their production facility in Bahia. Other firms that had already built production facilities, such as GM, were left to attempt to negotiate with the Rio Grande do Sul government, although from a less favorable bargaining position.

In the examples highlighted above, federal institutions had positive effects for multinationals, but also generated some political risks. State and local governments have the ability to offer tax incentives to multinationals, yet they also have the ability to renege on past promises after MNEs have invested. In chapter 3 I argued that political institutions can be important commitment mechanisms to market-friendly policies, and in chapter 5 I argued that democratic institutions have a positive impact on FDI inflows. In this chapter, I focus on how other types of political institutions affect FDI inflows. Specifically, I focus on how veto players and federal political institutions affect FDI inflows.

6.2 Veto Players

In an influential body of work, Tsebelis (1995, 2002) constructs a formal analysis of the relationship between veto players and policy stability. Defining veto players as individual or collective actors whose approval proves necessary for policy change, such as systems with a separation between the president and legislature, he constructs a simple model of policy change.

Using the actors' preferences (ideal points) and the formal voting rules, Tsebelis constructs what he calls the "winset."[3] This winset includes the set of policies, or the area of the policy space, which could defeat the status quo. In other words, the winset contains all of the potential policy changes from the status quo that all veto players would approve. This winset predicts future policy change.

The common interpretation of Tsebelis concludes that as the number of veto players increases, the size of this winset decreases. If we define policy stability as the range of possible policy changes, then it increases as the number of veto players increases. In simple terms, more veto players decrease the number of positions that all veto players can agree upon. For example, in systems such as the United States where there is a formal separation between the executive, legislative, and judicial branches of government, policy change is more difficult than in a system with fewer veto players, such as the British electoral system where there is no formal separation between the executive and legislative branches of government. Although this interpretation on the number of veto players generating policy stability generally seems fair, it fails to capture an important element of Tsebelis's argument.

For Tsebelis, not only does the number of veto players pose an important consideration, but so do the preferences of these veto players (the ideal points). In other words, it becomes possible for a country to have fewer veto players than another country, yet have higher degrees of policy stability (a smaller winset).[4] Therefore, not only does the number of veto players matter, but also their preferences in reference to each other matter as well. For example, the mere separation of powers between the legislative and executive offices doesn't take into account the preferences of these actors. If the legislature and the executive share similar preferences on legislation, for example if both the presidency and the legislative house(s) are controlled by the same party, the formal separation of powers may not decrease the ability to change policy. In the following section I expand on this simple example and discuss how differing preferences of actors within a political system are important to multinationals.

6.3 Veto Players and FDI

In the theoretical chapter of this book, I argue that policy stability does not provide an end in itself. Multinationals want commitments to "market-friendly policy," but this desire remains logically distinct from policy stability. Indeed, multinationals do not even necessarily prefer stable policies.

In chapter 3 I offered a simple argument. Multinationals prefer institutions that provide commitments to market-friendly policies and appear flexible enough to adapt to world economic and political conditions. In short, institutions must both generate some level of commitment to policy stability, and at the same time, offer an element of flexibility. Operationalizing this argument both in theoretical and empirical terms proves less simple. What type of institution can exhibit this mix of commitment and dynamism multinational corporations seek?

The argument I put forward in this chapter asserts that veto players in the political system can provide commitments and flexibility, but only under certain conditions. The preference structure of these veto players matters. For example, increasing the number of veto players could increase the level of policy stability, but this act does not correspond to preferring more market-friendly policies for multinationals. My argument suggests that only when some degree of convergence between the preferences of multinationals and the preference of one of the veto players exists do veto players help ensure market-friendly policies. Only when one of the veto players represents the interests of the multinationals more closely than that of the central government do veto players provide both the flexibility and credibility valued by multinational corporations.

If we have two hypothetical countries, one with no veto players (outside of the central government) and the other with one veto player (other than the central government), the logic of this argument becomes clear. Assume that the government (G) and the multinational (M) negotiate on one issue (I). The government has one preference (if this issue centers on taxes, the government prefers high taxes) and the multinational another (low taxes). Without going into a complex bargaining model, we may assume that the negotiated deal (D) between

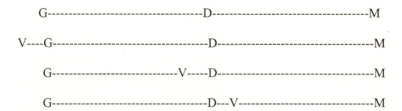

Figure 6.1. Veto Players and Policy Stability

the two actors will lie somewhere in between both of these ideal points, assuming unidimensionality (see fig. 6.1).

Once the multinational invests in the foreign country, the government has the incentive to alter the deal to move D closer to its ideal point. Now let us introduce a veto player. In this simple example, let us compare the potential policy changes with three different ideal points for the veto player.

Without discussing formalities, the predicted renegotiation in all three cases proves simple. Let us assume that the multinational and government first negotiate D. Next, the government can choose to alter the deal, but the government must obtain the approval of the veto player (V) to change from the status quo. The government acts as the agenda setter, proposing a change from the status quo (D), and the veto player can choose to accept the new deal or maintain the status quo.

In the second example in figure 6.1, the veto players' preferences lie farther to the "left" than that of the government or the status quo. The veto player will accept any renegotiation that moves the current deal closer to its ideal point. In this case, the veto players prefer any move left of the current deal (D). Knowing this, the government has the ability to renegotiate the terms, locating the new deal at its own ideal point. This move makes the veto player better off than the status quo, the government better off, and the multinational worse off.

In the third example, the veto player's preferences lie in between that of the status quo and the government's ideal point (interval GD). In this case, policy change should still favor the government over the multinational, but the degree of policy change depends on the exact location of the ideal point for the veto player. The government can propose a move from the status quo, but it can only go so far in altering the initial negotiated deal. Moving the status quo too far to the left will force the veto player to reject the policy change and maintain the status quo.

In the fourth example, when the preferences of the veto player lie to the right of the status quo (interval DM), the veto player will reject any proposed change in the status quo to the left. This observation proves critical. The veto player would oppose changes in the status quo that are closer to the ideal point of the central government. Thus, the government would not propose any policy change. A negotiation between a multinational and a government becomes credible when a veto player is on the same half of the policy space as the multinational (interval GM). In the theoretical section of this chapter I argue that this arrangement of ideal points is most likely in a politically federal system.

This situation could provide an important basis for a negotiation strategy for both a government and multinationals. A veto player can help make deals credible between firms and states. For example, if the veto player's preferences lie on the interval DM, then a government commitment to deal D remains credible. But I argue a more fundamental benefit to this analysis emerges.

Much of the interplay between multinationals and states does not relate to the explicit contract made, such as the level of taxation. Rather, multinationals care how the overall policy environment will affect multinational operations. Once again, will the government provide market-friendly policies?

This veto player analysis sheds some light on this issue. My argument centers on the fact that in political systems where one or more veto players share a similar preference structure with a multinational, or at least preferences closer than that of the central government, veto players can increase the probability of market-friendly policies. In a dynamic environment with multiple issues on the agenda, and only some explicitly negotiated, multinationals can have reasonable assurances on the future of economic policy with certain types of veto players. These players have similar preferences to multinationals, or have the incentive to cater to the interests of multinationals, and provide multinational firms with commitments to market-friendly policies.

In the following sections of this chapter, I will focus on the role of federalism in promoting FDI. This scenario provides just one example of a veto player that could provide benefits to multinationals. I contrast the institutional structure of political federal actors and their preferences to fiscally federal systems. I argue that subnational units in a politically federal system have similar preferences to multinationals on some issues, while fiscally federal subnational actors do not.

6.4 Federalism

Scholars have become increasingly interested in the study of federalism. Theorists have revived old debates on the effects of federal institutions on economic performance and have generated a number of new theories supported by formal models and empirical tests. Unfortunately, to date, no consensus has emerged in either the theoretical or the empirical analysis on federalism's effects on the economic performance.

Part of the reason for this theoretical and empirical confusion centers on the complexity of the concept of federalism. I argue that serious conceptual distinctions characterize different forms of federalism that affect economic performance. More precisely, this chapter explores the effects of federalism on the ability of countries to attract FDI by differentiating between three types of federalism: (1) fiscal federalism, (2) political federalism, and (3) political decentralization.

Using this conceptual distinction as a guide, we can more clearly examine the effects of federal political institutions on multinational investments. I test the differing effects of fiscal federalism and political federalism on FDI inflows for 124 countries from 1975 to 1995. The central finding of this chapter reflects that politically federal institutions correspond to higher inflows of FDI, while fiscal federalism has no statistically significant effect.

6.5 Federalism and Economic Performance

Although a complete review of the literature on federalism's effects on economic performance lies beyond the scope of this chapter, a number of notable scholars have examined the benefits of federal institutions on economic performance, enhancing our understanding of the impact federalism has on FDI. One thesis is that state actors are more knowledgeable about local tastes and business costs than the central government in a unitary state (Oates 1999). The "laboratory of federalism" concept stresses the role of federalism in finding innovative solutions to problems by allowing different states to experiment with different policy solutions. Rose-Ackerman (1980), however, posits that this tactic leads to free-riding by states.[5] Brennan and Buchanan (1980) argue that fiscal decentralization can help control public expenditures, although Oates (1985) finds no evidence to support this claim.[6] Moreover, federal institutions can provide competition for mobile factors between subnational units (Tiebout 1956). If mobile factors can "vote with their feet," subnational units will force market-enhancing competition, such as investments in growth-promoting infrastructure (Qian and Roland 1998).

Federal institutions can also have political advantages that lead to better macroeconomic performance. Most notably, Weingast (1995) argues that federal institutions ensure limited government, allowing nation-states to credibly commit to ensuring property rights. Moreover, a series of papers examine the role of federal institutions in promoting economic development (North and Weingast 1989; Montinola, Quian, and Weingast 1995).

Other theorists stress federalism's potential negative effects on economic performance. Subnational units may be more susceptible to corruption, particularly problematic in developing countries (Prud' homme 1995; Rodden and Rose-Ackerman 1997; Bardhan and Mookherjee 2000). Wibbels (2000) finds empirical evidence that politically federal institutions inhibit macroeconomic performance and economic reform in developing countries.

These differing empirical results on the impact of federalism in macroeconomic performance can partially be attributed to the complexity of federal institutions. Some recent works attempt to disaggregate the conceptual distinctions between different forms of federalism and empirically test these effects.[7] Before this step proves possible in our case, we need to review the different concepts of federalism.

6.6 Political Federalism, Political Decentralization, and Fiscal Federalism

Before embarking on a discussion of *political* federalism and *political* decentralization, one must contrast these arrangements with the growing literature on *fiscal* federalism/decentralization. Early scholars such as Tiebout (1956) and Oates (1972) constructed the foundation for the study of fiscal decentralization on economic performance. Fiscal federalism and fiscal decentralization entail a degree of regional government autonomy from the central government in both taxing and spending. Although these works on fiscal decentralization provide important academic contributions, they miss an important institutional element of federal systems.

As spelled out in chapter 1, Weingast (1995) amends the literature on fiscal federalism, arguing that for states to be "market-preserving" federal countries, five conditions must be met

1. A *hierarchy* of governments must exist, with a clear scope of authority.
2. The *autonomy* of each government is assured through some set of institutions.
3. The subnational governments become the primary agents responsible for *regulation* of the economy.
4. There must be a guaranteed *common market* of free trade between subnational units.
5. Subnational units face a *hard budget constraint*.

Weingast stresses that while the first two conditions may ensure a politically federal system as envisioned by Riker (1964), the final three conditions give the subnational units enough autonomy to constrain the central government.

This concept of market-preserving federalism has endured some criticism. Rodden and Rose-Ackerman (1997) stress that not only do almost all federal systems fall short of meeting this standard, this theory also does not address other political and electoral pressures within a political system. As Wibbels (2000) suggests, this literature has "failed to account for the differences in political incentives facing subnational leaders in federal and unitary nations. . . . The difficulty with this perspective is that it fails to account for the crucial role of political accountability."[8]

Moving away from fiscal federalism, the study of politically federal institutions provide an important element in understanding the relationships of political accountability between the central government and regional governments. These political relationships prove difficult to separate and classify. Daniel Elazar identifies a number of politically federal institutional arrangements, including, federations, confederations, unions, constitutionally decentralized unions, federacies, associated statehood, condominiums, leagues, and joint functional authorities.[9] For Lijphart (1999), these distinctions break down into two dimensions: federal/unitary and decentralized/centralized.[10] These two dimensions clearly point out that, at the very least, politically federal systems are not synonymous with politically decentralized systems.

The definition of politically federal systems employed in this analysis is based on political relationships between the central government and local/regional governments. Contrasting from Watts's (1999) definition of federalism as a combination of "shared-rule and regional self-rule," the working definition of political federalism is based solely on the first dimension.[11] Specifically, political systems where regional actors affect *national* policy are politically federal systems.

Political federalism contrasts with political decentralization, where decentralization encompasses the second part of Watts's definition, self-rule. Regional units are often given functional authority over certain policy areas. This includes "autonomous regions" within a polity that are given some degree of political autonomy but have no real effect on the crafting of national policy.

The working definitions of these three concepts are summarized as:

1. *Fiscal Federalism*: Subnational units are given primary responsibility of spending and raising revenue. These units have primary responsibility of regulating economic activity within their subnational territorial area.

2. *Political Federalism*: Subnational units do not have the primary responsibility of taxing and raising their own revenue but do have a hand in crafting

national policy. Subnational units are involved (in ways that will be described later) in legislation at the national level.

3. *Political Decentralization*: Subnational units are given autonomy over policy within their subnational territorial unit, short of taxing and spending their own revenue. Subnational units have no role in the crafting of national policy.

The debate on federalism's effects on macroeconomic performance centers on the first two concepts. For this study, I exclude further examination of political decentralization and focus on fiscal federalism and political federalism. Significantly, these two conceptions place different theoretical effects on flows of foreign direct investment.

6.7 Federalism and FDI

As highlighted in chapter 3, although investing in foreign production facilities provides substantial benefits, multinational corporations face high levels of risk in these investments. FDI projects enjoy relative liquidity ex ante; companies can make the decision to invest essentially anywhere in the world. Ex post, once multinationals have made the initial investment, constructed production facilities, imported machinery, and sunk fixed costs, their investments quickly become illiquid.

Numerous scholars identify federal institutions as a veto point within the political system. These institutions, such as a legislature that represents regional units, can block the passage of new legislation. Tsebelis (1995) argues that the existence of a larger number of veto points increases the probability of policy stability. From this logic, one could make the argument that federal systems increase the number of veto points in the political system, thus providing a more stable environment for FDI. Henisz (2000, 2002) constructs a measure of the number of veto points, including federal institutions, and argues that this characteristic affects the type of entry decision made by a multinational. Within this framework, federal institutions offer just another barrier to policy change, just as supreme courts, the number of legislative houses, and presidential systems do.

While federal institutions undoubtedly increase the number of veto points within the political system, their potential importance proves much richer and more varied. As Oates (1972) underscores, federal political systems can fit into the principal-agent framework, where the central government and the regional government represent actors with diverse preferences that can greatly affect multinationals.[12]

Federalism becomes a meaningful concept if we specify the preferences of the regional and central governments' actors. If these actors' preferences diverge, then, in the language of Tsebelis (1995, 2002), the size of the winset decreases and policy stability increases. If the preferences of the subnational units coincide perfectly with that of the central government, federalism will have less of an effect on policy stability. Most importantly, if subnational actors have similar preferences to multinationals, they have the incentive to provide market-promoting policies favored by multinationals.

Specifying these preferences facilitates understanding the role of federalism in attracting FDI, and more generally the effects of federalism on macroeconomic performance. The preference structure of the actors within a federal system depends on the formal institutional arrangement of the system. Subnational units that rely on the central government for tax revenue may have very different preferences than if they raise their own revenue. This same logic applies to spending decisions, the ability to regulate firms, and numerous other responsibilities that can be shifted between the central government and subnational units. The structural differences between the three types of federalism analyzed in this chapter—political federalism, political decentralization, and fiscal federalism—entail very different preferences for subnational units.

To highlight these different preference structures in the context of FDI, let us explore a simple example of multinational investment. Multinational investments provide countries with numerous benefits, ranging from national (economy wide) effects to more localized effects. The use of multinational exports to improve the trade balance of the country and generate foreign exchange offers an excellent example of a purely national effect.

Job creation provided by multinational investment supplies one of the most important local benefits. Multinationals create new jobs and in many countries pay higher wages than domestic firms.[13] These jobs barely affect the national economy, but they create a large localized pocket of employment. These jobs opportunities increase as multinationals expand operations, reinvest earnings, and contract with local providers for inputs and services.

By examining the distribution of these benefits, in terms of national and localized benefits, and specifying the institutional structure of the federal system, we can predict the degree of policy stability and the content of the policies. The next section will use the example of the taxation of multinational corporations to highlight the important distinctions between different institutional structures.

6.8 Unitary, Politically Federal, Fiscally Federal Systems and the Issue of Taxation

In chapter 4 I argued that levels of capital taxation have little impact on FDI inflows across countries. But multinationals do attempt to minimize their tax burden. Multinationals often negotiate taxation rates, exemptions levels, depreciation schedules, and tax holidays with host governments before investing. Once committing the investment, however, firms are susceptible to host governments changing their policies toward taxation. These changes can include a renegotiation of the original tax agreement, or may entail a more subtle change in government policy. Assets, for example, meet more favorable depreciation schedules, or specific requirements might allow for lower rates of taxation (such as export requirements).

In a unitary political system, the central government makes all decisions regarding the treatment of the multinational. In these unitary political systems, the government will obviously care about both localized and national benefits, but may have a strong preference toward maximizing national benefits at the expense of localized benefits.

In both politically and fiscally federal systems, on the other hand, actors with much stronger preferences on the maximization of localized FDI benefits will have some degree of power. In its ideal type, fiscally federal subnational units would be fiscally autonomous from the central government, raising and spending their own revenue. These subnational units would bargain directly with multinational corporations and could renegotiate with these firms once the initial investment started.

In politically federal systems, negotiations on taxation levels occur between the central government and the multinational firms. Subnational units pose no direct role in negotiations, but they do have a tremendous amount of political power in influencing the central government's policies. These subnational units can propose or stall legislation,[14] provide suspensive vetoes,[15] or veto legislation completely.[16] This institutional organization parallels a system of checks and balances between an executive and a legislature, requiring both bodies to agree on policy or legislation (Persson, Roland, and Tabellini 1997).

The important distinction between fiscally federal systems and politically federal systems stems from the fact that many of the national benefits of FDI *become localized* in fiscally federal systems. In both systems, pockets of employment benefit the subnational governments, but in the fiscally federal system, the benefits of taxation accrue to the subnational government. For this reason, subnational governments in fiscally federal systems will attempt to maximize the total benefits of employment and taxes from multinationals.

In many ways, a subnational unit within a fiscally federal system begins to look like a unitary state. Throughout the world, unitary states tax their citizens and spend their own revenue. While scholars often argue that the "hard-budget constraints" of subnational units within fiscally federal nations force subnational units into better behavior, unitary nation-states also face hard budget constraints. The competition between states within a federal system for international investment mirrors competition between nation-states for international investment within the international systems. In essence, since the degree of competition between states already proves high, the potential benefits of fiscal federalism in a world of capital mobility become small.

This scenario presents an obviously idealized conception of a fiscally federal system. In reality, no subnational government remains completely unconstrained in its dealing with multinational corporations. But, the important distinction is the degree to which the incentive structures of the subnational units diverge from the national government. In fiscally federal systems, in their less ideal type, subnational units generate tax revenue from multinational corporations. These subnational units will have preferences similar to the national government, or at least more similar than that of a politically federal nation-state.

Political federalism, on the other hand, could provide some benefits to multinational investors. The agency that negotiates and collects taxes from foreign investors supplies the central difference between fiscal federalism and political federalism. In politically federal systems, subnational units receive relatively few benefits from the taxation of multinational corporations. In these systems, tax revenues benefit the nation as a whole, and the central government attempts to maximize them.

Subnational units have little incentive to behave opportunistically in terms of striking tax deals with multinational corporations. They want to maximize the localized benefits of multinational investment. Moreover, subnational units would at the very least feel indifferent to the central government's interest in renegotiating a tax ex post. If this process entails some costs, either the credibility of the country or the relations with the existing multinationals that may affect localized benefits, then subnational units will attempt to block policy changes.

This argument on taxation provides just one of many examples of subnational actors' potential role in constraining the central government from enacting policies that would harm multinationals. Similar arguments could be made for the imposition of capital controls, changing legislation regarding business regulations, exchange rate decisions, or any host of policies that would be important to multinational corporations. Politically federal institutions can be advantageous to foreign investors because of the shared power between the central and subnational governments.

6.9 The Data

The terms political decentralization and fiscal federalism remain logically distinct from political federalism. While considerable overlap may exist between these systems, scholars by no means consider them synonymous. Since these analytical differences entail divergent underlying patterns of relationships, authority, and responsibility, we, as social scientists, must strive to create measures that capture these variances in our empirical tests. Although a number of academics separate the important features between political decentralization and fiscal decentralization and create corresponding measures, little work designs variables that capture the important distinctions between political federalism and the other alternatives.

The recent devolution of power to Scotland within the United Kingdom provides one example of a politically decentralized system that differs from a politically federal system. Although the creation of a separate parliament ensures Scotland a number of powers, this assembly holds little or no power over national policy. This illustration highlights the distinction between decentralization and the operationalization of "Political Federalism" in this data set.

The political federalism variable attempts to measure the political relationship between subnational units and central governments. In a political federal system, subnational actors help shape *national* policy. By this definition, countries with autonomous or semi-autonomous units do not hold federal status unless these autonomous units play a role in policies that affect the nation as a whole. Political systems where subnational actors join national politics are classified as federal.

I examined a number of institutional features to classify these political regimes. First, countries with bicameral legislatures with a "strong federal chamber" classify as federal.[17] In most cases, this characteristic consists of an upper house representing territorial units, although in some countries this federal dimension centers in the lower house. A formal federal constitution supplies a second important feature. Third, and most often ignored in the federalism literature, remains the ability of regional actors to veto or suspend legislation. For example, in Malaysia, regional elites can suspend central government legislation for thirty days.

This definition allows for the existence of federal systems in authoritarian or semi-democratic regimes. In both democratic and authoritarian systems, the ruling elite needs to maintain the support of some groups within society, whether the majority of the electorate, the military, or some other subset of the population.[18]

Given the heterogeneity of federal political systems, no better formulaic explanation of the construction of the variable emerges. Political federalism acts as an ordinal variable taking on the values of 0, 1, and 2 from the least federal to the most federal. While much finer gradations of federalism exist in the world, the use of this simple measure helps to limit subjectivity.

The time frame of this data set spans from 1975 to 1995. Some countries encountered institutional change within this time period. For countries with institutional change in the first half of the year, I code it as occurring in that year. For countries where institutional change occurred in the second half of the year, I record the institutional change in the following year. The appendix to this chapter describes all thirty federal systems and the timing of any institutional changes.

I relied on a large number of sources for the construction of this variable, including: *The Political Handbook of the World*; *Political Systems of the World*; Watts (1999); The World Bank's Database of Political Institutions; Lijphart (1999); and Wibbels (2000). Wibbels (2000) proved a tremendously informative source for classifying a number of developing countries. For some of these nations, a complete overlap exists between this data set and Wibbels (2000), for which he should receive credit for the country classification. This data set includes annual observations for 124 countries from both the developed and developing world from 1975 to 1995.

In the presentation of this data set, I attempt to limit both Type I and Type II errors. I minimize type II error, the possibility of incorrectly classifying a system as "federal," by giving detailed descriptions of all federal systems in the chapter appendix. Given the small universe of federal systems (30 countries), these accounts allow scholars to examine their institutional structure. Type I error, classifying a system as unitary instead of federal, proves slightly more difficult. Although impossible to examine every political system and explain their institutional features, table A6.1 presents the coding for all 124 countries.

6.10 Empirical Analysis

The empirical analysis of this chapter examines the effects of federal institutions on annual inflows of foreign direct investment. I employ a time-series-cross-sectional regression analysis from 1975 to 1995 for

124 countries, using the same baseline model constructed in chapter 3. I use the same empirical techniques as in chapter 4 and chapter 5: an OLS regression with panel-corrected standard errors, a lagged dependent variable, a one-year lag for all independent variables, and decade dummies.

The regressions equation appears as:

$$\text{Net FDI Inflows}_t = \alpha + \beta^i(\text{Net FDI}_{t-1}) + \beta^i(\text{Independent Varables}_{t-1}) + \varepsilon_i$$

I also include the polity measures of democracy as explained in chapter 5 and a measure of the number of "veto players" in the political system from the World Bank's *Database of Political Institutions*.[19] Including this variable illuminates the relationship between federalism and the number of veto points in the political system. The theory section of this book stresses that political federalism entails a richer conception than just the number of veto points it adds. I test this assertion and present the data in table 6.1.

To examine the effects of fiscally federal institutions on FDI inflows, I use a measure of fiscal federalism from the IMF's World Financial Statistics yearbook.[20] I rely on state and local revenue as a percentage of total revenue.[21] This variable proxies for state and local ability to tax multinational corporations.

In table 6.1 I present the empirical results of the basic model. I estimate both regressions with and without country dummies. Estimation with country dummies is an important robustness test, but it does prove problematic for empirical analysis of the impact of federalism on FDI inflows. In only eleven countries in my sample do we observe institutional change, with nine of these cases moveing toward higher degrees of federalism. This lack of variance on this key independent variable makes estimation of the impact of federalism on FDI inflows difficult to discern when including country dummies. I present both sets of models in table 6.1 with the caveat regarding the problems with the models that include country dummies.

In both sets of regressions, these baseline models produce results similar to the models presented in chapter 5. Higher levels of trade and economic growth are associated with more FDI inflows. Levels of government consumption have a modest negative impact on FDI inflows, while budget deficits have a positive impact. The size of the domestic market and the level of economic development have no statistically significant impact.

In Models 1, 2, 3 I include measures of veto players, political federalism, and fiscal federalism in the models without country dummy variables. In Model 1 I estimate the impact of the number of veto players on flows of FDI. I find that the number of veto players has no signifi-

TABLE 6.1
Federalism and FDI

Variable	Model 1	Model 2	Model 3	Model 4	Model 5	Model 6
Lagged FDI	0.576***	0.552***	0.660***	0.375***	0.356***	0.432***
	(9.08)	(8.31)	(7.62)	(5.29)	(4.81)	(3.65)
Market Size	0.007	−0.006	−0.013	−0.499	−0.448	1.266*
	(0.29)	(−0.20)	(−0.37)	(−1.12)	(−0.98)	(1.71)
Growth	0.026***	0.027***	0.026**	0.024***	0.024***	0.047***
	(3.32)	(3.17)	(2.13)	(2.95)	(2.80)	(3.59)
Trade	0.009***	0.009***	0.005**	0.005	0.006	−0.000
	(4.84)	(4.87)	(2.25)	(1.14)	(1.18)	(−0.04)
Level of	−0.001	0.010	0.020	0.749*	0.690	−0.734
Development	(−0.03)	(0.20)	(0.34)	(1.69)	(1.56)	(−0.89)
Budget	0.002	0.003	0.011	−0.025**	−0.023**	−0.014
Deficits	(0.21)	(0.27)	(1.06)	(−2.31)	(−2.05)	(−1.01)
Government	−0.013*	−0.014*	−0.011	−0.035**	−0.037**	−0.028
Consumption	(−1.67)	(−1.68)	(−1.11)	(−2.12)	(−2.14)	(−1.14)
Democracy	0.010*	0.010*	0.017**	0.016**	0.018**	0.019
	(1.78)	(1.83)	(2.06)	(2.00)	(2.04)	(1.27)
Veto Players	0.032			0.066**		
	(1.61)			(2.42)		
Political		0.102**			0.229	
Federalism		(2.37)			(1.40)	
Fiscal			−0.750			0.482
Federalism			(−1.26)			(0.22)
Constant	−0.297	0.173	0.043	11.126	10.35	−29.650**
	(−0.47)	(0.23)	(0.04)	(1.14)	(1.00)	(−2.01)
Time Dummies	Yes	Yes	Yes	Yes	Yes	Yes
Country	No	No	No	Yes	Yes	Yes
Dummies						
Observations	1619	1535	617	1619	1535	617
Countries	111	104	61	111	104	61
R-sq	0.54	0.54	0.58	0.61	0.61	0.66

*** = 99% confidence level, ** = 95% confidence level, * = 90% confidence level

cant impact on FDI inflows. Conversely, in Model 2 I find that political federalism has a positive and statistically significant impact on FDI inflows. The effects of federal institutions are substantial; a move from a unitary state to a federal state increases FDI inflows by 0.2 percent of GDP.[22] Given 1.3 percent of GDP as the average level of FDI inflows for this sample, the impact of federalism on FDI inflows is substantial. Model 3 includes the variable, fiscal federalism, defined as subnational revenues as a percentage of total revenues. Unfortunately, this decreases the sample size from 124 countries to 61. Fiscal federalism does not significantly affect FDI inflows. These empirical results are robust to changes in specifications and other control variables. For example, political federalism remains significant, even when I control for natural resource endowments and restrictions on FDI inflows.

I estimate Models 4, 5, 6 with country dummies. As expected, political federalism falls below statistical significance in Model 5, but remains positive. The results for fiscal federalism are the same as in Model 3, where fiscal federalism is statistically insignificant. Surprisingly, the number of veto players is positive and statistically significant in the regressions with country dummies. Veto players, when fixed country factors are controlled for, increase FDI inflows. Veto players do not seem to be a cross-national determinant of FDI inflows in the models without country dummies, but once we control for fixed country factors, increasing the number of veto players increases FDI inflows. I leave further conjectures on this result for future research.

These empirical results do not directly test the causal mechanism linking federalism to market-friendly policies. My argument asserts that federal institutions enable governments to provide credible commitments to multinational corporations, essentially providing environments that entail lower levels of political risk. By making these commitments credible, countries with federal institutions attract higher levels of FDI. The robust results on the ability of federal countries to attract higher levels of FDI coincide with this story, but not a direct test.

With a second set of tests, I explore how veto players and federal institutions affect the risks associated with sovereign lenders. The ex-post/ex-ante bargaining nature of FDI parallels the dilemma political leaders face when attempting to obtain loans from foreign lenders. Governments make promises on repayments, but once the loan is disbursed, these conditions may not be met. Tremendous reputation costs exist for default, but often the short-run political and economic incentives outweigh this negative.[23] Creditors must attempt to predict the potential of default by examining the country's economic conditions and political institutions along with future world macroeconomic conditions.

Once again, this factor does not directly test the credibility-improving character of federal institutions, but it proves useful in exploring how federalism helps improve the credibility of governments dealing with investors, multinationals or lenders. I use the same baseline model from chapter 5 that models country risk using the following control variables: level of development (GDP per capita), debt (central government debt/GDP), and current account balance (current account/GDP), all from the World Bank's World Development Indicators. For these regressions, I use both the Institutional Investor credit ratings and Euromoney as the dependent variables. Once again, the Euromoney credit rating scores are constructed by a panel of experts, while the Euromoney credit risk ratings come from a survey of roughly one hundred international banks on the probability of default. I use the logistic transformation of both ratings.[24]

TABLE 6.2
Federalism and Institutional Investors Credit Ratings

Variable	Model 7	Model 8	Model 9	Model 10
Development Level	0.877***	0.665***	0.944***	0.645***
	(19.937)	(13.461)	(19.222)	(13.873)
Current Account	0.001	0.005	0.001	0.005
	(0.486)	(0.669)	(0.623)	(0.744)
Debt	−0.002***	−0.001***	−0.001***	−0.002***
	(−3.767)	(−2.731)	(−2.797)	(−2.858)
Political Federalism	0.389***			0.224***
	(5.403)			(2.779)
Fiscal Federalism		6.187***		5.294***
		(14.543)		(8.539)
Veto Points			0.004	−0.008
			(0.434)	(−0.745)
Countries	73	45	78	42
Observations	680	339	738	327
R-sq	0.59	0.53	0.54	0.55

Note: I estimate all regressions using OLS with panel-corrected standard errors with an AR1 correction and decade dummies.
*** = 99% confidence level, ** = 95% confidence level, * = 90% confidence level

In tables 6.2 and 6.3 I present the results of a simple OLS time-series-cross-sectional regression for 73–81 countries from 1980 to 1995, using the Institutional Investor (table 6.3) and Euromoney (table 6.4) risk ratings as the dependent variable.[25] As predicted, political federalism proves positive and statistically significant in all regressions except for Model 14 in table 6.3. The variable veto points do not emerge as statistically significant in any of the regressions. Interestingly, fiscal federalism, contrary to the earlier FDI results, becomes positive and statistically significant in all regressions. Political federalism and fiscal federalism associate with higher sovereign risk ratings (lower default risk).[26] In tables 6.4 and 6.5 I include the Polity measure of democracy used in chapter 5. The results remain unchanged.

One potential concern is the potential high degree of correlation between political federalism and tax rates. Although I argued in chapter 4 that rates of capital taxation have little impact on FDI inflows, readers still skeptical of this may argue that politically federal countries are often fiscally federal (correlation of 0.36 in my data), and that fiscal federalism leads to tax competition. The variable on political federalism may be indirectly measuring low levels of capital taxation. To test this I examined the correlation between the rates of highest marginal capital taxation and political federalism. I find that there is a small but

TABLE 6.3
Federalism and Euromoney Credit Ratings

Variable	Model 11	Model 12	Model 13	Model 14
Development Level	0.914***	0.619***	0.979***	0.602***
	(10.781)	(5.755)	(10.695)	(5.827)
Current Account	0.003	0.022*	0.004	0.214**
	(0.625)	(1.955)	(0.865)	(1.968)
Debt	−0.002***	−0.003**	−0.002**	−0.003***
	(−3.051)	(−2.477)	(−2.495)	(−2.855)
Political Federalism	0.378***			0.088
	(4.640)			(0.983)
Fiscal Federalism		7.873***		7.384***
		(5.352)		(4.865)
Veto Points			0.002	0.034
			(0.082)	(1.311)
Countries	83	46	88	43
Observations	718	322	778	310
R-sq	0.43	0.44	0.36	0.46

Note: I estimate all regressions using OLS with panel-corrected standard errors with an AR1 correction and decade dummies.

*** = 99% confidence level, ** = 95% confidence level, * = 90% confidence level

positive correlation between political federalism and capital taxation (correlation of 0.18).[27] Politically federal countries have slightly higher levels of corporate taxation, yet still attract higher FDI inflows.

6.11 Qualitative Evidence

To examine the impact of veto players, political federalism, and fiscal federalism, I conducted interviews with investment promotion agencies, investment location consultants, political risk insurance agencies, and multinational corporations. These interviews provide further evidence of the complexities in the way foreign investors view political institutions below the regime level. Democracies are clearly preferred investment environments, but specific details on the other types of political institutions preferred by multinationals are less clear.

In no interview did the issue of "veto points" come up as an important determinant. No investment promotion agency stressed veto players, no location consultant made any claim that this affected country risk, no political risk insurer formally modeled the risk environment using this measure, and no multinational corporation made any

TABLE 6.4
Federalism, Democracy, and Institutional Investor Ratings

Variable	Model 15	Model 16	Model 17	Model 18
Development Level	0.847***	0.639***	0.897***	0.619***
	(22.147)	(12.651)	(21.241)	(13.039)
Current Account	0.001	0.005	0.002	0.006
	(0.424)	(0.746)	(0.629)	(0.811)
Debt	−0.002***	−0.002***	−0.002***	−0.002***
	(−4.017)	(−2.649)	(−3.185)	(−2.778)
Political Federalism	0.349***	0.206**		
	(4.918)	(2.519)		
Fiscal Federalism	6.153***	5.314***		
	(21.161)	(9.784)		
Veto Points	0.002	−0.007		
	(0.238)	(−0.639)		
Democracy	0.010**	0.008	0.014***	0.009
	(1.999)	(0.787)	(3.161)	(0.800)
Countries	70	44	74	41
Obs.	646	332	699	320
R-sq	0.61	0.55	0.58	0.58

Note: I estimate all regressions using OLS with panel-corrected standard errors with an AR1 correction and decade dummies.
*** = 99% confidence level, ** = 95% confidence level, * = 90% confidence level

claim that veto players played any role in their investment location decisions.

The evidence on the importance of political federalism is more mixed. In the content analysis of the investment promotion agencies, no agency promoted political federalism as a positive factor for FDI, and political federalism was not included in any of the political risk models. Conversely, some agencies did point out the strong relationship between local and state governments and multinationals. For example, the Canadian investment promotion agency argued that, historically, domestic and foreign oil companies used the government of Alberta to help lobby for policies at the national level.

Similar evidence was presented in the interviews with multinational corporations and investment location consultants. None of the companies formally argued that political federalism was a major determinant of FDI inflows, but they did argue that local and regional elites could serve as an important ally for policy change at the national level. One example is provincial governments in China lobbying on behalf of Alcan for national policy change.

TABLE 6.5
Federalism, Democracy, and Euromoney Ratings

Variable	Model 19	Model 20	Model 21	Model 22
Development Level	0.874***	0.547***	0.926***	0.520***
	(9.108)	(4.976)	(9.208)	(4.939)
Current Account	0.004	0.022*	0.004	0.021*
	(0.769)	(1.845)	(0.833)	(1.835)
Debt	−0.003***	−0.003***	−0.002***	−0.003***
	(−3.477)	(−2.936)	(−2.972)	(−3.445)
Political Federalism	0.294***			0.065
	(3.498)			(0.715)
Fiscal Federalism		7.196***		6.739***
		(4.971)		(4.660)
Veto Points			−0.010	0.034
			(−0.440)	(1.319)
Democracy	0.019***	0.028*	0.022***	0.032**
	(3.162)	(1.946)	(3.589)	(2.199)
Countries	76	45	80	41
Obs.	656	316	709	320
R-sq	0.46	0.46	0.42	0.58

Note: I estimate all regressions using OLS with panel-corrected standard errors with an AR1 correction and decade dummies.

*** = 99% confidence level, ** = 95% confidence level, * = 90% confidence level

The evidence for the importance of fiscal federalism was very weak. Although some investment promotion agencies pointed to the level of taxation or incentives offered, these agencies did not focus on fiscal federalism as important determinants of FDI flows. They argued that the total level of incentives offered was important, not whether these incentives were offered by the central or local governments.

Doesn't fiscal federalism lead to downward tax competition? Interestingly, the evidence is fairly mixed in this respect. Some agencies, such as Brazil's, give numerous examples of tax wars to attract FDI inflows, but these similar tax wars take place between countries as well. Unitary countries such as Costa Rica use tax incentives to attract FDI, just as provinces in Brazil and Canada use incentives to attract FDI. Does fiscal federalism lead to lower taxes and higher FDI inflows? According to Montreal's investment promotion agency, the rising use of financial incentives was not spurned by competition between states in Canada, it was simply a strategy that emerged through a learning process of attracting FDI. Provinces began using tax incentives for the same reasons that unitary states began using tax incentives—because they thought it would help attract FDI. This evidence, when coupled with the empirical results in chapter 4, makes fiscal federalism look like an ineffective mechanism to attract multinationals.

This qualitative evidence supports many of the theoretical points in this chapter. Veto players have no real impact on multinationals' decisions. Fiscal federalism has little impact on FDI inflows, where competition across countries is sufficient for countries to use policy levers to attract FDI inflows. Finally, there is limited support that political federalism can lead to higher FDI inflows. Multinationals often use state and local governments to lobby for change at the national level.

6.12 Conclusion

In this chapter I argue that the existing literature on federalism generally fails to make careful distinctions between the structure of political and economic relationships within a federal system. These conceptual distinctions facilitate understanding the effect of federal institutions on economic performance. I conclude that, while politically federal institutions can have positive effects on FDI inflows, the same does not hold true for fiscal federalism. The benefits of federalism in attracting multinational corporations stem from the political relationships between the national government and subnational units, not from fiscal relationships. Once again, political institutions enormously impact FDI inflows. The following chapter will explore how international institutions can also affect FDI inflows.

APPENDIX: POLITICAL FEDERALISM

Federal Systems

ARGENTINA (MIXED 1975–1981; FEDERAL 1982–1995)

Argentina classifies as a mixed political system from 1975 to 1982, during the period of authoritarian rule. Argentina became a federal system after 1983, where a sixty-nine-member upper house represents the twenty-nine provinces, with each provincial assembly nominating two members and a third member representing minorities.

AUSTRALIA (FEDERAL 1975–1995)

The seventy-six-member Senate (12 seats for each of the 6 states, 2 for the Northern Territory, and 2 for the Australian Capital Territory) represents the provinces.

AUSTRIA (MIXED 1975–1995)

The sixty-four-member Bundesrat represents the Lander. The state assemblies elect candidates. Each Lander provides a chair for the Bundesrat for a six-month term.

BELGIUM (MIXED 1975–1995)

The seventy-one-member Senate consists of forty directly elected members (15 from Wallonia and 25 from Flanders), twenty-one indirectly elected (10 by the Flemish Council, 10 by the French Council, and 1 by the German Council), and ten appointed by the elected senators. Some institutional changes occurred in 1993, giving regions more autonomy, although this change did not significantly alter the role of regions in central government legislation.

BRAZIL (MIXED 1975–1981; FEDERAL 1982–1995)

The twenty-six states and the district of Brasilia attain representation in the upper house. From 1975 to 1981, candidates' selection was through partially fair elections, and from 1982 to 1988, by the state legislators. The 1988 Constitution further strengthened the federal system maintaining the election of senators (1 per state) and Chamber of Deputies (by population and 1 deputy representing each state).

CANADA (FEDERAL 1975–1995)

The 104-member Senate represents the provinces.

COLOMBIA (MIXED 1975–1990; FEDERAL 1991–1995)

From 1975 to 1990, the twenty-three national departments elect the 114-member Senate. The country ratified a new constitution in July 1991, which included a directly elected bicameral legislature. The 163-member House of Representatives includes two representatives from each of the twenty-three national departments.

ETHIOPIA (UNITARY 1975–1993; FEDERAL 1994–1995)

Ethiopia existed as a federal system from 1952 until it returned to unitary status in 1962. I coded it as a unitary system until 1994. The new 1994 Constitutions returned Ethiopia to federal status by granting the nine states a number of powers, including the right to secede through referendum. I coded Ethiopia as a federal system for 1994 and 1995.

GAMBIA (UNITARY 1975–1981; MIXED 1982–1989; UNITARY 1990–1995)

Gambia exists as a unitary system except in the period 1982 to 1989, during the Senegambian Confederation, the merger of Senegal and Gambia. This confederation dissolved on September 30, 1989.

GERMANY (FEDERAL 1975–1995)

The Lander (10 prior to unification, 16 since unification) enjoys representation in the sixty-eight-member Bundesrat, holding three to six seats (according to population).

INDIA (FEDERAL 1975–1995)

The 245-member Council of States (Rajya Sabha) represents the twenty-five states. The state assemblies choose members. The central government has the ability to impose "Presidential Rule" on the states during periods of turmoil, although this proves quite uncommon.

MALAYSIA (FEDERAL 1975–1995)

I code Malaysia as federal from 1975 to 1995. The states have representation in the Senate. Sixty percent of the candidates are selected state assemblies. The remaining 40 percent of the seats are reserved for minorities. The states also hold a suspensive veto (6 months) over central government legislation.

MEXICO (FEDERAL 1975–1995)

Mexico codes as a federal system from 1975 to 1995. The 128-member Senate represents the states.

NETHERLANDS (UNITARY 1975–1982; MIXED 1983–1995)

Constitutional change in 1983 specified that representatives of twelve provincial councils elect members of the first chamber.

NIGERIA (MIXED 1975–1977; FEDERAL 1978–1983; MIXED 1984–1989; FEDERAL 1990–1993; MIXED 1994–1995)

Constitutional change in 1978 stated that the states elected the Senate, until the military government suspended the federal constitution from 1984 to 1989. In late 1993 the government suspended the parliament.

PAKISTAN (MIXED 1975–1984; FEDERAL 1985–1995)

I classify Pakistan as a Mixed political system when the federal constitution remained suspended from 1973 to 1984. In 1985, the original constitution reemerged and that restored the provinces to indirectly elect the upper house.

PAPUA New Guinea (UNITARY 1975; MIXED 1976–1995)

Papua New Guinea classifies as a Mixed political system after constitutional change in September 1975. The single-chamber parliament, the National Assembly, consists of eighty local, single-member constituencies, and twenty provincial constituencies. Each elector has one vote for the local seat and one vote for the provincial seat.

SOUTH AFRICA (UNITARY 1975–1993; FEDERAL 1994–1995)

The 1994 Constitution specifies that the Senate consists of ten members from each of the nine regional legislatures.

SPAIN (UNITARY 1975–1978; MIXED 1979–1995)

The 1978 Constitution specifies that 49 of the 257 Senators represent the regions.

SUDAN (MIXED 1975 to 1995)

Sudan formally has a federal constitution that changed and suffered suspension from 1975 to 1995. The size and composition of the unicameral legislature varied from 1975 to 1985.

SWITZERLAND (FEDERAL 1975–1995)

Switzerland exists as a federation of twenty-six cantons. The cantons wield a tremendous amount of influence in the central government, indirectly through the Nationalrat, and directly through the use of referenda which can veto central government legislation.

UNITED ARAB EMIRATES (FEDERAL 1975–1995)

This federal system of seven sheikhdoms grants the sheikh hereditary rule over his own emirate.

UNITED STATES (FEDERAL 1975–1995)

The fifty states enjoy representation in the Senate with two senators per state, appointed through direct election.

VENEZUELA (FEDERAL 1975–1995)

Venezuela exists as a federal system with each of the twenty-three states and the Federal District appointing two members to the Senate.

TABLE A6.1.
Political Federalism

Country	System	Entry	Exit	Country	System	Entry	Exit
Afghanistan	unitary	1975	1995	Costa Rica	unitary	1975	1995
Albania	unitary	1975	1995	Côte d'Ivoire	unitary	1975	1995
Algeria	unitary	1975	1995	Cuba	unitary	1975	1995
Angola	unitary	1975	1995	Denmark	unitary	1975	1995
Argentina	mixed	1975	1981	Djibouti	unitary	1975	1995
	federal	1982	1995	Dominican	unitary	1975	1995
Australia	federal	1975	1995	Republic			
Austria	mixed	1975	1995	Ecuador	unitary	1975	1995
Bahamas	unitary	1975	1995	El Salvador	unitary	1975	1995
Bahrain	unitary	1975	1995	Egypt	unitary	1975	1995
Bangladesh	unitary	1975	1995	Ethiopia	unitary	1975	1993
Barbados	unitary	1975	1995		federal	1994	1995
Belgium	mixed	1975	1995	Fiji	unitary	1975	1995
Belize	unitary	1975	1995	Finland	unitary	1975	1995
Benin	unitary	1975	1995	France	unitary	1975	1995
Bhutan	unitary	1975	1995	Gabon	unitary	1975	1995
Bolivia	unitary	1975	1995	Gambia	unitary	1975	1981
Botswana	unitary	1975	1995		mixed	1982	1989
Brazil	mixed	1975	1981		unitary	1990	1995
	federal	1982	1995	Germany	federal	1975	1995
Brunei	unitary	1975	1995	Ghana	unitary	1975	1995
Burkina Faso	unitary	1975	1995	Greece	unitary	1975	1995
Burundi	unitary	1975	1995	Grenada	unitary	1975	1995
Cape Verde	unitary	1975	1995	Guatemala	unitary	1975	1995
Cambodia	unitary	1975	1995	Guinea	unitary	1975	1995
Cameroon	unitary	1975	1995	Guinea-Bissau	unitary	1975	1995
Canada	federal	1975	1995	Guyana	unitary	1975	1995
Central African	unitary	1975	1995	Haiti	unitary	1975	1995
Republic				Honduras	unitary	1975	1995
Chad	unitary	1975	1995	Hungary	unitary	1975	1995
Chile	unitary	1975	1995	Iceland	unitary	1975	1995
Colombia	mixed	1975	1990	India	federal	1975	1995
	federal	1991	1995	Indonesia	unitary	1975	1995
Congo, Republic of	unitary	1975	1995	Iran	unitary	1975	1995

TABLE A6.1. (*cont'd*)
Political Federalism

Country	System	Entry	Exit	Country	System	Entry	Exit
Iraq	unitary	1975	1995	Nicaragua	unitary	1975	1995
Ireland	unitary	1975	1995	Niger	unitary	1975	1995
Israel	unitary	1975	1995	Nigeria	mixed	1975	1977
Italy	unitary	1975	1995		federal	1978	1983
					mixed	1984	1989
Jamaica	unitary	1975	1995		federal	1990	1993
Japan	unitary	1975	1995		mixed	1994	1995
Jordan	unitary	1975	1995	Norway	unitary	1975	1995
Kenya	unitary	1975	1995	Oman	unitary	1975	1995
Korea, Republic of	unitary	1975	1995	Pakistan	mixed	1975	1984
Kuwait	unitary	1975	1995		federal	1985	1995
Laos	unitary	1975	1995	Panama	unitary	1975	1995
Lebanon	unitary	1975	1995	Paraguay	unitary	1975	1995
Lesotho	unitary	1975	1995	Papua New Guinea	unitary	1975	1975
Liberia	unitary	1975	1995		mixed	1976	1995
Libya	unitary	1975	1995	Peru	unitary	1975	1995
Luxembourg	unitary	1975	1995	Philippines	unitary	1975	1995
Madagascar	unitary	1975	1995	Poland	unitary	1975	1995
Malawi	unitary	1975	1995	Portugal	unitary	1975	1995
Malaysia	federal	1975	1995	Qatar	unitary	1975	1995
Maldives	unitary	1975	1995	Rwanda	unitary	1975	1995
Mali	unitary	1975	1995	Saudi Arabia	unitary	1975	1995
Malta	unitary	1975	1995	Senegal	unitary	1975	1995
Mauritania	unitary	1975	1995	Sierra Leon	unitary	1975	1995
Mauritius	unitary	1975	1995	Singapore	unitary	1975	1995
Mexico	federal	1975	1995	South Africa	unitary	1975	1993
Mongolia	unitary	1975	1995		federal	1994	1995
Morocco	unitary	1975	1995	Solomon Islands	unitary	1975	1995
Mozambique	unitary	1975	1995	Spain	unitary	1975	1978
Myanmar	unitary	1975	1995		mixed	1979	1995
Namibia	unitary	1975	1995	Sri Lanka	unitary	1975	1995
Nepal	unitary	1975	1995	St. Lucia	unitary	1975	1995
Netherlands	unitary	1975	1982	Sudan	mixed	1975	1995
	mixed	1983	1995	Swaziland	unitary	1975	1995
				Sweden	unitary	1975	1995
New Zealand	unitary	1975	1995	Switzerland	federal	1975	1995

TABLE A6.1. (*cont'd*)
Political Federalism

Country	System	Entry	Exit	Country	System	Entry	Exit
Syria	unitary	1975	1995	United Kingdom	unitary	1975	1995
Taiwan	unitary	1975	1995	United States	federal	1975	1995
Tanzania	unitary	1975	1995	Uruguay	unitary	1975	1995
Thailand	unitary	1975	1995	Vanuatu	unitary	1975	1995
Togo	unitary	1975	1995	Venezuela	federal	1975	1995
Trinidad and Tobago	unitary	1975	1995	Vietnam	unitary	1975	1995
Tunisia	unitary	1975	1995	Yemen	unitary	1975	1995
Turkey	unitary	1975	1995	Zaire	unitary	1975	1995
United Arab Emirates	federal	1975	1995	Zambia	unitary	1975	1995
Uganda	unitary	1975	1995	Zimbabwe	unitary	1975	1995

7

The IMF and FDI Inflows

7.1 Introduction

In the previous two chapters I explored how domestic political institutions affect FDI inflows. I argue that political institutions that provide an appropriate degree of credibility to multinational investors and still maintain policy flexibility are preferred by multinational investors. Countries with these political institutions attract higher levels of FDI inflows.

This study of the influence of political institutions on FDI inflows need not be limited to domestic institutions. International institutions, specifically the International Monetary Fund, could theoretically provide this same mix of both policy credibility and policy flexibility that multinationals prefer.

In this chapter I examine the link between IMF agreements and the conditions associated with IMF agreements to inflows of foreign direct investment. The conventional wisdom posits that IMF programs, and IMF conditionality, should positively affect FDI inflows.[1] If these agreements provide both capital and commitments to market-promoting economic reform, multinational investors would prefer IMF agreements. This logic suggests that IMF programs should be associated with higher inflows of FDI, when we control for the factors that lead countries to seek financing from the IMF. Ceteris paribus, countries in financial crisis improve their ability to attract FDI inflows by signing IMF agreements.

I propose that a number of theoretical reasons might cause IMF programs to have a negative impact on FDI inflows. Although IMF conditionality undoubtedly entails a commitment to a specific package of economic reforms, the value of these reforms to multinationals remains debatable. IMF agreements, and IMF conditions, may have harmful consequences for multinational investors.

As I argue in the theory section of this book, institutions that provide credible commitments to a policy equilibrium do not always offer value to multinationals. Institutions that lock countries into policies that hurt the domestic market will attract less FDI. In the empirical analysis of this chapter I test the effects of IMF programs on FDI inflows by using a treatment effects selection model for sixty-eight countries from 1970 to 1998. This model allows us to control for the factors that lead countries to seek IMF support, correcting the selection bias of participation in IMF programs, and to estimate the unbiased impact of IMF programs on FDI inflows. The central finding of this chapter concludes that IMF programs leads to lower levels of FDI inflows. A country signing an agreement with the IMF, ceteris paribus, attracts roughly 28 percent less FDI inflows than a country not doing so.

7.2 The IMF: Structure, History, and Conditionality

The IMF, and its sister institution, the World Bank, emerged as part of the Bretton Woods agreement at the end of the Second World War. Designers set up the World Bank as an institution to funnel economic assistance into developing countries, specifically by making project finance available to nations unable to attract capital through market mechanisms.[2] The IMF, on the other hand, originally oversaw the fixed exchange rate arrangements between countries and provided short-term capital for balance-of-payment crises.[3]

The collapse of the Bretton Woods exchange rate mechanism, coupled with the largely unforeseen explosion in world capital markets, threw the IMF into uncharted territory. The seemingly automatic role of the IMF became muddled after the end of the system of fixed exchange rates. It continued to function as the "lender of last resort," but this role changed fundamentally under the complex web of fixed and floating exchange rates after 1971. This alteration necessitated a fundamental shift from the management of fixed exchange rates to the "firm surveillance" of countries' exchange rate policies (James 1996, 592).

Although originally viewed as an automatic response mechanism in the management of fixed exchange rates, with a fixed exchange rate system, "inappropriate policies" would trigger balance-of-payments deficits under the IMF (James 1996, 588). Domestic governments were pressured (both by markets and the IMF) to alter policy to fix these imbalances. IMF funding would then provide short-term support.

Countries in the new financial system often ran current account deficits, but the IMF needed to determine whether these deficits stemmed from short-term fluctuations or misguided economic policies. The IMF had to move from lending countries capital to manage short-term losses, to examining the economic policies of host countries to determine if fluctuations or policy created the shortage of capital and what type of policies would ensure economic recovery. Thus, the organization's concerns evolved from simply current account deficits to overall macroeconomic performance.

With this change in organizational focus came a shift in IMF conditionality. IMF conditionality simply means the set of policies or "conditions" that the IMF requires in exchange for funding.[4] If countries do not meet these conditions, future disbursements of IMF funds may be withheld. The IMF provides domestic governments important financial incentives to ensure that they do.

In terms of assuring repayment of the loan, conditionality can serve an important function. In private lending markets, creditors require some form of collateral to ensure that the loan gets paid. For obvious reasons the IMF does not require collateral from countries; rather, it requires the government seeking financing to take actions to correct macroeconomic imbalances, thus increasing the probability that the loan will be repaid.[5] In this regard, macroeconomic reforms serve as "collateral" for IMF loans.

Conditionality has become a complex and changing concept. A growing consensus exists that the balance-of-payments position of a country strongly relates to the overall macroeconomic environment. Recognizing this fact, the IMF broadened the concept of conditionality to include macroeconomic reforms not directly related to the balance-of-payments position. Killick (1995, 25) argues that this led to a dramatic shift to "structural conditionality" in recent years and three main objectives of IMF conditionality emerged:[6]

1. To increase the role of markets and private enterprises relative to the public sector and to improve incentive structures.
2. To improve the efficiency of the public sector.
3. To mobilize additional domestic resources.

The IMF enforces conditionality through the Fund's "standby arrangements" and "extended fund facility"—essentially, loans meant for longer terms of support. Thus the IMF ties the meeting of specific conditions with future disbursements of the agreed upon loan. "If the executive directors are satisfied that the reforms will solve the problem," according to the IMF, "the loan is disbursed in installments (usually over one to three years) tied to the member's progress in putting the reforms into effect. If all goes well, the loan will be repaid on time, and the member, with necessary reforms now in place, will come out of the experience economically stronger" (IMF 1999a, 19).

The IMF maintains that conditionality does not rest on a set of rigid criteria, but rather relies on a set of general concepts to guide it. These measures include:

• Encouraging members to adopt corrective measures at an early stage.
• Stressing that the IMF pay due regard to members' domestic social and political objectives, as well as economic priorities and circumstances.

- Permitting flexibility in determining the number and content of performance criteria.
- Emphasizing that IMF arrangements are decisions of the IMF that set out—in consultation with members—the conditions for its financial assistance (IMF 1999b, 68).

In practice, the IMF stresses a number of specific macroeconomic policies. Although the conditionality of IMF lending generally isn't publicly available, the consensus suggests that the IMF focuses on controlling the size of the budget deficit. This leaves the politically sensitive issues of cutting spending or raising taxes to domestic governments (Krueger 1988). The IMF specifies criteria in other areas beyond the budget deficit as well, such as their insistence on trade reform and liberalization. These conditions, along with the funds made available through the IMF, can potentially have major effects on domestic economies.

7.3 The International Monetary Fund and Foreign Direct Investment

To my knowledge, no cross-national studies explore the effects of IMF programs on foreign direct investment. This omission appears striking, given the vast econometric literature on the importance of FDI for developing countries, and the growing scholarship on the effects of IMF programs on economic growth.[7] Understanding the effects of IMF programs on FDI inflows becomes an important public policy question, as countries in economic crisis attempt to calm foreign investors. More importantly, by understanding firms' responses to IMF programs, we might have more insight into the overall effects of IMF programs on macroeconomic performance. Do firms perceive IMF programs as increasing the attractiveness of a host country's market and business climate?

Empirically, little consensus exists about the role of the IMF in stabilizing countries in crisis. The effect of IMF programs on the current account balance and overall balance of payments provides one link between IMF loans and macroeconomic performance. In a comprehensive survey, Haque and Khan (1998) conclude that in most cases the IMF helped improve both current account balance and the overall balance of payments. Prezworski and Vreeland (2000) find more pessimistic results, citing the work of Reichmann and Stillson (1978) and Connors (1979) as examples of studies that discover IMF programs have no effect on the balance of payments.

The most damaging criticism comes from the recent evidence on the impact of IMF programs on economic growth. Vreeland (2002) provides the most recent major contribution on the subject. Using a dynamic bivariate probit model with partial observability, he finds that when controlling for both observed and unobserved selection factors, IMF programs correspond to lower levels of economic growth.[8] This result confirms the early result from Przeworski and Vreeland (2000) regarding the negative impact of IMF participation on economic growth.[9]

One compelling argument regarding the link between IMF programs and weak macroeconomic performance concludes that the IMF may prescribe inappropriate policies. With a modest budget and staff, the international organization attempts to monitor the economic conditions of over 180 countries. James (1996) argues that the Western educated elites at the IMF could be unfamiliar with local economic conditions, cultures, and environments. Gould (2003) claims that IMF conditions are partly driven by private banks attaching their loans to those of the Fund. Dreher and Jensen (2003) argue that strong allies of the IMF's primary stakeholders (U.S., EU, and Japan) receive looser conditions on loans, especially in the period prior to democratic elections.

Jeffrey Sachs provides an interesting example of the IMF's inability to predict the Asian Financial Crisis:

> Consider what the fund said about Korea just three months ago (September 1997) in its 1997 annual report. "Directors welcomed Korea's continued impressive macroeconomic performance and praised the authorities for their enviable fiscal record." Three months ago there was not a hint of alarm, only a call for further financial sector reform—incidentally without mentioning the *chaebols* (conglomerates) or the issue of foreign ownership of banks or banking supervisions that now figure so prominently in the IMF's Korea Program.

> In the same report, the IMF had this to say about Thailand, at the moment on the edge of the financial abyss. "Directors strongly praised Thailand's remarkable economic performance and the authorities' consistent record of sound macroeconomic policies."

> With a straight face, Michel Camdessus, the IMF managing director, now blames Asian governments for the deep failures of macroeconomic and financial policies that the IMF has discovered. It would have been more useful, instead, for the IMF to ponder why the situation looked so much better three months ago, for therein lies a basic truth about the situation in Asia. (Sachs 1999, 116–117)

Lack of understanding of this financial crisis ultimately led to bad public policy prescriptions, such as pushing for fiscal policies that proved "too tight" in a number of countries (Lane et al. 1999).

The G-24 summarizes its view of the effects of IMF programs:

The experience of developing countries that have undertaken Fund supported adjustment programs has not generally been satisfactory. The Fund approach to adjustment has had severe economic costs for many of these countries in terms of declines in the levels of outputs and growth rates, reductions in employment and adverse effects on income distribution. A typical Fund program prescribes measures that require excessive compression of domestic demand, cuts in real wages, and reductions in government expenditures; these are frequently accompanied by sharp exchange rate depreciation and import liberalization measures, without due regard to their potentially disruptive effects on the domestic economy. (G-24 1987, 9)

At best, no conclusive evidence exists that IMF programs greatly affect macroeconomic performance. At worst, IMF programs correspond to worse performance.

A related argument asserts that the signing of IMF agreements with conditionality may entail political costs for domestic governments. In exchange for IMF funds, recipient governments sacrifice policy autonomy. The contractionary policies prescribed by the IMF can generate political costs for host governments.[10] Citizens may take to the streets or punish governments at the polls. The signing of IMF agreements may trade an increase in economic stability with a potential increase in political instability. This overall relationship appears complex; in some cases IMF loans can stabilize economies and provide citizens with an improved economic environment, in other cases the IMF-imposed conditions can cause political instability.

One possible scenario suggests that a developing country may have a sustainable fiscal deficit, but IMF conditionality forces a lowering of the real urban wage (via devaluation) that may cause political protests (Bird 1995). Pastor (1987) and Vreeland's (2002) findings that IMF programs are associated with a decline in labors' share of national income correspond to this thesis. Sidell (1988) surprisingly finds little relationship between IMF programs and stability across countries from 1976 to 1985.

Political stability does not mean the same thing as political risk. Even if IMF programs do not generate large street riots, they may have political consequences negatively perceived by multinational investors. One distinct possibility implies that IMF programs could increase the level of leadership turnover as political leaders suffer electoral backlashes against the prescribed IMF conditions. This leadership turnover can translate into dramatic policy changes, which could harm multinational investors.

Although these theoretical arguments prove persuasive, little support in the empirical literature exists for this higher leadership turnover conjecture. Killick (1995) argues that in more cases than not, IMF programs helped existing governments to maintain offices rather than to increase their slide out of power. Sidell (1988) draws a similar conclusion. Overall, although considerable evidence exists that IMF programs can negatively impact macroeconomic performance, but there seems little conclusive proof that IMF programs prove politically destabilizing.

Moreover, IMF agreements could also lead domestic governments to take policy positions directly impacting multinational operations. Multinationals may be leery of investing in countries under IMF programs, fearing that these agreements may lock governments into taking policy positions that will harm multinational operations. Alternatively, IMF programs may offer multinational producers direct benefits through the policy changes induced through IMF conditionality.

I argue that IMF conditions can affect multinationals through the three following mechanisms: (1) changing the set of buying opportunities in foreign markets, (2) changing the profits and prices for multinationals, (3) changing the level of public goods available to the economy (and multinationals).

The first mechanism proves the most obvious. One potential set of IMF conditions provides an agreement to privatize state-run firms and allow for foreign entry in closed sectors of the economy. This dictate provides more opportunities for multinationals to make greenfield or brownfield (through privatization) investments. By increasing the available opportunities for multinationals, IMF agreements could attract higher levels of FDI inflows.

The second mechanism appears more complex, but equally important. IMF conditions may affect a multinational's profitability either directly or indirectly. The simplest mechanism changes corporate taxes either directly lobbied for by the IMF, or more likely a domestic government's response to IMF spending or deficit conditions. Domestic firms must react to IMF-imposed spending and deficit ceilings by making changes in taxation and spending that will directly impact firms, both domestic and foreign.

Multinational profitability can also be influenced by less direct policy changes, such as a change in tariffs, a currency devaluation, labor wages, or taxation (such as the value-added tax). For example, the IMF argues that controlling budget deficits could be done through increased levels of taxation, such as when the IMF lobbied for increases in the value-added tax under Argentina's Menem administration (Bandow 1994).[11] Alternatively, IMF encouragement of easing of tariffs could decrease the costs of inputs for multinationals, leading to higher profit margins. These changes in taxation can have an immediate impact on multinational operations. Other policy changes, although not directly targeted to multinationals' profits, can affect both the prices of inputs (imported goods, labor, etc.) or outputs (exports or domestic goods).

It remains unclear whether these indirect impacts will have an overall positive or negative effect on multinationals. For example, a multinational may perceive a currency devaluation as positive because it will decrease the cost of the initial investment in a new production facility, and make exports from this foreign market more competitive. Alternatively, multinationals investing to serve the domestic market will find that the profits remitted back to the host country will do so at a less favorable exchange rate, leading to lower operating profits. In summary, these indirect impacts could lead to either a positive or a negative impact on multinationals.

The effect of IMF conditions on the provision of public goods provides a third mechanism. For example, IMF conditionality often imposes spending constraints on domestic governments. Governments must slash spending to conform to agreed upon budget deficit levels and the IMF increasingly discusses the composition of government spending, even in realms as politically sensitive as military spending (Killick 1995, 20). This decrease in spending in certain areas can translate into a lower provision of public goods, such as decreased spending on education and physical infrastructure. These public goods are valuable to multinationals' operations, and to the domestic market generally.

If IMF programs promote markets, multinational corporations should prefer to invest in countries under IMF agreements, holding all political and economic factors equal. IMF agreements could then produce "catalytic effects" on financial markets, where the IMF could restore confidence and lead to higher levels of FDI inflows.[12] Conversely, IMF conditions could lead to lower levels of FDI inflows either by imposing costs directly on multinationals or by indirectly affecting multinationals by worsening the macroeconomic performance of the country.

Although no studies to date empirically test the effects of IMF programs on FDI inflows, a number of analyses provide some insights on the influence of IMF programs on financial markets. Hajivassiliou (1987) and Faini et al. (1991) find a negative or no relationship between IMF programs and flows of private debt. Brune, Garrett, and Kogut (2004) explore the relationship between IMF programs and the number or value of privatization of state's assets. They find that IMF programs are associated with both more privatizations and much higher privatization revenues. Mody and Saravia (2003) find that in circumstances where the IMF can influence politics IMF loans do serve as catalysts for private capital flows. The following section examines this relationship between IMF programs and FDI inflows.

7.4 Empirical Analysis

To examine the influence of IMF agreements on FDI, I first employ an ordinary least squares (OLS) regression with panel-corrected standard errors as recommended by Beck and Katz (1995) for annual observations of FDI inflows from 1970 to 1998 for sixty-eight countries.[13] I used the theoretical model constructed in chapter 3 for the baseline regressions. I ran all regressions with both a lagged dependent variable and decade dummies. The time-series-cross-sectional econometric equation is:

$$\text{Net FDI Inflows}_t = \alpha + \beta_1(\text{Net FDI}_{t-1}) + \beta_i(\text{Independent Variables}_{t-1}) + \varepsilon_i$$

The variable IMF Participation determines if a country is currently under an IMF agreement at any time during the year. Vreeland (2002) constructs this dichotomous measure of IMF participation for 183 countries from 1970 to 2000. I make no attempt to differentiate between various types of IMF agreements or the actual conditions imposed.

As a first cut, I simply examine the relationship between IMF participation and net FDI inflows. In table 7.1, I present a standard OLS regression with panel-corrected standard errors using the same baseline regressions as chapter 3 and both without country dummy variables (Model 1) and with country dummy variables (Model 2) from 1970 to 1998. The regression results for most of the control variables are similar to the models presented in chapters 4, 5, and 6. The key independent variables from chapters 5 and 6, democracy and federalism, are statistically significant in Model 1, while only democracy remains significant in Model 2. As argued in chapter 6, the insignificance of the federalism variable is due to the lack of variation in federalism over time. In both models IMF programs have a negative, but not statistically significant, impact on FDI inflows in this regression. This result is robust to other specifications, including using measures of natural resource endowments, controls on FDI inflows, and dropping both democracy and federalism variables.

This finding using a standard OLS regression should not surprise us. Tremendous selection bias appears in the countries that participate in IMF programs. Not all countries participate equally in IMF programs. For example, Bird (1995) argues that less developed countries more likely seek IMF funding. These countries often hold lower per-

TABLE 7.1.
The Effects of IMF Programs on FDI Inflows

Variable	Model 1	Model 2
Lagged FDI	0.550***	0.356***
	(8.20)	(4.78)
Trade	0.009***	0.006
	(3.11)	(1.12)
Market Size	−0.005	−0.498
	(−0.16)	(−1.05)
Development	−0.007	0.752
	(−0.14)	(1.59)
Growth	0.027***	0.025***
	(3.11)	(2.80)
Deficit	0.003	−0.023**
	(0.28)	(−2.04)
Government Spending	−0.014*	−0.038**
	(−1.65)	(−2.16)
Democracy	0.011*	0.017**
	(1.88)	(2.00)
Federalism	0.084*	0.232
	(1.86)	(1.42)
Constant	0.307	11.334
	(0.40)	(1.08)
IMF	−0.074	0.028
	(−0.98)	(0.28)
Trend Variable	Yes	Yes
Country Dummy	No	Yes
Observations	1511	1511
Countries	103	103
R-sq	0.54	0.61

*** = 99% confidence level, ** = 95% confidence level,
* = 90% confidence level

centages of foreign reserves, have balance-of-payment deficits, and generally have higher foreign debts.

Even more importantly, countries in serious financial crises, those with adverse conditions for foreign investors, also more often seek IMF support. If this IMF variable simply proxies for "financial crises," then the standard OLS regressions do not accurately portray the effects of IMF programs on FDI inflows. Only by properly controlling for these selection effects can we explore the real relationship between IMF flows and multinationals' investment decisions.

To control for these selection effects, I draw upon the empirical techniques used by Przeworski et al. (2000) and Vreeland (2002). Most simi-

TABLE 7.2.
The Determinants of IMF Participation

Variable	Model 3
Lagged IMF Participation	1.945***
	(18.22)
Political Regime	0.005
	(0.06)
GDP Per Capita	0.005
	(0.06)
GDP Growth	−0.025**
	(−2.18)
Budget Deficit	−0.005
	(−0.41)
Central Government Debt	0.015***
	(3.76)
Inflation	−0.000
	(−0.63)
Domestic Investment	−0.011
	(−1.32)
Foreign Reserves (Months of Exports)	−0.084***
	(−3.86)
Constant	−0.748
	(−1.41)
Number of Countries	69
Number of Observations	916

*** = 99% confidence level, ** = 95% confidence level,
* = 90% confidence level

lar to this problem, Vreeland (2002) uses a number of advanced Heckman models to control for the selection effects of participation in IMF programs.

I use the same technique from chapter 5, a treatment effects selection model that predicts participation in IMF programs using a recipient country's economic performance and political institutions. Essentially, I construct a probit model using IMF participation as the dependent variable, generate a predicted IMF participation variable, and use this variable to examine the selection-corrected effects of IMF participation on FDI inflows.

Table 7.2 presents a probit analysis of the determinants of IMF participation for sixty-eight countries from 1970 to 2000. The dependent variable represents participation in IMF programs, and all independent variables lag one year. Past participation in IMF programs proves the strongest predictor of current IMF participation. Countries already under IMF agreements will more likely continue to do so or sign onto new agreements. A country that enters into an IMF agreement may need to continue since economic conditions may not have improved. The conditions that drove the country to seek IMF funding may still persist.

Vreeland (2002) offers another explanation. He argues that signing IMF agreements entails sovereignty costs for the domestic government. By agreeing to IMF financing, the country has bowed to a number of IMF conditions. The country now remains constrained in their macroeconomic policies. Once a government pays these sovereignty costs (by signing an agreement last year), the marginal cost of another IMF agreement, and set of conditions, becomes relatively low.

Beyond recidivism, the total debt burden of the government and the level of foreign exchange reserves are important predictors of IMF participation. Countries with low levels of foreign exchange reserves and high debt burden prove more likely to seek and obtain IMF financing.

Similar to Vreeland (2002), I discover that the level of economic development and inflation level do not significantly determine IMF participation. Contrary to Vreeland (2002), however, I find the rate of economic growth to be a significant determinant of IMF participation. Countries with lower levels of economic growth more likely obtain IMF funding.

Interestingly, I find that democratic political regimes, the existence of democracy, do not affect IMF participation, contrary to Vreeland (2002). This difference stems from different empirical methods.[14] Vreeland (2002) argues that the sovereignty costs of signing IMF agreements remain especially high for democratic leaders, making democratic countries less likely to seek IMF funding. But Vreeland argues that political regimes do not prove a significant factor in the continuation of IMF programs, and that only economic factors explain a country's continuation in IMF agreements.

In figure 7.1, I present the predicted values of country participation in IMF programs for 916 observations using the model in table 7.2. The model accurately predicts participation in IMF programs. Out of the 464 observations of IMF agreements, this model correctly predicts participation in 434 of these cases. Of the years of nonparticipation in IMF programs in the 453 countries, this model accurately predicts 393 of these cases. Overall, this model accurately predicts over 83 percent of the cases in the sample.

Next I produce a selection model using the selection equation from table 7.2 and the standard FDI determinant equation from table 7.1. This model relies on predicted values of IMF participation to find the unbiased effect of IMF agreements on FDI inflows. Unfortunately the sample size decreases substantially due to data availability, from 1,511 observations in 103 countries to 916 observations in 68 countries. This

		Actual		
		Yes	*No*	*Total*
Predicted	*Yes*	374	60	434
	No	90	393	483
	Total	464	453	

Figure 7.1. Actual Participation versus Predicted Participation in IMF Programs

subset of countries does not include many of the low FDI recipient countries that tend to be authoritarian and unitary. Thus, the variation in the key control variables, democracy and federalism, is greatly reduced, and that sample is skewed toward higher FDI countries.

Given this caveat, exploring how IMF programs affect FDI inflows in the remaining sixty-eight countries remains an important test of the impact of IMF programs on multinational investors' expectations. Empirical results are provided in table 7.3.

In Model 4 I present a simple OLS model of FDI inflows and in Model 5 I present the selection-corrected model. In both regressions, most of the results on the control variables remain unchanged. Using the predicted IMF participation variable, I find the OLS results in Model 4 biased and I find that they understate the true impact of IMF programs on FDI inflows. IMF participation, when I control for selection in Model 5, proves both negative and statistically significant.

These results appear substantial. The average level of FDI inflows in this sample equals roughly 1.3 percent of GDP. The estimated difference in FDI inflows between countries under IMF agreements versus those countries not under IMF agreements roughly amounts to a difference of 0.36 percent of GDP. Countries under IMF agreements ceteris paribus attract 28 percent less FDI than countries that opt not to seek IMF financing. IMF agreements lead to substantially lower levels of FDI inflows.

In Models 6 and 7 I include control variables for the level of democracy and federalism. In both models neither democracy nor federalism

TABLE 7.3.
The Effects of IMF Programs on FDI Inflows

Variable	Model 4 (OLS)	Model 5 (Selection)	Model 6 (OLS)	Model 7 (Selection)
Past FDI	0.546***	0.0543***	0.522***	0.520***
	(6.81)	(18.39)	(6.03)	(16.81)
Market Size	−0.035	−0.039	−0.094	−0.092
	(−0.76)	(−0.85)	(−1.49)	(−1.67)
Growth	0.040***	0.040***	0.045***	0.045***
	(3.88)	(3.81)	(4.01)	(4.02)
Trade	0.007***	0.007***	0.008***	0.008***
	(2.81)	(3.28)	(2.78)	(3.21)
Level of Development	0.181**	0.180**	0.196***	0.189*
	(2.52)	(2.12)	(2.66)	(1.96)
Budget Deficit	0.000	−0.003	0.001	−0.002
	(0.02)	(−0.27)	(0.08)	(−0.13)
Government Consumption	−0.014	−0.016	−0.016	−0.017
	(−0.97)	(−1.30)	(−1.00)	(−1.32)
IMF	−0.129	−0.365**	−0.102	−0.313*
	(−1.23)	(−2.21)	(−0.95)	(−1.78)
Democracy			−0.000	0.000
			(−0.01)	(0.04)
Federalism			0.167*	0.151
			(1.92)	(1.51)
Constant	−0.092	−0.667	1.034	1.32
	(−0.06)	(−1.19)	(0.62)	(1.04)
Time Dummies	Yes	Yes	Yes	Yes
Number of Countries	68	68	67	67
Number of Observations	814	814	764	764

Note: Rho 0.165 (0.087), Sigma 1.480 (0.037), Lambda 0.244 (0.132).
*** = 99% confidence level, ** = 95% confidence level, * = 90% confidence level

are statistically significant. As argued earlier, this is due to the decrease in the sample size, dropping many low FDI countries that are both authoritarian and unitary. More importantly, the IMF variable remains robust with the inclusion of these controls. IMF programs, after controlling for the factors that lead multinationals to seek IMF support, have a negative impact on FDI inflows.

7.5 Qualitative Evidence

Interviews with investment promotion agencies confirm the results in this chapter. In the content analysis of 115 agency's Web sites, no agency made specific references to IMF programs as leading to a better investment environment. In interviews with most investment promotion agencies, they argued that IMF programs had no impact on multinationals or their investment strategies. For example, according to Thailand's investment promotion agency, investors are not generally concerned with the details of the IMF package, even after the 1998 financial crisis.

The two exceptions are two countries that recently had substantial financial crises. In interviews with representatives of the economics department at Citigroup, a investor relations representative of the Brazilian Central Bank, and the projects and economic advisory manager of Brazil's largest stock exchange (BOVESPA), a few themes became apparent. First, IMF reforms have some impact on investors' perceptions during the crisis, but the main impact was the infusion of capital to stave off the crisis. All three interviewees agreed that the current IMF conditions are actually reforms the government would have enacted anyway. Far more significant were domestic events and policies, such as leftist presidential candidate Lula's visiting the stock exchange or appointing a relatively orthodox cabinet. They argued that IMF capital had a positive impact on investors, but IMF conditions did not.

Even stronger support for the empirical results on the negative impact of IMF programs on FDI inflows was present in interviews with Malaysia's investment promotion agency. Malaysia is now famous for rebuffing the IMF's advice not to impose capital controls after the 1998 financial crisis and emerging from the financial crisis in better shape than many of its neighbors. A representative of Malaysia's investment promotion agency argued that most multinational investors understood Malaysia's policy position during the financial crisis and argued that the policies taken by Malaysia, not the ones prescribed by the IMF, maximized FDI inflows.

This point underscores interview evidence with location consultants B-G Consulting and IBM's Plant Location International (IBM-PLI). According to the president of B-G Consulting, in some cases IMF programs promote market-friendly policies, such as some market reforms in Bolivia, while in many other cases the IMF prescribes "one-size-fits-all" packages that are often not conducive for attracting multinationals. The IMF did not build a consensus around the economic reforms, leading to political instability and ineffective economic reforms. A representative of IBM-PLI took a similar position, where in some cases IMF programs make the country more attractive to multinationals while in other cases they have a negative impact.

According to the political risk insurers and analysts, IMF programs do have some impact on country risks, specifically currency and inconvertibility risk. For example, Export Development Canada considers relations with the IMF as an important determinant of currency risks, but these relations exist whether or not the country has access to IMF capital to shore up reserves. Once again, IMF capital, not IMF conditions, is valuable.

Interviews with representatives of multinational corporations yield similar results. Representatives of some multinationals, such as deputy head of the Latin American Research Department at UBS, a global financial firm, argued that IMF capital can be an important factor for developing countries, but IMF conditions have no real impact. This is due to the IMF specifying targets rather than instruments, and simply attempting to solve political problems with economic solutions. For many other companies, IMF programs do not have a major impact on multinationals' operations, even in crisis-prone countries. For example, representatives of Alcan Corporation stated that IMF conditionality had little impact on investment decisions. No company argued that IMF conditionality was seen as having a positive impact on the investment environment.

This qualitative evidence all points to both potential positives and negatives of IMF programs on multinationals' investment strategies. The clear positive is that access to IMF capital can be an important determinant of FDI inflows, but there is little systematic evidence that links IMF conditions to higher FDI inflows. In many cases, interviewees highlighted the same problems with IMF conditionality stressed in the theory section of this chapter. IMF conditions can potentially have a positive impact, but they have a negative impact if applied in a one-size-fits-all fashion, make loans conditional on specific targets rather than appropriate policies, or do not build a domestic base of support for economic reforms.

7.6 Conclusion

In this chapter, I explore the effects of IMF programs on inflows of foreign direct investment. Theoretically, distinct arguments could link IMF programs to either higher or lower levels of FDI inflows. On one hand, IMF programs may prescribe economic reform packages conducive to multinational investors, resulting in higher levels of economic stability and strong macroeconomic performance. Conversely, these IMF reform packages could lead to worse macroeconomic performance and higher levels of economic and political instability. Most specific to multinationals, IMF conditionality might cause an underprovision of market-enhancing public goods.

In the empirical section of this chapter, after controlling for selection, I find strong evidence linking IMF participation to lower levels of FDI inflows. Countries in economic crisis that turn to IMF support inhibit their ability to attract multinational investors. These results help illuminate a new set of challenges for countries in financial crisis attempting to calm foreign investors. IMF support, sometimes essential to crisis prevention and alleviation, produces policies that decrease inflows of foreign direct investment and perhaps worsens overall long-run macroeconomic performance.

This quantitative evidence, when coupled with the qualitative evidence in this chapter, paints an interesting picture of the net impact of IMF support on FDI inflows. In some cases the IMF can have a positive impact on FDI inflows. This is mostly due to access to IMF capital for crisis-prone countries. Contrary to claims on the market-improving impact of IMF conditions on domestic economies, there is little support for the claim that IMF conditions promote FDI inflows. My empirical estimates actually find that, even after controlling for the underlying factors that lead a country to seek IMF loans, IMF support is associated with lower FDI inflows. While theoretically IMF support could be market promoting, the empirical evidence is rather compelling. Signing onto IMF packages leads to 28 percent less FDI inflows.

8

Conclusion

8.1 Introduction

This book focuses on the economic, political, and policy factors that influence foreign direct investment across countries. Understanding these determinants of FDI provides important insights into how countries attract capital flows that have become associated with higher levels of economic growth, employment creation, and technology transfer. As countries in the developed and developing world embrace foreign investment promotion strategies as part of a larger strategy of macroeconomic development, an understanding of the determinants of FDI inflows holds important academic and public policy ramifications.

These capital flows also serve as a barometer of firms' perceptions of domestic governments' policies and institutions. By exploring how capital flows react to policies and institutions, we can develop a greater knowledge of how politics and policy affect macroeconomic performance generally. The findings of this book may have broader implications for the study of the impact of political institutions on macroeconomic performance.

Finally, and perhaps most timely, as protestors and citizens have become increasingly disenchanted with the activities and actions of multinational corporations abroad, a deeper understanding of these firms and their investment decisions becomes increasingly important. Only by analyzing multinationals and their investments can we learn how to maximize the benefits of multinational production and to minimize the adverse effects.

In this study, I generate four sets of empirical tests of the determinants of FDI inflows. First, I explore fiscal policy determinants of FDI. Second, I explore the complex relationship between democratic institutions and FDI. Next, I examine the relationship between political veto players and FDI. Finally, I assess the net impact of International Monetary Fund involvement in countries and the influence of IMF programs on FDI inflows.

8.2 Economic Policy: Race to the Bottom

According to the race to the bottom perspective, multinationals search the world for investment opportunities, playing governments against one another, entering and exiting domestic markets at will in an attempt to obtain higher returns. I argue in chapter 3 that this view of capital mobility—of frictionless investment across national borders— contradicts decades of research on FDI that focuses on *imperfect* market approaches to the study of multinational firms. The race to the bottom thesis rests on this myth of capital mobility.

In chapter 4, I explore the fiscal competition among fifteen OECD countries and the impact of these policies on FDI inflows. My results conclude:

- Levels of government consumption *across* countries do not affect FDI inflows, while some evidence exists that a decline in the level of government consumption *within* a country can increase FDI inflows.
- The level of social security transfers does not affect FDI inflows.
- Levels of capital taxation insignificantly impact FDI inflows.
- No evidence emerges that FDI flows react positively to a shift in taxation from capital to labor.
- I find no support that left governments decrease inflows of FDI.

In summary, I find very little support for the race to the bottom thesis.

8.3 Political Institutions as a Commitment Mechanism

As I outlined in chapter 3, multinational investments, while relatively liquid ex ante, prove much more illiquid ex post. Once a multinational corporation commits resources to an investment location, the investment becomes relatively immobile. Although multinationals may hold considerable bargaining power prior to investment, a large degree of power shifts to the host government after investment.

This ex-post immobility of multinationals forces firms to try to predict the future policies of host governments. Politicians may attempt to make assurances on future policies, but governments have the incentive to change policy once a multinational commits substantial resources to the project. Governments that can credibly commit to a policy equilibrium, ensuring policy stability, attract higher levels of FDI by lowering political risks for multinationals. More importantly, governments that can commit to market-friendly policies can assure multinationals of a favorable policy environment for their operations. This ability to provide assurances to multinationals on future policy proves central to attracting FDI. Political institutions can serve as these commitment mechanisms. I identify three sets of institutions that could affect FDI inflows: veto player institutions, democratic institutions, and the International Monetary Fund.

8.4 Democratic Institutions

Scholars and pundits assume that multinationals prefer to invest in dictatorships. They argue that dictators are not responsible to an electorate, allowing authoritarian leaders more room to maneuver and negotiate with multinationals. Even if one assumes the argument that multinationals may prefer to bargain with authoritarian leaders, there are a number of other channels through which democracy could affect FDI inflows.

Profit-maximizing multinational enterprises will weigh the varying factors that impact operations in host countries. Contrary to the pessimism about the link between authoritarian regimes and foreign direct investment, in this book I identify three mechanisms through which democratic institutions would be the preferred institutional structure for their investments, and I argue that the last of these mechanisms, the role of political institutions on government policy, has large influences on FDI inflows. These three mechanisms are:

Information: Multinationals are attracted to democratic countries because of the better information available on government policy and current political and economic conditions.

Representation: Foreign investors can more easily influence policy in democracies through institutionalized mechanisms than in authoritarian regimes. MNCs may find vested interests in democratic systems already in place.

Credibility: Although the effects of democracy on information and representation are important, in this project I stress the policy-enhancing nature of democracy. Two sub-mechanisms provide multinationals with market-promoting policies. One mechanism that leads democratic governments to higher levels of credibility in terms of economic policy is based on the number of veto points in a democratic political system. Democratic governments have these institutional constraints in place, making the possibility of policy reversal more difficult. Multinationals investing in large illiquid projects will prefer to invest in countries where there is a lower probability of policy reversal once the investment has been made.

Even more important for multinationals, democratic institutions provide multinationals benefits through the existence of "audience costs." If governments make agreements with multinational firms and renege on the contracts after the investment has been made, democratic leaders may be punished at the polls. The potential for these electoral backlashes constrains democratic leaders in their policies toward multinational corporations. Democratic governments may provide more market-friendly policies for multinational investors.

Given the market-promoting nature of democratic institutions, I predict that democratic nations will attract higher levels of FDI than their authoritarian counterparts. I test this theory in chapter 5 using cross-sectional, time-series-cross-sectional, and treatment effects selection regressions on the determinants of FDI inflows.

The first set of regressions utilizes cross-sectional data for eighty countries on the determinants of FDI in the 1990s. These regressions find that democratic political institutions are associated with as much as 78 percent more FDI flows than authoritarian regimes. These results are robust when other political factors are controlled for.

The second set of regressions utilizes panel data to explore the effects of democratic institutions on FDI inflows from 1970 to 1998 for over one hundred countries. In this set of tests I construct a number of Ordinary Least Squares regressions with robust standard errors using annual FDI inflows as a percentage of GDP as the dependent variable. As with the cross-sectional results, these time-series-cross-sectional regressions find that democratic institutions have a positive and statistically significant effect on FDI inflows. The magnitude of these flows is massive—democratic institutions attract 70 percent more FDI as a percentage of GDP. The cumulated effect of democratic institutions after ten years of continuous democracy amounts to an added stock of FDI of roughly 20 percent of GDP.

The third set of empirical tests corrects for the selection bias in democratic institutions by utilizing a selection model, controlling for the limited number of observations of democracies in low-income countries. I find that the OLS regressions were biased and that the effects of democratic institutions on FDI are vastly underestimated. The selection-corrected estimates of the effects of democracy are roughly three times larger than the OLS results. Democratic institutions have an even more massive positive effect on FDI inflows than originally estimated.

In a final set of empirical tests I explore the credibility-enhancing nature of democratic institutions by exploring the effects of democracy on country sovereign debt ratings for eighty countries from 1980 to 1998. The empirical results find a strong positive and statistically significant effect of democracy on sovereign debt ratings. In summary, democratic institutions are associated with higher levels of FDI inflows and lower levels of sovereign debt risk.

8.5 Veto Players

In chapter 3 I argue that multinational corporations, investing in large illiquid projects, become susceptible to enormous political risks. Certain political institutions, such as institutional veto players, limit a country's ability to enact sweeping policy reforms. Unfortunately, policy stability does not provide an end in itself. Multinational corporations want governments to enact policies that provide environments that will be conducive for their investments to prosper. This means that governments, operating in a world of constant change, must also have the ability to alter policy.

I establish in chapter 6 that federal institutions can be associated with higher flows of FDI. Federal institutions can provide benefits to multinationals by enhancing policy stability and providing multinational-friendly policies. Subnational actors can potentially provide veto points within the political system that enhance the credibility of host governments. The value of these "veto points" depends on the exact type of federal institutions.

I argue that a careful theoretical distinction between political federalism, political decentralization, and fiscal federalism must be developed to understand the independent effects of these institutions on multinational production. In politically federal systems, subnational units can provide a de facto veto on central government legislation. This increase in the number of veto players provides higher levels of policy stability in a Tsebelis-style framework. More importantly, I argue that these veto players in federal systems have the incentives and the power to protect the operations of multinational firms.

In a model constructed in chapter 6, I show that these differing incentives of the central government and subnational governments can provide multinationals with a credible commitment to market-friendly policies. This "market-preserving federalism" only occurs within systems where the power of taxation rests in the hands of the central government and subnational units have some degree of political power. Only *politically* federal systems provide commitments to market-promoting policies. These political systems attract higher levels of FDI.

Empirically, I find the effects of political federalism on FDI positive and statistically significant. Politically federal countries attract higher levels of FDI, even when I control for other political and economic factors. The effects on fiscal federalism prove neither consistently positive nor statistically significant. In a test of sovereign debt ratings, I find both political and fiscal federalism are associated with higher sovereign debt ratings.

8.6 The International Monetary Fund

Although domestic political institutions can have major effects on government policy, and ultimately FDI, international institutions can also affect policy in ways that affect FDI inflows. In chapter 7 I explore the effects of signing agreements with the International Monetary Fund on FDI inflows. Countries in severe economic crisis turn to the IMF for "lender of last resort" funds. These funds are often provided with explicit IMF conditionality, where disbursements of IMF funds are contingent on specific macroeconomic reforms.

The signing of a loan agreement with the IMF can provide international investors with a limited credible commitment to a specific package of future economic policies. Countries signing IMF agreements face more than just reputation costs; they will incur actual fiscal costs in terms of lower levels of funding from the IMF for reversing policy. IMF packages should decrease the level of policy risk.

Unlike democratic institutions and federal institutions, IMF packages, while decreasing policy instability, do not ensure market-friendly policies. I argue that the effect of IMF agreements on FDI is strictly an empirical question. Financial markets, in this case FDI flows, should provide the answer as to whether foreign investors value these reforms. Economic reforms that will stabilize the economy and provide the foundation for robust future macroeconomic performance should be valuable to multinational corporations. Countries that sign IMF agreements should then be associated with higher FDI inflows.

At the same time the possibility exists that IMF programs could have a detrimental effect on multinational investors. Signing of IMF agreements could also lock governments into an inefficient policy equilibrium. If the conditionality associated with IMF loans is worse than the current economic policies, foreign investors will react negatively to IMF agreements.

Using a treatment effects selection model to control for the factors that lead countries to be under IMF agreements, I find that IMF programs do not help restore the confidence of multinationals during an economic crisis. In fact, I find that IMF programs are associated with a significant reduction in FDI inflows for a host country. Countries that sign IMF agreements, even after controlling for selection, attract 28 percent less FDI than countries that do not obtain IMF support. This leads to the conjecture that IMF conditions, usually austerity policies, are viewed unfavorably by multinational corporations.

8.7 Qualitative Evidence

In this book I present evidence from twenty-nine interviews with representatives from country investment promotion agencies, location consultants, political risk insurers/analysts, and multinational firms. These interviews support the findings from the empirical section. Levels of corporate taxation and tax incentives are not the major determinants of FDI, and in many cases they had no impact on firms' investment location decisions. Institutions that lower political risks for multinationals, on the other hand, are more hospitable to multinational investors. Democratic governments are hands down the top choice for multinational investors, while institutional structures such as the number of veto players have no impact on FDI decisions. There is limited support that federal institutions also provide avenues for multinationals to reduce their political risks. Finally, the conditionality associated with IMF programs does not provide commitments to market-friendly policy; in some cases it may actually worsen the macroeconomic situation and increase the political risks to which multinationals are exposed. These interviews confirm the empirical analysis presented in this book, and provide causal tests on the impact of political institutions on multinational investment decisions.

In summary, the empirical chapters of this book find that the public policy factors related to FDI, such as levels of government spending and taxation, have been overemphasized as important determinants of FDI inflows. Alternatively, political institutions, in our case levels of democracy, forms of federal institutions, and agreements with the International Monetary Fund, all have significant effects on FDI inflows.

Understanding the impact of these political institutions is necessary to understand the investments of multinational corporations worldwide.

8.8 Public Policy Ramifications

This book, while academic in focus, informs four public policy debates.

1. *Fiscal policy has little impact on FDI inflows.* Countries in developed and developing countries that are attempting to attract multinationals should focus on the crafting of broad institutions that are conducive to strong macroeconomic performance rather than a narrow focus on fiscal policy to induce investment.

2. *Scholars have overemphasized the tension between democracy and the attraction of FDI inflows.* Although a number of cases may be made regarding the tensions between democracy and economic development, this study finds no evidence that multinational corporations prefer to invest in authoritarian regimes. In fact, I find that democratic institutions can provide important benefits to multinational corporations, specifically in lowering levels of political risk for investors.

In parts of the world that have been plagued with low levels of FDI, such as Sub-Saharan Africa, the importance of these institutions as central to attracting FDI inflows cannot be overemphasized. Although democratic institutions are not a panacea for development, for these countries, fundamental economic and political reforms are a necessary condition in attracting FDI. Specifically, the consolidation and maintenance of democratic institutions are an important economic development strategy, not to mention a potential mechanism for dealing with civil conflict and governing natural resources endowments.[1]

In other areas of the globe that have been more successful in attracting FDI, such as the post-Communist states of Eastern and Central Europe along with the former Soviet Union, this study illuminates the dangers of executive discretion in a world of global capital markets. Political leaders in a number of countries, such as Slovakia and Russia, wield tremendous influence in their countries' domestic policy and international relationships. This executive discretion is not only dangerous to the democratic process; it may also entail serious economic costs.

3. Relationships between political actors within a nation-state can affect a country's ability to attract multinational corporations. In this book I stress that the patterns of political accountability between central and subnational governments can lead to higher levels of FDI inflows. More generally, governance relationships between actors within nation-states can help provide a more conducive environment for multinationals. A careful consideration of political relationships between the executive and other political actors (legislatures, courts, etc.) can be an important component of economic development strategies for developing countries. Getting "institutions right," both domestic and international, has become more important in a world of multinational production.

4. IMF Programs do not restore the confidence of multinational investors. IMF conditions in their present form do not have a positive impact on FDI inflows. The fact that forward-looking investors do not consider IMF programs valuable to countries in economic crisis leads us to doubt the overall value of IMF programs and conditions. Reform of the IMF and IMF conditionality should be in the interest of governments, citizens, and multinational corporations.

8.9 Caveats

This book, while attempting to remain objective and empirical, generates results that speak to both academic and public policy debates.

- Governments' fiscal policies are not constrained by capital mobility.

- Democracy is not under threat by foreign markets; markets only strengthen the case for democratic institutions.
- Certain types of federal systems may provide even more benefits to domestic governments by lowering levels of political risk.
- IMF reforms that would most likely be less draconian in the eyes of the populace would also most likely be more conducive to multinational investors. The austerity packages promoted by the IMF, so often opposed by the citizenry, are indeed not market promoting.

Have the critics of multinationals, the opponents of globalization, the pessimists about the race to the bottom, and the supporters of the IMF got it all wrong? Not exactly.

First, it is important to note that while this study finds that multinationals do not challenge economic policy autonomy or democratic governance, I am by no means advocating that MNEs can not, or do not, have negative impacts on government. In this book I simply assume that MNEs are profit-maximizing enterprises, neither demons nor angels, only firms that answer to investors. There are economic benefits to democratic institutions, and there seem to be few economic consequences to government fiscal autonomy. Unfortunately, there are a number of areas where some pessimism is in order.

Perhaps the greatest challenge to domestic governments in a world of free trade and mobile capital is to foster economic development and the protection of property without further damaging the physical environment. Environmental protection, a textbook example of a public good, is generally underprovided through market mechanisms. Environmental protection, a benefit to consumers and citizens, has little value to multinational investors. Countries in the developing and developed world may lower standards on the protection of the environment in order to attract multinationals that are hampered by high environmental standards.

Sadly, many of the international institutions, regional trade associations, and international agreements have not only failed to adequately protect the environment in the face of these pressures, they have made the domestic regulation of environmental standards even more difficult. One glaring example is chapter 11 of the NAFTA agreement that has been used by multinationals to challenge domestic environmental legislation and standards. Similar examples can be found in the WTO, EU, and the proposed (and failed) Multilateral Agreement on Investment. Multinational investment, and international financial flows generally, can pose real and serious challenges to the environment.

Second, the findings on the impact of federal political systems on FDI inflows stresses that specific institutional arrangements can produce lower levels of political risk and increase FDI inflows. Unfortunately, few federal systems meet these criteria in the real world, and federal institutional arrangements can have serious effects on other aspects of economic policy and the political process. This book attempts to sort out part of the confusion on the effects of federalism on macroeconomic performance by differentiating between different types of federalism. I am in no position to advocate unitary systems in developing countries to adopt politically federal constitutions.

More importantly, the fiscal reforms most recently promoted by the World Bank in developing countries do not fit into this set of "market-promoting institutions." In chapter 6 I find some evidence that fiscal federalism may be associated with lower levels of political risk, but I find no evidence that fiscal federalism is associated with higher levels of FDI inflows. Coupled with the existing literature on the potential negative effects of fiscal federalism on macroeconomic performance, the emphasis on fiscal federalism seems less appropriate for fostering economic development.

Finally, in chapter 7, I showed the negative impact of IMF agreements on multinational corporations. There is also a growing literature on the negative impact of IMF programs on economic performance and domestic societies. At the same time I think one can make a strong case for a larger, better funded IMF. The qualitative evidence indicates that multinationals find little value in IMF conditions, but access to IMF capital can be an important determinant of FDI decisions. The true problem with the current IMF may be its form, not its function.

With the end of the gold standard and fixed exchange rates, the complexity and responsibilities of the IMF increased without an increase in resources. Many of the criticisms of the IMF, and many of their policy mistakes, have their roots in the lack of resources at the disposal of the IMF. To make informed decisions and provide adequate support for countries in economic crisis, the IMF needs more staff and resources.

The IMF also needs a fundamental transformation in the role and form of conditionality in the lending process. IMF conditions can be linked to a number of negative economic consequences. At the same time, the funds provided by the IMF can help save countries in economic crisis and more generally promote world financial stability. In short, the IMF may need to get out of the economic growth business, but not out of the lending business altogether.

8.10 Conclusion

In sum, multinational corporations still pose tremendous possibilities and enormous challenges to governments and citizens. This book makes a serious attempt to understand multinational corporations and their investment decisions. The main point of the book is that political institutions, both domestic and international, have major effects on multinational investors. This understanding can serve as a foundation for both enabling and regulating multinationals to serve the needs of governments and citizens in countries around the world.

Notes

Chapter 1
Introduction

1. See Lohmann (1992).

2. I examine the importance of public goods to multinationals in my discussion of the extensive literature on the determinants of FDI inflows in chapter 2.

3. For an extensive discussion of the links between democracy and economic growth and development, see Przeworski et al. (2000); for federalism and economic performance, see Oats (1999) and Rodden and Rose-Ackerman (1997); for IMF programs and economic performance, see Przeworski and Vreeland (2000) and Vreeland (2002).

4. Influential works such as Andrews (1994), Cerny (1990), and Kurzer (1993) all argue that global markets seriously pressure governments to lower levels of capital taxation and government spending.

5. Even the assumption that multinationals are liquid ex ante appears questionable. Past studies of MNEs focus on imperfect market approaches. See chapter 2.

6. The degree of ex-post liquidity varies by industry. In capital-intensive industries, firms often invest in massive production facilities which are difficult to liquidate. In other labor-intensive industries, such as textiles, firms only commit limited capital and are more liquid after investment.

7. I discuss this time inconsistency of government policy as originally theorized by Kydland and Prescott (1977) in more detail in chapter 2.

8. Oneal (1994); Jessup (1999). For a more recent test of the link between democracy and FDI, see Li and Resnick (2003).

9. I further discuss the preferences of multinationals in chapter 3.

10. For a review of the most recent literature, see Schultz (1999).

11. Hillman and Ursprung (1988), 730.

12. This logic aligns theoretically with the work done by Frieden (1991) where he distinguishes between different types of capital based on their mobility. Milner (1988) argues that companies with an international focus share similar preferences on trade protection policy. One example of this is a recent power dispute between aluminum manufacturer Alcan and the government of Brazil. Alcan is lobbying the Brazilian government through a Brazilian consortium of foreign and domestic manufacturers.

13. Henisz (2000) argues that foreign firms change their entrance strategies into domestic markets in response to the number of veto players.

14. Watts (1999), p. 6.

15. In a recent work, Przeworski and Vreeland (2000) found that IMF policies lead to lower levels of long-run economic growth for countries.

16. This time period was selected in order to replicate the results of Garrett and Mitchell's (2001) work.

17. Rosenthal (1991); Bulow and Rogoff (1989).

18. Thanks to Jonathan Rodden for this data.

19. These agencies were selected by their country coverage. All organizations selected covered a large number of both developed and developing countries.

Chapter 2
Multinational Firms and Domestic Governments

1. See Lipsey (1999) for a discussion of the stability of FDI flows relative to other investment flows.

2. The IMF uses these statistical rules. See IFC (1997), 9.

3. Survey evidence suggests that the average time horizon from decision to investment is 12–24 months (MIGA 2002, 15).

4. IFC (1997), 14.

5. Mallampally and Sauvant (1999).

6. The one exception is natural resource–seeking FDI flows to developing countries in the 1970s.

7. Interview with Costa Rica's investment promotion agency (CINDE) on June 10, 2004, and July 27, 2004.

8. Interviews #25 and #26.

9. Markusen (1995), 172.

10. See Wang (1990) and Grossman and Helpman (1991).

11. See Görg and Strobl (2001) and Lipsy (2002).

12. This model generated a tremendous amount of theoretical and empirical analysis of the relationship between trade and investment.

13. Agosin (1995).

14. Some evidence exists that increased trade barriers may be related to increased "tariff-jumping" FDI. See Bhagwati (1985) and Barrell and Pain (1999).

15. One recent example of increases in oil production due to multinational investments appears in Equatorial Guinea.

16. This view of capital accumulation began with Harrod (1939), culminating into the famous Solow growth model. See Solow (1956).

17. Balasubramanyam, Salisu, and Sapsford (1999), 28.

18. IFC (1997), 51.

19. See http://www.svtc.org/listserv/leter12a.htm.

20. Interview #26.

21. This is not to say that multinationals don't have negative consequences for host countries. The Union Carbide gas leak in Bhopal, India, that was responsible for an estimated 15,000 deaths and 578,000 injuries, is perhaps the most striking example of this.

22. Drezner (2001) provides an excellent overview and analysis of this literature.

23. Andrews (1994); Cerny (1990); Kurzer (1993). See Garrett (1998) for a discussion of the literature. See Hayes (2003) and Basinger and Hallerberg (2004)

for recent contributions on how domestic political institutions affect a country's ability to lower capital taxation rates.

24. Bennell (1997), 133–134.

25. Chudnovsky, Lopez, and Porta. (1995), 41–42.

26. The GATT provisions concerning National Treatment (Article III), reaffirmed by the Agreement on Trade-Related Investment Matters (TRIMs), explicitly prohibits these trade-balancing requirements.

Chapter 3
Theory

1. "Western Companies Warm to Russia." *New York Times*, May 30, 2002.

2. Other notable contributions include Vernon's (1966) product life cycle, Buckley and Casson (1976) on internalization, Magee (1977) on information, Rugman (1979) on international diversification, Lamfalussy (1961) on defensive FDI, and Williamson (1975) on transaction costs. For a recent contribution see Moran (2001).

3. Dunning (1981). For an interesting discussion on the OLI framework and recent work done in relation to it, see Markusen (1995).

4. See Markusen and Maskus (1999a, 1999b).

5. For a review of the literature, see Markusen and Maskus (1999a).

6. Brewer (1993a) reviews much of the existing literature on the political determinants of FDI flows in developing countries.

7. The debate on FDI investment and trade policy centers on international trade as a complement or substitute for FDI, with the consensus shifting toward FDI as a complement.

8. Martin and Velazquez (1997) also found that "endowments of transport and human capital infrastructure" have a positive effect on FDI inflow. These factors have begun to find themselves within the FDI models of economic theorists, where Zhang and Markusen (1999) develop a theoretical model that argues that MNEs need skilled labor, and that public and private services (telecom, laws, etc.) drive FDI flows.

9. For a brief review, see Markusen (1995). For interesting work on the level of tax rates under conditions of capital mobility, see Swank (1998) and Garrett and Mitchell (2001).

10. For a review, see Brewer (1993a).

11. Ibid. For an examination of contract risks and MNE activities, see Lehmann (1999) and Henisz (2000, 2002).

12. UNCTC (1991) examines 46 countries from 1977 to 1987 and finds that government policy had an effect on FDI inflows, but these policies alone do not attract FDI. Markets and economic conditions matter more. Ganesan (1998) argues that "while an MAI (multilateral agreement on investment) may contribute to an improvement in the investment climate of a country, it will not be the dominant factor in directing FDI flows to developing countries."

13. I provide a more comprehensive definition of foreign direct investment in the next section.

14. See Harms (2000) for a review of the political risk literature.

15. See also Minor (1994).

16. David (1985) argues that political risk assessment often hinges on an American-centric view of world business.

17. See Osebhale (1993) for more on creeping expropriation.

18. For example, see Erb, Harvey, and Viskanta (1996).

19. "Administration to U.S. Oil Giants: Reconsider Russian Investment," *Energy Daily*, October 4, 2002.

20. Transcript from "Weekend All Things Considered," October 5, 2002.

21. "Iraq the Threat of War: Energy," *The Independent*, September 26, 2002.

22. Some organizations such as MIGA use four categories, while others such as EDC lump expropriation and breach of contract into the same category.

23. Interview #17.

24. In some cases, investors may opt for arbitration through the International Centre for Settlement of Investment Disputes (ICSID), but as noted by García-Bolívar (2004) this jurisdiction is very limited.

Chapter 4
The Race to the Bottom Thesis and FDI

1. Christopher Brown-Humes, "Finland's high tax, high-wage economy fights to stay high in the global competitiveness stakes," *Financial Times* May 15/16, 2004, 4.

2. Outsourcing is not the same as outward FDI. The common usage of "outsourcing" refers to the closing of U.S. production facilities or service centers and moving these operations abroad. Outward FDI is any investment of a multinational that is not in the host country.

3. At JohnKerry.com.

4. See UNCTAD (2003) for a more detailed treatment of the issue. See also Vernon (1998).

5. For an excellent recent contribution see Mutti (2003).

6. For an excellent contribution on taxation and international capital in non-OECD countries see Wibbels and Arce (2003).

7. This trend toward investment promotion programs extends to developing countries also. See Moran (1998).

8. See chapter 2.

9. Solow (1956).

10. Markusen (1995).

11. Drezner (2001) offers an excellent overview of this literature.

12. Andrews (1994); Cerny (1990); Kurzer (1993). See Garrett (1998) and Swank (2002) for a discussion of the literature. See Basinger and Hallerberg (2004) for a discussion of how transaction costs and constituency costs affects tax policy.

13. Cameron (1978); Garrett (1998); Swank (2002). See Basinger and Hallerberg (2004) and Hayes (2004) on how domestic politics affects capital taxation.

14. Rodrik (1997).

15. Rodden and Rose-Ackerman (1997).

16. See Hayes (2003) for a discussion of this literature.

17. Tiebout (1956).

18. Multinationals also make choices on investment levels and the forms of entry into foreign markets. For an interesting examination of multinational entry decisions, see Henisz (2000).

19. This corresponds to the works in "new growth theory." See Lucas (1988); Barro (1990); and Romer (1990).

20. In many ways these theories remain compatible with each other. The race to the bottom thesis could be seen as the "lean government" thesis plus competition among countries.

21. For all regressions, I used Stata 6.0 with the xtpcse option.

22. Interviews with firms and investment promotion agencies argued that past FDI serve as a signal of the business environment.

23. See IFC (1997), 9.

24. See Markusen (1998a, 1998b); Markusen and Maskus (1999a, 1999b).

25. Kurzer (1993) argues that financial markets punish states enacting social welfare policies and public spending expansion.

26. See Gravelle and Smetters (2001) for a review of the literature and a theoretical examination of the burden of taxation in a simple open-economy model.

27. This epitomizes a classical free-rider problem. See Olsen (1965).

28. Labor taxation comes from the effective labor tax rate from Mendoza et al. (1997).

29. Even in systems where multinationals negotiate investment incentives, the statutory tax rate is the starting point for these negotiations. According to Mutti (2003, 31), "statutory rates certainly influence effect rates calculated from company tax returns, but they also have a separate effect on the incentives firms have to declare double taxable income in one jurisdiction or another."

30. I also ran a simple OLS regression with 2002 FDI inflows as the dependent variable, and control variables for the level of economic development, economic growth, trade, and the corporate tax rates. Corporate tax rate was not statistically significant.

31. Interview #20.

32. Interview #21.

33. To qualify for Free Zone status, companies must invest a minimum of $150,000 in fixed assets and export 50% of their final product. Interview #10.

Chapter 5
Democracy and FDI

Portions of this chapter are from Jensen (2003a).

1. Details on Alcan's operations can be found in the Alcan Inc. 2003 Annual Report and at alcan.com.

2. Interview #20.

3. Jessup (1999) asserts that authoritarian regimes in developing countries attract more international investment. Oneal (1994) finds that authoritarian regimes provide investors with higher returns in developing countries, although overall investment flows do not relate to regime type. Li and Resnick (2003) find that in the long run, democracies are associated with lower FDI inflows.

4. Of course, a large number of definitions of democracy exist. Robert Dahl (1971), one of the most influential democratic theorists of our time, defines democracies as countries where: (1) citizens can vote; (2) the government comes to power in a freely contested election where two or more parties compete; and (3) the executive is held either directly accountable through direct elections (presidential systems) or indirectly by the legislature (parliamentary systems). A more minimalist theory of democracy, employed by Przeworski et al. (2000), distinguishes between "(1) regimes that allow some, even limited, regularized competition among conflicting visions and interests and (2) regimes in which some values or interests enjoy a monopoly buttressed by the threat or the actual use of force. Thus democracy, for us, is a regime in which those who govern are selected through contested elections" (Przeworski et al. 2000, 15).

5. See Brooks (2005) on the relationship between multinational corporations and international conflict.

6. Russett (2001), 53.

7. One comprehensive game-theoretic study by Bueno de Mesquita and Lalman (1992) incorporates both of these concepts into one model.

8. For a review of the most recent literature, see Schultz (1999).

9. Hillman and Ursprung (1988), 730.

10. *The Economist*, February 17, 2001, 43.

11. This comports theoretically with the work done by Frieden (1991), where he distinguishes between different types of capital based on their mobility. Milner (1988) argues that companies with an international focus share similar preferences on trade protection policy.

12. One interesting example pointed out to me by the manager of the Investor Relations Group at the Central Bank of Brazil was the public outcry when the government of Brazil attempted to suspend the autonomy of the national telecommunications regulation agency. Popular pressure by citizens helped protect the autonomy of this agency.

13. Interviews with investment promotion agencies and multinationals support this view that wage rates, independent of labor force quality, are not major determinants of FDI.

14. The 2002 Brazilian and 2004 Indian national elections are both examples of how financial markets can influence the choices of political leaders. In Brazil, following negative reactions of financial markets to trade unionist Luiz Inácio Lula da Silva's lead in presidential polls, Lula moderated his policy positions, appointed a relatively economically conservative cabinet, and visited the stock exchange. In India, the Bharatiya Janata Party's surprising loss in the national elections was followed by a 10% slide in stock market prices. Sonia Ghandhi stepped down as candidate for prime minister and endorsed the more economically orthodox Manmohan Singh. Markets rebounded.

15. For an interesting discussion of expropriation, see Thomas and Worrall (1994).

16. See Bueno de Mesquita et al. (1999). The most logical extension of their theory suggests that expropriation would more likely occur in systems with smaller selectorates (authoritarian regimes). In systems with large selectorates (democracies), political leaders would have to spread the benefits of expropriation over a larger percentage of the citizenry, making it a less viable option.

17. I do not include transition economies in this sample.

18. Given the democratizations in the 1990s, the 1990 measure of democracy provides a more representative measure of political institutions during the period of FDI investment. As an alternative specification, I also tested all models with the average level of democracy in the 1980s. These results proved slightly weaker.

19. The correlation between the Polity III democracy measure and the Alvarez et al. (1996) democracy score equals 0.92. This measure obviously ignores important variation in institutional features and public policy between dictatorships. See Gandhi (2004) for a discussion.

20. For some examples of the effects of natural resources on political institutions, see Wantchekon and Jensen (2000), Ross (2000), Wantchekon and Jensen (2004).

21. The basis of the concept of convergence comes from the Solow (1956). See Barro (1996) for a discussion of conditional convergence and empirical results.

22. The empirical results are essentially unchanged under different measures of democracy. See Jensen 2003a.

23. Easterly (1999). These variables are all highly correlated with each other, with correlations ranging from 0.63 to 0.81.

24. I have also tested this result without a lagged dependent variable, but with AR1 correlations. The results are essentially unchanged.

25. Long-run estimates derive the formula for calculating the present value of perpetuity: (Democracy Coefficient*Democracy Score)/(1 - Coefficient on the Lagged FDI). After 10 years of continuous democracy, a country will have an added stock of FDI that amounts to over 5% of GDP.

26. I have also checked the robustness of the empirical results by dropping each independent variable individually. The results on democracy unchanged.

27. See Alvarez et al. (1996) and Przeworski et al. (2000) for a more detailed discussion of the variable.

28. This is the similar empirical technique employed by Przeworski et al. (2000). They find that the level of economic development and the number of transitions from authoritarian rule correctly classify 77.7% of the political regimes from 1950 to 1990.

29. Both Lambda and the LR test confirm the significance of the selection model. See table 5.4.

30. Rosenthal (1991) and Bulow and Rogoff (1989).

31. See Feder and Uy (1985); Cosset and Roy (1990); and Lee (1993).

32. The formula for the transformation appears as: Dependent variable = $ln[R/(1 - R)]$ where R represents the Institutional Investor or Euromoney Rating divided by 100.

33. I tested all models with controls for the average annual consumer price inflation and the real effect exchange rate using World Bank World Development Indicators data.

34. I included all national investment promotion agencies with English language Web sites list either at the MIGA Web site or the World Investment Promotion Agency Web site (WIPA).

35. At www.belizeinvest.org.bz.

36. At www.fdi.gov.cn.

37. At www.iesingapore.com.

38. The example the interviewee gave of an immature democracy was Iraq.

39. At http://www.prsgroup.com/icrg/icrg.html.

Chapter 6
Veto Players and FDI

1. Mutti (2003, 11).

2. Nelson Silveira, "Ford Promove Festa Política na Bahia," *Journal do Brasil*, June 29, 1999, 16.

3. He constructs a model with multiple veto players with Euclidian preferences in a two-dimensional policy space.

4. See Tsebelis (1995), Proposition 2.

5. See Oats (1999) for a review of this literature.

6. See also Rodden and Wibbels (2002) and Rodden (2003).

7. See Treisman (2000b).

8. Wibbels (2000), 690.

9. Elazar (1994).

10. Lijphart (1999), 185.

11. Watts (1999), 6.

12. In democratic systems, the regional units represent the citizens of the region and the central government the whole country. In authoritarian countries, the central and regional elites become different principals.

13. The topic of relative wages of workers employed by multinationals involves complex issues that lie beyond the scope of this chapter.

14. Most federal systems have bicameral legislatures with at least one house representing the territorial units.

15. Malaysia is an example of this type of system.

16. Authoritarian federal systems such as the United Arab Emirates could rely on this tactic.

17. Lijphart (1999), 187.

18. Bueno de Mesquita et al. (1999) label this group the selectorate.

19. According to their definition, veto players are political actors that have heterogeneous preferences. See Beck et al. (2000) for a discussion of the project. I use the recommended veto player variable, Checks2a.

20. I thank Jonathan Rodden for this data.

21. Using state expenditures as a percentage of GDP produces similar results.

22. It is important to note that political federalism is positively correlated with market size (0.46).

23. Rosenthal (1991) and Bulow and Rogoff (1989).

24. The formula for the transformation appears as: Dependent variable = $ln[R/(1 - R)]$ where R represents the Institutional Investor or Euromoney Rating divided by 100.

25. I lag all independent variables one year.

26. The positive relationship between fiscal federalism and sovereign debt ratings is beyond the scope of this chapter.

27. This correlation is based on the maximum corporate tax rates from the World Bank's World Development Indicators 2003.

Chapter 7
The IMF and FDI Inflows

1. For a discussion of IMF conditionality and its impact on capital markets, see http://www.imf.org/external/np/exr/facts/crises.htm.

2. De Gregorio et al. (1999) argue that with the availability of capital to most middle-income countries, the role of the World Bank has diminished considerably in recent years.

3. I admittedly ignore the complex governance structure of the IMF. Instead, I simply discuss the IMF as a single international organization. In reality, the mechanism for governance of the IMF is relatively complex.

4. IMF conditionality became part of the IMF's lending scheme in 1952 (Sidell 1988), and later codified in the charter in 1968. After the 1976 Annual Meeting, the concept of conditionality further evolved, and the 1979 IMF Guidelines on Conditionality dubbed it "strict conditionality" (James 1996, 322–323). These conditions became more detailed in the 1960s and 1970s.

5. See Khan and Sharma (2001).

6. Other scholars argue for a greater differentiation in the level of conditionality. See Dell (1982) and Williamson (1983).

7. See chapter 2.

8. This model uses a version of a dynamic probit model to predict IMF participation. In this dynamic, bivariate probit, Vreeland controls for selection both (1) the types of countries that seek IMF support and (2) the types of countries that receive support. In the real world we only observe when a country has an IMF agreement (both condition 1 and condition 2 are satisfied) or when a country does not (either one or both conditions are not met).

9. Even some IMF research shows programs could have a negative impact on output (Kahn et al. 1986; Vines 1990).

10. The political costs to reform can prove extremely high in countries with a large debt overhang (Sachs 1989; Krugman 1988).

11. Another possibility suggests that developing countries dependent on tariffs for government revenue may see a marked decrease in revenues during

a devaluation. Government deficits will rise further or the burden of taxation must be shifted to another source.

12. Bird and Rowlands (1997), Krueger (1988), and Rodrik (1996) all criticize these catalytic effects.

13. The selection of cases is based on data availability.

14. Vreeland uses a dynamic model, while I employ a static model.

Chapter 8
Conclusion

1. Wantchekon and Jensen (2000).

References

Agosin, Manuel R. 1995. *Foreign Investment in Latin America*. Washington, D.C.: Inter-American Development Bank.

Alesina, Alberto, and David Dollar. 1998. "Who Gives Foreign Aid to Whom and Why?" *National Bureau of Economic Research Working Paper Series*. Working Paper 6612. Copyright © 1998, Alberto Alesina and David Dollar.

Alesina, Alberto, and Roberto Perotti. 1996. "Income Distribution, Political Instability, and Investment." *European Economic Review* 40:1203–1228.

Alesina, Alberto, and Dani Rodrik. 1994. "Distributive Politics and Economic Growth." *Quarterly Journal of Economics* 109:465–490.

Aliber, Robert Z. 1971. "The Multinational Enterprise in a Multiple Currency World." In John H. Dunning, ed., *The Multinational Enterprise*. London: Allen & Unwin.

Altshuler, Rosanne. 2001. Forthcoming chapter in James R. Hines, ed., *International Taxation and Multinational Activity*. Chicago: University of Chicago Press.

Alvarez, Michael, Antonio Cheibub, Fernando Limongi, and Adam Przeworski. 1996. "Classifying Political Regimes." *Studies in Comparative International Development* (31) 2:3–36.

Alvarez, Michael R., Geoffrey Garrett, and Peter Lange. 1991. "Government Partisanship, Labor Organization and Macroeconomic Performance." *American Political Science Review* 85:541–556.

Andrews, David. 1994. "Capital Mobility and State Autonomy: Toward a Structural Theory of International Relations." *International Studies Quarterly* 38 (2):193–218.

Baker, James C. 1999. *Foreign Direct Investment in Less Developed Countries: The Role of ICSID and MIGA*. Westport, Conn.: Quorum Books.

Balasubramanyam, V. N., M. Salisu, and David Sapsford. 1996. "Foreign Direct Investment and Growth in EP and IS Countries." *Economic Journal* 106 (434):95–105.

Balasubramantan, V. N., M. Salisu, and David Sapsford. 1999. "Foreign Direct Investment as an Engine of Growth." *Journal of International Trade and Economic Development* 8 (1):27–40.

Bandow, Doug. 1994. "The IMF: A Record of Addiction and Failure." In Doug Bandow and Ian Vasquez, eds., *Perpetuating Poverty: The World Bank, the IMF, and the Developing World*. Washington, D.C.: Cato Institute.

Banks, Arthur S. (various years). *The Political Handbook of the World*. Binghampton: CSA Publications.

Bardhan, Pranab, and Dilip Mookherjee. 2000. "Capture and Governance at Local and National Levels." *American Economic Review* 90 (2):35–39.

Barrell, Ray, and Nigel Pain. 1999. "Domestic Institutions, Agglomerations and Foreign Direct Investments in Europe." *European Economic Review* 43 (4): 925–934.

Barro, Robert. 1990. "Government Spending in a Simple Model of Endogenous Growth." *Journal of Political Economy* 98 (5):S103–S126.

Barro, Robert. 1996. "Democracy and Growth." *Journal of Economic Growth* 1: 1–27.

Barro, Robert, and J. W. Lee. 1993. "International Measures of Schooling Years and Schooling Quality." *American Economic Review.* 86 (2):218–223.

Bartlett, David, and Anna Seleny. 1998. "The Political Enforcement of Liberalism: Bargaining, Institutions, and Auto Multinationals in Hungary." *International Studies Quarterly* 42:319–338.

Basinger, Scott J., and Mark Hallerberg. 2004. "Remodeling the Competition for Capital: How Domestic Politics Erases the Race to the Bottom." *American Political Science Review* (98) 2:261–291.

Beck, Nathaniel, and Jonathan Katz. 1995. "What to Do (and Not to Do) with Time-Series-Cross-Sectional Data in Comparative Politics." *American Political Science Review* 89:634–647.

Beck, Thorsten, George Clarke, Alberto Groff, Philip Keefer, and Patrick Walsh. 2000. "New Tools and New Tests in Comparative Political Economy: The Database of Political Institutions." *World Bank Research Paper*, 2283.

Beetsma, Roel M.W.J., and Harald Uhlig. 1999. "An Analysis of the Stability and Growth Pact." *Economic Journal* 109:546–571.

Bende-Nabende, Anthony. 1999. *FDI, Regionalism, Government Policy, and Endogenous Growth.* Aldershot: Ashgate.

Bennell, Paul. 1997. "Foreign Direct Investment in Africa: Rhetoric and Reality." *SAIS Review* (September):127–139.

Bennett, D. Scott. 1997. Testing Alternative Models of Alliance Duration 1816–1985. *American Journal of Political Science* 41 (3):846–878.

Bhagwati, Jagdish N. 1978. *Anatomy and Consequences of Exchange Rate Control Regimes.* Vol. 1 of *Studies in International Economic Relations, No. 10.* New York: National Bureau of Economic Research.

Bhagwati, Jagdish N. 1985. Esmee Fairbain Lecture, University of Lancaster, UK. In *Political Economy and International Trade,* ed. Douglas Irvin and J. N. Bhagwati, 309–339. Cambridge, Mass.: MIT Press, 1991.

Bhagwati, Jagdish, Elias Dinopoulos, and Kar-Yiu Wong. 1992. "Quid Pro Quo Foreign Investment." *American Economic Review* 82:186–190.

Bird, Graham. 1995. *IMF Lending to Developing Countries.* London: Routledge.

Bird, Graham. 1996. "Borrowing from the IMF: The Policy Implications of Recent Empirical Research." *World Development* 24 (11):1753–1760.

Bird, Graham, and D. Rowlands. 1997. "The Catalytic Effects of Lending by the International Financial Institutions." *The World Economy* 20 (7):967–991.

Blomstrom, Magnus, and Ari Kokko. 1997. "How Foreign Investment Affects Host Countries." *World Bank Policy Research Working Paper*, 1745.

Blonigen, Bruce, and Robert Feenstra. 1996. "Protectionist Threats and Foreign Direct Investment." *Nation Bureau of Economic Research Working Paper*, 5475.

Boix, Carles. 1998. *Political Parties, Growth, and Equality.* Cambridge: Cambridge University Press.

Borensztein, E., J. DeGregorio, and J.-W. Lee. 1998. "How Does Foreign Direct Investment Affect Economic Growth?" *Journal of International Economics* 45(1):115–135.

Bremer, Stuart A. 1992. "Dangerous Dyads: Conditions Affecting the Likelihood of Interstate War, 1816–1965." *Journal of Conflict Resolution.* 36(2): 309–341.

Brennan, Geoffrey, and James M. Buchanan. 1980. *The Power to Tax: Analytic Foundations of a Fiscal Constitution.* New York: Cambridge University Press.

Brewer, Thomas L. 1983. "The Instability of Governments and the Instability of Controls on Funds Transfers by Multinational Enterprises: Implications for Political Risk Analysis." *Journal of International Business Studies* 14: 147–157.

Brewer, Thomas L. 1993a. "Government Policies, Market Imperfections, and Foreign Direct Investment." *Journal of International Business Studies* 24:67–80.

Brewer, Thomas L. 1993b. "Foreign Direct Investment in Emerging Market Countries." In Oxelheim, Lars, ed., *The Global Race for Foreign Direct Investment: Prospects for the Future.* New York: Springer.

Brooks, Steven. 2005. *Producing Security: Multinational Corporations and the Changing Calculus of Conflict.* Princeton, N.J.: Princeton University Press.

Bruce, Neil. 1995. "A Fiscal Federalism Analysis of Debt Policies by Sovereign Regional Governments." *Canadian Journal of Economics* 28:S195–S206.

Brune, Nancy, Geoffrey Garrett, Alexandra Guisinger, and Jason Sorens. 2001. "The Political Economy of Capital Account Liberalization." Paper presented at the 2001 Annual Meeting of the American Political Science Association, San Francisco.

Brune, Nancy, Geoffrey Garrett, and Bruce Kogut. 2004. "The IMF and the Global Spread of Privatization." *IMF Staff Papers* 51 (2):195–219.

Buckley, Peter J., and Mark Casson. 1976. *The Future of the Multinational Enterprise.* New York: Holmes and Meiers.

Bueno de Mesquita, Bruce, and David Lalman. 1992. *War and Reason: Domestic and International Imperatives.* New Haven, Conn.: Yale University Press.

Bueno de Mesquita, Bruce, James D. Morrow, Randolph M. Siverson, and Alastair Smith. 1999. "An Institutional Explanation of the Democratic Peace." *American Political Science Review.* 93 (4):791–808.

Bulow, Jeremy, and Kenneth Rogoff. 1989. "Sovereign Debt: Is to Forgive to Forget?" *America Economic Review* 79 (1):43–50.

Cameron, David R. 1978. "The Expansion of the Public Economy: A Comparative Analysis." *American Political Science Review* 72 (4):1243–1261.

Caves, Richard E. 1971. "International Corporations: The Industrial Economics of Foreign Investment." *Economica* 38 (1):1–27.

Cerny, Philip G. 1990. *The Changing Architecture of Politics.* London: Sage.

Chudnovsky, Daniel, Andres Lopez, and Fernando Porta. 1995. "New Foreign Direct Investment in Argentina: Privatization, the Domestic Market, and Regional Integration." In ed. Manuel R. Agosin, *Foreign Direct Investment in Latin America.* Washington, D.C.: Inter-American Development Bank.

Clegg, Jeremy, and Susan Scott-Green. 1999. "The Determinants of New FDI Capital Flows into the EC: A Statistical Comparison of the USA and Japan." *Journal of Common Market Studies* 37 (4):597–616.

Connors, T. A. 1979. "The Apparent Effects of Recent IMF Stabilization Programs." *International Finance Discussion Paper* 135. Board of Governors of the Federal Reserve System.

Cosset, Jean-Claude, and Jean Roy. 1990. "The Determinants of Country Risk Ratings." *Journal of International Business Studies* 1:135–142.

Cowhey, Peter F. 1993. "Domestic Institutions and the Credibility of International Commitments: Japan and the United States." *International Organization* 50:109–139.

Dahl, Robert 1971. *Polyarchy: Participation and Opposition.* New Haven, Conn.: Yale University Press.

David, Kenneth. 1985. "Home Country Policy and International Competitive Performance of Third World Corporations: A Study of Indian and Korean Services Industries." In Thomas L. Brewer, ed.. *Political Risk in International Business.* New York: Praeger.

De Gregorio, José, Barry Eichengreen, Takatoshi Ito, and Charles Wyplosz. 1999. *An Independent and Accountable IMF.* Geneva: International Center for Monetary and Banking Studies.

Dell, S. 1982. "Stabilization: The Political Economy of Overkill." *World Development.* August. 10 (8):597–687.

De Mello, Luiz R. Jr. 1999. "Foreign Direct Investment-Led Growth: Evidence from Time Series and Panel Data." *Oxford Economic Papers* 51 (1):133–151.

Derbyshire, J. Denis, and Ian Derbyshire. *Political Systems of the World.* New York: St. Martin's Press.

Dewenter, Kathryn L. 1995. "Do Exchange Rate Changes Drive Foreign Direct Investment?" *Journal of Business* 68 (3):405–434.

Dreher, Axel, and Nathan M. Jensen. 2003. "Independent Actor or Agent? An Empirical Analysis of the Impact of U.S. Interests on IMF Conditions." Yale University Leitner Working Paper 2003–04.

Drèze, Jean, and Amartya Sen. 1989. *Hunger and Public Action.* Oxford: Oxford University Press.

Drezner, Daniel W. 2001. "Globalization and Policy Convergence." *International Studies Review* 3 (1):53–78.

Dunning, John H. 1971. "Trade, Location of Economic Activity and the MNE: A Search for an Eclectic Approach." In B. Ohlin, ed., *The International Allocation of Economic Activity, Proceedings of a Nobel Symposium held at Stockholm.* London: Macmillan.

Dunning, John H. 1977. *The Multinational Enterprise.* London: Allen & Unwin.

Dunning, John H. 1981. *International Production and the Multinational Enterprise.* London: Allen & Unwin.

Durham, Benson J. 1999. "Economic Growth and Political Regimes." *Journal of Economic Growth* 4 (3):81–111.

Easterly, William J. 1999. "Life During Growth." *Journal of Economic Growth* 4 (3):239–276.

Eaton, Jonathan, and Mark Gersovitz. 1981. "Debt with Political Reputation: Theoretical and Empirical Analysis." *Review of Economic Studies* 48:289–309.

Edwards, Sebastion. 1999. "How Effective Are Capital Controls?" *Journal of Economic Perspectives* 13 (4):65–84.

Elazar, Daniel J. 1994. *Federal Systems of the World: A Handbook of Federal, Confederal and Autonomy Arrangements*. New York: Longman Press.

Ellingsen, Tore, and Karl Wärneryd. 1999. "Foreign Direct Investment and the Political Economy of Protection." *International Economic Review* 40 (2): 357–379.

Erb, Claude B., Campbell R. Harvey, and Tadas E. Viskanta. 1996. "Political Risk, Economic Risk, and Financial Risk." *Financial Analysts Journal* (Nov./ Dec.):29–46.

Ethier, Wilfred, and James R. Markusen. 1996. "Multinational Firms, Technology Diffusion and Trade." *Journal of International Economics* 41:1–28.

Ethier, Wilfred, and Lars E. O. Svensson. 1986. "Theorems of International Trade with Factor Mobility." *Journal of International Economics* 20:21–42.

Evans, Peter. 1979. *Dependency Development: The Alliance of Multinational, State, and Local Capital in Brazil*. Princeton, N.J.: Princeton University Press.

Faini, R., J. De Melo, A. Senhadji-Semlal, and J. Stanton. 1991. "Macro Performance under Adjustment Lending." In Vinod Thomas et al., eds. *Restructuring Economies in Distress: Policy Reform and the World Bank*. Oxford: Oxford University Press.

Farber, Henry, and Joanne Gowa. 1995. "Politics and Peace." *International Security* 20 (2):123–146.

Farber, Henry, and Joanne Gowa. 1997. "Common Interests or Common Polities?" *Journal of Politics* 57 (3):393–417.

Fearon, James D. 1994. "Domestic Political Audiences and the Escalation of International Disputes." *American Political Science Review* 88:577–592.

Feder, Gershon, and Lily Uy. 1985. "The Determinants of International Creditworthiness and their Policy Implications." *Journal of Policy Modeling* 7: 133–156.

Frankel, Jeffrey A., and Sergio L. Schmukler, 1996. "Country Fund Discounts, Asymmetric Information and the Mexican Crisis of 1994: Did Local Residents Turn Pessimistic Before International Investors?" NBER Working Papers 5714, National Bureau of Economic Research.

Freeman, C. 1982. *The Economics of Industrial Innovation*. London: Francis Pinter.

Frieden, Jeffrey A. 1991. "Invested Interests: The Politics of National Economic Policies in a World of Global Finance." *International Organization* 45 (4): 425–453.

Friedman, Thomas L. 1999. *The Lexus and the Olive Tree*. New York: Anchor Books.

Froot, Kenneth, 1993. *Foreign Direct Investment*. Chicago: University of Chicago Press.

Froot, Kenneth, and Jeremy C. Stein. 1991. "Exchange Rates and Foreign Direct Investment: An Imperfect Capital Markets Approach." *Quarterly Journal of Economics* 106 (4):191–217.

Frynas, Jedrzej George. 1998. "Political Instability and Business: Focus on Shell in Nigeria." *Third World Quarterly* 19 (3):457–478.

Gandhi, Jennifer. 2004. *Political Institutions Under Dictatorship*. Ph.D. diss., New York University.

Ganesan, A. V. 1998. "Strategic Options Available to Developing Countries with Regard to a Multilateral Agreement on Investment." *UNCTAD Discussion Paper* No. 134.

García-Bolívar, Omar E. 2004. "Foreign Investment Disputes under ICSID: A Review of Its Decisions on Jurisdiction." *Journal of World Investment* 5 (1):187–214.

Garrett, Geoffrey. 1998. *Partisan Politics in the Global Economy*. Cambridge: Cambridge University Press.

Garrett, Geoffrey. 2001. "Globalization and Spending around the World." *Studies in Comparative Political Development* 35 (4):3–29.

Garrett, Geoffrey, and Debra Mitchell. 2001. "Globalization, Government Spending and Taxation in OECD Countries." *European Journal of Political Research* 39 (3):145–177.

Gatignon, Hubert, and Erin Anderson. 1988. "The Multinational Corporation's Degree of Control over Foreign Subsidies: An Empirical Test of a Transaction Cost Explanation." *Journal of Law, Economics, and Organization* 4 (2):305–336.

Gaubatz, Kurt Taylor. 1996. "Democratic States and Commitment in International Relations." *International Organization* 50:109–139.

Gereffi, Gary. 1983. *The Pharmaceutical Industry and Dependency in the Third World*. Princeton, N.J.: Princeton University Press.

Gilady, Lilach, and Nathan M. Jensen. 2002. "The Peace Dividend and Globalization: Military Expenditures and Multinational Investments." Paper presented at the American Political Science Association Annual Conference.

Gleditsch, Kristian, and Michael D. Ward. 2000. "War and Peace in Space and Time: The Role of Democratization." *International Studies Quarterly* 44 (1):1–29.

Goldberg, Linda S., and Michael Klein. 1998. "Foreign Investment, Trade and Real Exchange Rate Linkages in Developing Countries." In Reuven Glick, ed., *Managing Capital Flows and Exchange Rates: Lessons from the Pacific Basin*. Cambridge: Cambridge University Press.

Goldberg, Linda S., and Michael Klein. 1999. "International Trade and Factor Mobility: An Empirical Investigation." *National Bureau of Economic Research Working Paper*, 7196. Copyright © 1999, Linda S. Goldberg and Michael W. Klein.

Goodman, Louis Wolf. 1976. "The Social Organization of Decision-Making in the Multinational Corporation." In David E. Apter and Louis Wolf Goodman, eds., *The Multinational Corporation and Social Change*. New York: Praeger.

Görg, Holger, and Eric Strobl. 2001. "Multinational Companies and Productivity Spillovers: A Meta-Analysis." *Economic Journal* 111 (475):723–739.

Gould, Erica R. 2003. "Money Talks: Supplementary Financiers and International Monetary Fund Conditionality." *International Organization* 57 (3):551–587.

Gravelle, Jane G., and Kent Smetters. 2001. "Who Bears the Burden of Corporate Taxation in the Open Economy?" *National Bureau of Economic Research Working Paper*, 8280.

Gropp, Reint, and Kristina Kostial. 2001. "FDI and Corporate Tax Revenue: Tax Harmonization or Competition?" *Finance and Development* 38(2).

Grossman, Gene M., and Elhanan Helpman. 1991. *Innovation and Growth in the Global Economy.* Cambridge, Mass.: MIT Press.

Grossman, Herschel I., and John B. Van Huyck. 1988. "Sovereign Debt as a Contingent Claim: Excusable Default, Repudiation, and Reputation." *American Economic Review* 78 (5):1088–1097.

Group of Twenty-Four (G-24) 1987. *The Role of the IMF in Adjustment with Growth. Report of a Working Group.* Washington, D.C.: Group of 24, March.

Gruben, William C., and Darryl McLeod. 1998. "Capital Flows, Savings, and Growth in the 1990s." *The Quarterly Review of Economics and Finance* 38 (3):287–301.

Haggard, Stephan. 1989. "The Political Economy of Foreign Direct Investment in Latin America." *Latin American Research Review* 24 (1):184–208.

Hajivassiliou, V. A. 1987. "The External Debt Repayment Problems of LDCs: An Econometric Model Based on Panel Data." *Journal of Econometrics* 36: 205–230.

Hansen, Wendy L., and Neil J. Mitchell. 2000. "Disaggregating and Explaining Corporate Political Activity: Domestic and Foreign Corporations in National Politics." *American Political Science Review* 94 (4):891–903.

Haque, Nadeem, and Moshin S. Khan. 1998. "Do IMF-Supported Programs Work? A Survey of the Cross-Country Empirical Evidence." *International Monetary Fund Working Paper*, WP/98/169.

Harms, Philipp. 2000. *International Investment, Political Risk, and Growth.* Boston: Kluwer Academic.

Harrod, Roy F. 1939. "An Essay in Dynamic Theory." *The Economic Journal* 49:14–33.

Hayes, Jude C. 2003. "Globalization and Capital Taxation in Consensus and Majoritarian Democracies." *World Politics* 56 (1):79–113.

Helpman, Elhanan. 1984. "A Simple Theory of International Trade with Multinational Corporations." *Journal of Political Economy* 92 (3):451–471.

Henisz, Witold J. 2000. "The Institutional Environment for Multinational Investment." *Journal of Law, Economics and Organization* 16 (2):334–364.

Henisz, Witold. 2002. *Politics and International Investment.* Cheltenham, UK: Edward Elgar.

Hillman, Arye L., and Heinrich W. Ursprung. 1988. "Domestic Politics, Foreign Interests, and International Trade Policy. *American Economic Review* 78 (4):729–745.

Huntington, Samuel P. 1968. *Political Order and Changing Societies.* New Haven, Conn.: Yale University Press.

Hymer, Stephan H. 1976. *The International Operations of National Firms: A Study of Direct Foreign Investment.* Cambridge, Mass.: MIT Press.

International Finance Corporation (IFC). 1997. *Foreign Direct Investment: Lessons from Experience.* Washington, D.C.: International Finance Corporation and Foreign Investment Advisory Service.

International Monetary Fund (IMF). 1989. *Exchange Arrangements and Exchange Restrictions.* Washington, D.C.: International Monetary Fund.

International Monetary Fund (IMF). 1999a. *What Is the International Monetary Fund?* Washington, D.C: International Monetary Fund.

International Monetary Fund. 1999b. *Conditionality: Fostering Sustained Policy Implementation.* Washington, D.C: International Monetary Fund.

Jaggers, Keith, and Ted Robert Gurr. 1996. "Polity III: Regime Change and Political Authority, 1800–1994." ICPSR Study Number 6695. Ann Arbor, Mich.: Inter-University Consortium for Political and Social Research. At www.icpsr.umich.edu.

James, Harold. 1996. *International Monetary Cooperation Since Bretton Woods.* Washington, D.C.: International Monetary Fund.

Javorcik, Beata Smarzynska. 2004. "Does Foreign Direct Investment Increase the Productivity of Domestic Firms? In Search of Spillovers Through Backward Linkages." *American Economic Review* 94 (3):605–627.

Jensen, Nathan M. 2002. "Economic Reform, State Capture, and International Investment in Transition Economies." *Journal of International Development* 14:973–977.

Jensen, Nathan M. 2003a. "Democratic Governance and Multinational Corporations: Political Regimes and Inflows of Foreign Direct Investment." *International Organization* 57 (3):587–616.

Jensen, Nathan M. 2003b. "Rational Citizens Against Reform: Poverty and Economic Reform in Transition Economies." *Comparative Political Studies* 36 (9):1092–1111.

Jensen, Nathan M. 2004. "Crisis, Conditions, and Capital: The Effects of International Monetary Fund Agreements on Foreign Direct Investment Inflows." *Journal of Conflict Resolution* 48 (2):194–210.

Jensen, Nathan M., and Fiona McGillivrary. 2000. "The Political Determinants of Foreign Direct Investment." Paper presented at the 2000 American Political Science Association Conference.

Jessup, David. 1999. *Dollars and Democracy.* Document from the New Economy Information Service. At www.newecon.org.

Jones, Ronald W. 1967. "International Capital Movements and the Theory of Tariffs and Trade." *Quarterly Journal of Economics* 81 (Feb.):1–38.

Kapstein, Ethan B. 2000. "Winners and Losers in the Global Economy." *International Organization* 54 (2):359–384.

Kemp, Murray C. 1966. "The Gains from International Trade and Investment: A Neo-Heckscher-Ohlin Approach." *American Economic Review* 61 (Sept.):788–809.

Khan, Mohsin, Peter Montiel, and Nadeem Ul Haque. 1986. "Adjustment with Growth: Relating the Analytical Approaches of the World Bank and the IMF." *World Bank Discussion Paper.* Washington, D.C.: World Bank.

Khan, Mohsin S., and Sunil Sharma. 2001. "IMF Conditionality and Country Ownership of Programs." *IMF Working Paper,* 142.

Killick, Tony. 1995. *IMF Programmes in Developing Countries.* London: Routledge.

Kindleberger, Charles P. 1969. *American Business Abroad*. New Haven, Conn.: Yale University Press.

Kletzer, Kenneth M. 1984. "Asymmetries in Information and LDC Borrowing with Sovereign Risk." *Economic Journal* 94:287–307.

Knack, Stephen, and Philip Keefer. 1995. "Institutions and Economic Performance: Cross-Country Tests Using Alternative Institutional Measures." *Economics and Politics* 7:207–227.

Kobrin, Stephen J. 1979. "Political Risk: A Review and Reconsideration." *Journal of International Business Studies* 10 (Spring):67–80.

Kobrin, Stephen J. 1982. *Managing Political Risk Assessment: A Strategic Response to Environmental Change*. Berkeley: University of California Press.

Kobrin, Stephen. 1984. "Expropriation as an Attempt to Control Foreign Firms in LDCs: Trends from 1960–1979." *International Studies Quarterly* 28 (3): 329–348.

Kobrin, Stephen J. 1985. "Expropriation as an Attempt to Control Foreign Firms in Developing Countries: Trends from 1960–1979." In Thomas L. Brewer, eds., *Political Risk in International Business*. New York: Praeger.

Krueger, Ann. 1988. "Whither the World Bank and the IMF." *Journal of Economic Literature* 36 (4):1983–2020.

Krugman, Paul. 1988. "Financing versus Forgiving a Debt Overhang." *Journal of Development Economics* 29:253–268.

Kurzer, Paulette. 1993. *Business and Banking: Political Change and Economic Integration in Western Europe*. Ithaca, N.Y.: Cornell University Press.

Kydland F., and E. Prescott. 1977. "Rules Rather than Discretion: The Inconsistency of Optimal Plans." *Journal of Political Economy* 85:473–491.

Lamfalussy, Alexandre. 1961. *Investment and Growth in Mature Economies*. London: Basil Blackwell and Mott.

Lane T., A. R. Ghosh, J. Hamann, S. Phillips, M. Schultz-Ghattas, and T. Tsikata. 1999. *IMF-Supported Programmes in Indonesia, Korean and Thailand: A Preliminary Assessment*, mimeo.

Lanton, Stuart, and Constance E. Smith. 2000. "Government Debt Spillovers and Creditworthiness in a Federation." *Canadian Journal of Economics* 33 (3):634–661.

Lee, Sunk Hun. 1993. "Relative Importance of Political Instability and Economic Variables on Perceived Country Creditworthiness." *Journal of International Business Studies* 4:801–812.

Leeds, Brett Ashley. 1999. "Domestic Political Institutions, Credible Commitments, and International Cooperation." *American Journal of Political Science* 42 (4):979–1002.

Lehmann, Alexander. 1999. "Country Risks and the Investment Activity of U.S. Multinationals in Developing Countries." *IMF Working Paper*, WP/99/133.

Li, Quan, and Adam Resnick. 2003. "Reversal of Fortunes: Democratic Institutions and Foreign Direct Investment Inflows to Developing Countries." *International Organization* 57 (1):175–212.

Lijphart, Arend. 1999. *Patterns of Democracy*. New Haven, Conn.: Yale University Press.

Lindblom, Charles E. 1977. *Politics and Markets: The World's Political-Economic Systems.* New York: Basic Books.

Lipset, Seymour Martin. 1959. "Some Social Requisites of Democracy: Economic Development and Political Legitimacy." *American Political Science Review* 53 (1):69–105.

Lipsey, Robert E. 1999. "The Role of Foreign Direct Investment in International Capital Flows." *National Bureau of Economic Research Working Paper,* 7094.

Lipsey, Robert E. 2002. "Home and Host Country Effects of FDI." *National Bureau of Economic Research Working Paper,* 9293.

Lohmann, Susan. 1992. "Optimal Commitment in Monetary Policy: Credibility versus Flexibility." *American Economic Review* 82 (1):273–286.

Lohmann, Susan. 1998. "Federalism and Central Bank Independence: The Politics of German Monetary Policy 1957–92." *World Politics* 50 (3):401–446.

Lucas, Robert E. 1988. "On the Mechanics of Economic Development." *Journal of Monetary Economics* 22:3–42.

Magee, Stephan P. 1977. "Information and the Multinational Corporation: An Appropriability Theory of Direct Foreign Investment." In J. N. Bhagwati, ed., *The New International Economic Order.* Cambridge, Mass.: MIT Press.

Mallampally, Padma, and Karl P. Sauvant. 1999. "Foreign Direct Investment in Developing Countries." *Finance and Development* (March):34–37.

Mankiw, N. Gregory, David Romer, and David N. Weil. 1992. "A Contribution to the Empirics of Economic Growth." *Quarterly Journal of Economics* 107 (2):407–438.

Mansfield, Edward, and Jack Snyder. 1995. "Democratization and the Danger of War." *International Security* 20 (1):5–38.

Markusen, James R. 1983. "Factor Movements and Commodity Trade as Compliments." *Journal of International Economics* 13:341–356.

Markusen, James R. 1984. "Multinationals, Multi-Plant Economies, and the Gains from Trade." *Journal of International Economics* 16 (3–4):205–226.

Markusen, James R. 1985. "Trade in Goods and Factors with International Differences in Technology." *International Economic Review* 26:175–192.

Markusen, James R. 1995. "The Boundaries of Multinational Enterprises and the Theory of International Trade." *Journal of Economic Perspectives* 9 (2): 169–189.

Markusen, James R. 1997. "Trade versus Investment Liberalization." *National Bureau of Economic Research Working Paper,* 6231.

Markusen, James R. 1998a. "Contracts, Intellectual Property Rights and Multinational Investments in Developing Countries." *National Bureau of Economic Research Working Paper,* 6448.

Markusen, James R. 1998b. "Multinational Firms, Location and Trade." *World Economy* 21:733–756.

Markusen, James R., and Wilfred Ethier. 1996. "Multinationals, Technical Diffusion, and Trade." *Journal of International Economics* 41 (1–2):1–28.

Markusen, James R., and Keith E. Maskus. 1999a. "Multinational Firms: Reconciling Theory and Evidence." *National Bureau of Economic Research Working Paper,* 7163.

Markusen, James R., and Keith E. Maskus. 1999b. "Discriminating Among Alternative Theories of the Multinational Enterprise." *National Bureau of Economic Research Working Paper*, 7164.

Markusen, James R., and Lars E. O. Svensson. 1985. "Trade in Goods and Factors with International Differences in Technology." *International Economic Review* 26:175–192.

Markusen, James R., and Anthony J. Venables. 1999. "Foreign Direct Investment as a Catalyst for Industrial Development." *European Economic Review* 43 (2):335–356.

Marshall, Monty G., and Keith Jaggers. 2000. Polity IV Project: Political Regime Characteristics and Transitions, 1800–1999. Center for International Development and Conflict Management, University of Maryland.

Martin, Carmela, and Francisco J. Velázquez. 1997. "The Determining Factors of Foreign Direct Investment in Spain and the Rest of the OECD: Lessons from the CEECS." *Center for Economic Policy Research*, Discussion Paper 1637.

McGillivray, Fiona, and Alastair Smith. 1998. "Cooperating Democrats, Defecting Autocrats." Working Paper, Yale University.

McGillivray, Fiona, and Alastair Smith. 2000. "Trust and Cooperation through Agent Specific Punishments." *International Organization* 54 (4):809–824.

Mendoza, Enrique, Giancarlo Milesi-Ferreti, and Patrick Asea. 1997. "On the Ineffectiveness of Tax Policy in Altering Long-Run Growth." *Journal of Public Economics* 66:99–126.

Miller, Gary. 1992. *Managerial Dilemmas: The Political Economy of Hierarchy.* Cambridge: Cambridge University Press.

Milner, Helen V. 1988. *Resisting Protectionism: Global Industries and the Politics of International Trade.* Princeton, N.J.: Princeton University Press.

Minor, Michael S. 1994. "The Demise of Expropriation as an Instrument of LDC Policy, 1980–1992." *Journal of International Business Studies* 25 (1):177–188.

Mody, Ashoka, and Diego Saravia. 2003. "Catalysing Capital Flows: Do IMF Programs Work as Commitment Devices?" *IMF Working Paper* 03/100.

Montinola, Gabriella, Yingyi Quian, and Barry R. Weingast. 1995. "Federalism, Chinese Style: The Political Basis for Economic Success in China." *World Politics* 50:50–81.

Moran, Theodore H. 1998. *Foreign Direct Investment and Development.* Washington, D.C.: Institute for International Economics.

Moran, Theodore H. 2001. *Parental Supervision: The New Paradigm for Foreign Direct Investment and Development.* Washington, D.C.: Institute for International Economies.

Moran, Theodore H. 2002. *Beyond Sweatshops: Foreign Direct Investment and Globalization in Developing Countries.* Washington, D.C.: Brookings Institution Press.

Morck, Randall, and Bernard Yeung. 1991. "Why Investors Value Multinationality." *Journal of Business* 64 (2):165–187.

Mosley, Layna. 2000. "Room to Move: International Financial Markets and National Welfare States." *International Organization* 54 (4):737–773.

Mosley, Layna. 2003. *Global Capital and National Governments.* Cambridge: Cambridge University Press.

Mowery, D. C., and N. Rosenberg. 1989. *Technology and the Pursuit of Economic Growth*. Cambridge: Cambridge University Press.

Multilateral Investment Guarantee Agency (MIGA). 2002. *Foreign Direct Investment Survey*. Washington, D.C.: World Bank/MIGA.

Multilateral Investment Guarantee Agency (MIGA). 2004a. *Investment Guarantee Guide*. Washington, D.C.: World Bank Group.

Multilateral Investment Guarantee Agency (MIGA). 2004b. "Political Risk Insurance Costing/Pricing: Methodology and Applications." Presentation given May 5, 2004.

Mundell, Robert. 1957. "International Trade and Factor Mobility." *American Economic Review* 47:321–335.

Murtha, Thomas. 1991. "Surviving Industrial Targeting: State Credibility and Public Policy Competencies in Multinational Subcontracting." *Journal of Law, Economics, and Organization* 7 (1):117–143.

Mutti, John H. 2003. *Foreign Direct Investment and Tax Competition*. Washington, D.C.: Institute for International Economics.

North, Douglass C. 1990. *Institutions, Institutional Change and Economic Performance*. Cambridge: Cambridge University Press.

North, Douglass C., and Barry Weingast. 1989. "Constitutions and Credible Commitments: The Evolution of the Institutions of Public Choice in 17th Century England." *Journal of Economic History* 49:803–832.

Oatley, Thomas. 1999. "How Constraining Is Capital Mobility? The Partisan Hypothesis in an Open Economy." *American Journal of Political Science* 43 (4):1003–1027.

Oates, Wallace E. 1972. *The Political Economy of Fiscal Federalism*. Lexington, U.K.: D.C. Heath and Company.

Oates, Wallace E. 1985. "Searching for Leviathan: An Empirical Study." *American Economic Review* 75: 748–757.

Oates, Wallace E. 1999. "An Essay on Fiscal Federalism." *Journal of Economic Literature* 37 (3):1120–1149.

Ohmae, Kenichi. 1991. *The Borderless World*. New York: Harper Business.

Ohmae, Kenichi. 1995. *The End of the Nation State: The Rise of Regional Economies*. New York: Simon & Schuster.

Olsen, Mancur. 1965. *The Logic of Collective Action*. New Haven, Conn.: Yale University Press.

Oman, Charles. 2000. *Policy Competition for Foreign Direct Investment*. Paris: Organization for Economic Co-operation and Development.

Oneal, John R. 1994. "The Affinity of Foreign Investors for Authoritarian Regimes." *Political Research Quarterly* 47 (3):565–588.

Oneal, John R., and Bruce Russett. 1997. "The Classic Liberals Were Right: Democracy, Interdependence, and Conflict, 1950–1985." *International Studies Quarterly* 41 (2):267–294.

Organization for Economic Co-operation and Development (OECD). 1995. *Foreign Direct Investment, Trade and Employment*. Paris: Organization for Economic Co-operation and Development.

Organization for Economic Co-operation and Development (OECD). 1998. "Survey of OECD Work on International Investment." *OECD Working Papers on International Investment*.

Osebhale, B. D. 1993. *Political Instability, Interstate Conflict, Adverse Change in Host Government Policies and Foreign Direct Investment. A Sensitivity Analysis*. New York: Garland.

Oxley, Joanne E. 1997. "Appropriability Hazards and Governance in Strategic Alliances: A Transaction Cost Approach." *Journal of Law, Economics, and Organization* 13 (2):387–409.

Pain, Nigel, and Katherine Wakelin. 1998. "Export Performance and the Role of Foreign Direct Investment." *Manchester School* 66 (0):62–88.

Pastor, Manuel Jr. 1987. "The Effects of IMF Participation in the Third World: Debate and Evidence from Latin American." *World Development* 15 (2): 249–262.

Persson, Torsten, and Guido Tabellini. 1994. "Is Inequality Harmful for Growth?" *American Economic Review* 84 (3):600–619.

Persson, Torsten, Gerard Roland, and Guido Tabellini. 1997. "Separation of Powers and Political Accountability." *Quarterly Journal of Economics* 3:1163–1202.

Polak, Jacques. 1991. "The Changing Nature of IMF Conditionality." *Princeton Essays in International Finance*, no. 184. Princeton, N.J.: Princeton University Press.

PriceWaterhouseCoopers. 2001. *Investigating the Costs of Opacity: Deterred Foreign Direct Investment*. Available online at www.opacityindex.com.

Prud'homme, Remy. 1995. "On the Dangers of Decentralization." *World Bank Research Observer* 10 (2):201–210.

Przeworski, Adam, Michael E. Alvarez, José Antonio Cheibub, and Fernando Limongi. 2000. *Democracy and Development: Political Institutions and Material Well-Being in the World, 1950–1990*. Cambridge: Cambridge University Press.

Przeworski, Adam, and Fernando Limongi. 1997. "Modernization: Theories and Facts." *World Politics* 49:155–183.

Przeworski, Adam, and James Vreeland. 2000. "The Effects of IMF Programs on Growth." *Journal of Development Economics* 62 (2):385–421.

Purvis, Douglas D. 1972. "Technology, Trade and Factor Mobility." *Economic Journal* 82:991–999.

Putnam, Robert D. 1988. "Diplomacy and Domestic Politics: The Logic of Two-Level Games." *International Organization* 42 (Summer):51–69.

Qian, Yingyi, and Barry R. Weingast. 1997. "Federalism as a Commitment to Preserving Market Incentives." *Journal of Economic Perspectives* 11 (4):83–92.

Qian, Yingyi, and Gérard Roland. 1998. "Federalism and the Soft Budget Constraint." *American Economic Review* 88 (5):1143–1162.

Quinn, Dennis. 1997. "The Correlates of Changes in International Financial Regulation." *American Political Science Review* 91:531–552.

Rangan, Subramanian. 1998. "Do Multinationals Operate Flexibly? Theory and Evidence." *Journal of International Business Studies* 29 (2):217–237.

Reichmann, T. M., and R. T. Stillson. 1978. "Experiences with Programs of Balance of Payments Adjustment: Stand-by Arrangements in the Highest Tranches, 1963–72." *IMF Staff Papers* 25:292–310.

Riker, William H. 1964. *Federalism: Origin, Operation, and Significance.* Boston: Little Brown.

Rioux, Jean-Sebastien. 1998. "A Crisis-Based Evaluation of the Democratic Peace Proposition." *Canadian Journal of Political Science* 31 (2):263–283.

Robock, Stefan H. 1971. "Political Risk: Identification and Assessment." *Columbia Journal of World Business* (July–Aug.):6–20.

Rodden, Jonathan. 2003. "Reviving Leviathan: Fiscal Federalism and the Growth of Government." *International Organization* 57:695–729.

Rodden, Jonathan, and Susan Rose-Ackerman. 1997. "Does Federalism Preserve Markets?" *Virginia Law Review* 83 (7):1521–1572.

Rodden, Jonathan, and Erik Wibbles. 2002. "Beyond the Fiction of Federalism: Macroeconomic Management in Multitiered Systems." *World Politics* 54:494–531.

Rodrik, Dani. 1996. "Understanding Economic Policy Reform." *Journal of Economic Literature* 34 (1):9–41.

Rodrik, Dani. 1997. *Has Globalization Gone Too Far?* Washington, D.C.: Institute for International Economics.

Rodrik, Dani. 1999. "Democracies Pay Higher Wages." *Quarterly Journal of Economics* 114 (3):707–738.

Romer, Paul M. 1986. "Increasing Returns and Long-Run Growth." *Journal of Political Economy* 94:1002–1037.

Romer, Paul M. 1990. "Endogenous Technical Change." *Journal of Political Economy* 98:79–102.

Rose-Ackerman, Susan. 1980. "Risk Taking and Reelection: Does Federalism Promote Innovation?" *Journal of Legal Studies* 9:593–616.

Rosen, Daniel. 2001. *Behind the Open Door: Foreign Enterprises in the Chinese Marketplace.* Washington, D.C.: Institute for International Economics.

Rosenthal, R. W. 1991. "On the Incentives Associated with Foreign Debt." *Journal of International Economics* 30:167–176.

Ross, Michael. 2001. "Does Oil Hinder Democracy?" *World Politics* 53:325–361.

Rousseau, David. 1996. *Domestic Institutions and the Evolution of International Conflict.* Ph.D. diss., University of Michigan.

Rousseau, David, Christopher Gelpi, Dan Reiter, and Paul Huth. 1996. "Assessing the Dyadic Nature of the Democratic Peace, 1918–1988." *American Political Science Review* 90 (3):512–533.

Rugman, Alan M. 1979. *International Diversification and the Multinational Enterprise.* Lexington, U.K.: D.C. Heath.

Russett, Bruce M., and John Oneal. 2001. *Triangulating Peace: Democracy, Interdependence, and International Organizations.* New York: W.W. Norton.

Sachs, Jeffrey. 1989. "Strengthening IMF Programmes in Highly Indebted Countries." In C. Gwin and R. Feinberd, eds., *The International Monetary Fund in a Multipolar World: Pulling Together.* U.S.-Third World Policy Perspectives No. 13. Washington, D.C.: Overseas Development Council.

Sachs, Jeffrey. 1999. "Power Unto Itself." In L. McQuillan and P. Montgomery, eds., *International Monetary Fund: Financial Medic to the World?* Stanford: Hoover Institution Press.

Sachs, Jeffrey, and Andrew Warner. 1995. "Natural Resource Abundance and Economic Growth." *National Bureau of Economic Research Working Paper*, 5398.

Schelling, Thomas C. 1956. "An Essay on Bargaining." *American Economic Review* 46 (June):281–306.

Schultz, Kenneth A. 1999. "Do Democratic Institutions Constrain or Inform? Contrasting Two Institutional Perspectives on Democracy and War." *International Organization* 53 (2):233–266.

Sidell, Scott R. 1988. *The IMF and Third World Instability: Is There a Connection?* Basingstoke: Macmillian.

Small, Melvin, and David Singer. 1976. "The War-Proneness of Democratic Regimes." *Jerusalem Journal of International Relations* 1 (1):50–69.

Sobel, Andrew. 1999. *State Institutions, Private Incentives, Global Capital.* Ann Arbor: University of Michigan Press.

Solow, Robert. 1956. "A Contribution to the Theory of Economic Growth." *Quarterly Journal of Economics* 70 (1):65–94.

Strange, Susan. 1996. *The Retreat of the State: The Diffusion of Power in the World Economy.* Cambridge: Cambridge University Press.

Svensson, Lars E. O. 1984. "Factor Trade and Goods Trade." *Journal of International Economics* 16:365–378.

Swank, Duane. 1998. "Funding the Welfare States." *Political Studies* 46:672–692.

Swank. Duane. 2002. *Global Capital, Political Institutions, and Policy Change in Developed Democracies.* Cambridge: Cambridge University Press.

Therborn, Goran. 1977. "The Rule of Capital and the Rise of Democracy." *New Left Review* 103 (May–June):3–41.

Thomas, Jonathan, and Tim Worrall. 1994. "Foreign Direct Investment and the Risk of Expropriation." *Review of Economic Studies* 61:81–108.

Tiebout, Charles. 1956. "A Pure Theory of Local Expenditures." *Journal of Political Economy* 64 (October):416–424.

Treisman, Daniel. 2000a. "Decentralization and Inflation: Commitment, Collective Action, or Continuity?" *American Political Science Review* 94(4):837–857.

Treisman, Daniel. 2000b. "Decentralization and the Quality of Government." Paper presented at the Political Economy of Development Conference, Yale University.

Tsebelis, George. 1995. "Decision Making in Political Systems: Veto Players in Presidentialism, Parliamentarism, Multicameralism and Multipartyism." *British Journal of Political Science* 25:289–325.

Tsebelis, George. 2002. *Veto Players: How Political Institutions Work.* New York and Princeton, N.J.: Russell Sage Foundation and Princeton University Press.

United Nations Conference on Transnational Corporations (UNCTAD). 1991. *World Investment Report.* New York: United Nations.

UNCTAD 2000. *World Investment Report.* New York: United Nations.

UNCTAD. 2003. *World Investment Report.* New York: United Nations.

Vernon, Raymond. 1966. "International Investment and International Trade in the Product Cycle." *Quarterly Journal of Economics* 30 (May):190–207.

Vernon, Raymond. 1971. *Sovereignty at Bay*. New York: Basic Books.

Vernon, Raymond. 1998. *In the Hurricane's Eye: The Troubled Prospects of Multinational Enterprises*. Cambridge: Cambridge University Press.

Vines, David. 1990. "Growth Oriented Adjustment Programmes: A Reconsideration." London: Centre for Economic Policy Research Discussion Paper, No. 406.

Vreeland, James. 2002. *The IMF and Economic Development*. Cambridge: Cambridge University Press.

Vreeland, James R. 2002. "The Effect of IMF Programs on Labor." *World Development* 30(1):121–139.

Wang, J.-Y. 1990. "Growth, Technology Transfer, and the Long-Run Theory of International Capital Movements." *Journal of International Economics* 29 (2):255–271.

Wantchekon, Leonard, and Nathan M. Jensen. 2000. "Resource Wealth and Political Regimes in Africa." *African Studies Research Working Paper*, Yale University.

Wantchekon, Leonard, and Nathan M. Jensen. 2004. "Resource Wealth and Political Regimes in Africa." *Comparative Political Studies* 37 (7):816–841.

Wantchekon, Leonard, and Ricky Lam. 1998. "Dictatorship as a Political Dutch Disease." Yale University, mimeo.

Ward, Michael D. and Kristian Gleditsch. 1998. "Democratizing for Peace." *American Political Science Review* 92 (1):51–62.

Watts, Ronald. 1999. *Comparing Federal Systems*. Montreal: McGill-Queen's University Press.

Wei, Shang-Jin. 2000. "How Taxing Is Corruption on International Investors?" *Review of Economics and Statistics* 82 (1):1–11.

Weingast, Barry. 1995. "The Economic Role of Political Institutions: Market-Preserving Federalism and Economic Development." *The Journal of Law, Economics, and Organization* 11 (1):1–32.

Wheeler, David, and Ashokoa Mody. 1992. "International Investment Location Decisions: The Case of US Firms." *Journal of International Economics* 33:57–76.

Wibbels, Erik. 2000. "Federalism and the Politics of Macroeconomic Policy and Performance." *America Journal of Political Science* 44 (4):687–702.

Wibbels, Erik, and Moisés Arce. 2003. "Globalization, Taxation, and Burden-Shifting in Latin America." *International Organization* 57(1):111–136.

Williamson, John R. 1983. "The Lending Policies of the International Monetary Fund." In John R. Williamson, *IMF Conditionality*. Washington, D.C.: Institute for International Economics.

Williamson, Oliver E. 1975. *Markets and Hierarchies: Analysis and Antitrust Implication*. New York: Free Press.

Williamson, Oliver E. 1996. *The Mechanisms of Governance*. Oxford: Oxford University Press.

Wong, Kar-Yui. 1986. "Are International Trade and Factor Mobility Substitutes?" *Journal of International Economics* 20:25–44.

World Bank. 1997. *Private Capital Flows to Developing Countries: The Road to Financial Integration*. A World Bank Policy Research Report. Washington, D.C.: World Bank.

World Bank. 1999. *World Development Indicators*. CD-ROM.

World Bank. 2000. *Global Development Finance*. Washington, D.C.: World Bank.

World Bank. 2003. *World Development Indicators*. CD-ROM.

Zhang, Kevin Honglin and James R. Markusen. 1999. "Vertical Multinationals and Host Country Characteristics." *Journal of Developmental Economics* 59:233–252.

Interviews

Interview	Date	Investment Promotion Agency/Government Agency
1	3/17/04	Banco Central do Brasil
2	3/18/04	BOVESPA (Brazilian Stock Exchange)
3	5/10/04	Office of the Hungarian Trade Commission
4	5/10/04	Malaysian Industrial Development Authority
5	5/28/04	Investment and Development Agency Ireland
6	6/10/04	Investment Partnerships Canada
7	6/11/04	Investissement Québec
8	7/11/04	Thailand Board of Investment
9	7/27/04	Costa Rican Investment Board
1	7/28/04	The Foreign Trade Corporation of Costa Rica (Procomer)

Interview	Date	Investment Location Consultant
11	6/29/04	IBM Plant Location International (IBM-PLI)
12	7/2/04	B-G Consulting
13	8/11/04	Baker, Donelson, Bearman, Caldwell & Berkowitz P.C.

Interview	Date	Risk Insurance/Analysis Agency
14	5/27/04	ERisk
15	6/11/04	Export Development Canada (EDC)
16	7/21/04	Multilateral Investment Guarantee Agency (MIGA)
17	8/24/04	Overseas Investment Protection Agency (OPIC)

Interview	Date	Company	Sector
18	3/17/04	Citigroup	Financial Services
19	3/20/04	UBS	Financial Services
20	6/10/04	Alcan	Manufacturing
21	7/13/04	Daimler Chrysler	Manufacturing
22	7/27/04	Weststar	Manufacturing

23	7/27/04	Inamed	Manufacturing
24	7/28/04	L.L. Bean	Distribution
25	7/28/04	Multi-mix	Manufacturing
26	7/29/04	Intel	Manufacturing/R&D

Index

188

INDEX

Freeman, C., 47
free-riding, 105
Free Zone Company, 69
Frieden, Jeffrey A., 157n12, 162n11
Friedman, Thomas L., 56
Frito-Lay, 40
Frynas, Jedrej George, 48

G-24, 134
Gambia, 123
Ganesan, A. V., 159n12
Garrett, Geoffrey, 58, 60–61, 85, 136
Gatignon, Hubert, 46, 48
Gaubatz, Kurt Taylor, 7–8, 77, 80
General Electric, xi, 26
General Motors, xi, 40, 100
Gereffi, Gary, 33
Germany, 28, 75, 123
Ghandhi, Sonia, 162n14
Gleditsch, Kristian, 76
globalization, 154; compensation issues
   and, 56–57; efficiency hypothesis and,
   57; race to the bottom (RTB) thesis and,
   53–71
Goldberg, Linda S., 30
Goodman, Louis Wolf, 57
Gould, Erica R., 133
governments, 42, 147; authoritarian regimes and, 7–8, 17–19, 77–80, 96–97,
   112–13, 148, 162n3, 163n16; autonomy
   and, 11, 106–8; central, 4; compensation
   issues and, 56–57; contract renegotiation and, 46; credibility and, 8–9, 50–52;
   decentralization and, 105–8, 112; democracy and, 72–99 (see also democracy);
   dictatorships and, 7, 75, 97; domestic
   politics and, 55–59; employment and,
   31; federalism and, 10–12, 16, 104–12,
   122–28; fiscal competition and, 1 (see
   also competition); hierarchy and, 11,
   106; incentive structure and, 4–5; international law changes and, 35–38; International Monetary Fund (IMF) and, 13,
   130; leadership turnover and, 134–35;
   lean, 58, 65–68; military costs and, 136;
   national representation and, 4–5; privatization and, 136–37; renege and, 100–
   101; representation and, 8; risk and, 46–
   50, 100–101; social democratic, 65–68,
   94; social security and, 62–63; sovereignty costs and, 140; spending by, 58–
   62, 71, 83, 86–87, 99, 136; stability and,

44; state-run enterprises and, 24; subnational, 11, 111–12; taxes and, 63–65 (see
   also taxes); total debt burden and, 140;
   veto players and, 10–12, 100–121
Gowa, Joanne, 75
greenfield investments, 23
Gropp, Reint, 64
Gross Domestic Product (GDP) measurement, 14–15, 141, 149; Argentina and,
   74; democracy and, 73, 82–83, 89–90;
   federalism and, 115–16; foreign direct
   investment (FDI) percentage and, 25;
   government spending and, 62; IMF
   data and, 16; low-income countries
   and, 25–26; race to the bottome (RTB)
   thesis and, 55, 60; social security and,
   63; sovereign debt risk and, 91–93;
   world trade data and, 24
Gross National Product (GNP) measurement, 96
Guisinger, Alexandra, 85

Haggard, Stephen, 34
Hajivassiliou, V. A., 136
Hansen, Wendy L., 8, 78
Haque, Nadeem, 132
Heckscher-Olin-Samuelson model, 30
Helpman, Elhanan, 43
Henisz, Witold J., 10, 44, 48, 80, 108
Hewlett-Packard, 26
Hillman, Arye L., 8, 78–79
horizontal firms, 43
Horn, Gyula, xi
Hungary, xi–xii, 28, 38, 68, 94
Huntington, Samuel P., 74
Hussein, Saddam, 48
Hymer, Stephan H., 41–42, 57

IBM Plant Location International, 68, 143
Iceland, 72
ICRG Political Stability, 96
ideal points, 101–4
imperfect market approach, 42, 57, 147
India, 26–27, 40, 93, 123, 162n14
Indonesia, 97
inflation, 10
inflows. See foreign direct investment
   (FDI)
informational mechanisms, 7, 43, 77–78,
   148
institutions, 2; checks and balances, 80; as
   commitment mechanism, 147; con-